Strategic Management and Public Service Performance

Strategic Management and Public Service Performance

Rhys Andrews

George A. Boyne

Jennifer Law

and

Richard M. Walker

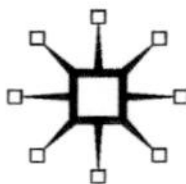

First published 2012 by
PALGRAVE MACMILLAN

Palgrave Macmillan in the UK is an imprint of Macmillan Publishers Limited, registered in England, company number 785998, of Houndmills, Basingstoke, Hampshire RG21 6XS.

Palgrave Macmillan in the US is a division of St Martin's Press LLC, 175 Fifth Avenue, New York, NY 10010.

Palgrave Macmillan is the global academic imprint of the above companies and has companies and representatives throughout the world.

Palgrave® and Macmillan® are registered trademarks in the United States, the United Kingdom, Europe and other countries.

ISBN 978–0–230–25242–4

This book is printed on paper suitable for recycling and made from fully managed and sustained forest sources. Logging, pulping and manufacturing processes are expected to conform to the environmental regulations of the country of origin.

A catalogue record for this book is available from the British Library.

Library of Congress Cataloging-in-Publication Data
Strategic management and public service
performance / Rhys Andrews . . . [et al.].
p. cm.
Includes index.
ISBN 978–0–230–25242–4 (hardback)
1. Strategic planning. 2. Organizational change.
3. Public administration. I. Andrews, Rhys.
HD30.28.S7294 2011
352.3′4—dc23 2011029560

10 9 8 7 6 5 4 3 2 1
21 20 19 18 17 16 15 14 13 12

Printed and bound in Great Britain by
CPI Antony Rowe, Chippenham and Eastbourne

Contents

List of Figures and Tables

Figures

Tables

Foreword by Professor Charles C. Snow

Mellon Foundation Faculty Fellow, Smeal College of Business, Pennsylvania State University

When Raymond Miles and I, along with our colleagues Alan Meyer and Henry Coleman, did our original research in the 1970s, the field of strategic management did not yet exist as a formal academic discipline. The Miles and Snow (1978) strategy typology helped to establish the field by integrating the literature on managerial strategizing and planning with the literature on organization theory. Our empirical studies included firms from an industry undergoing a major transformation (college textbook publishing), two industries adapting to various new technologies (microelectronics and hospitals) and a stable industry (food processing). In each industry, we identified similar patterns in firms' strategic choices which we labelled Prospector, Analyzer and Defender. (We also identified ineffective patterns of strategic choices which we labelled the Reactor.) Each of these labels indicates the strategy the firm uses to compete in its chosen markets, and each type has its own organization structure and management system that is specifically suited to its strategy. Subsequently, Miles and Snow (1984) argued that a firm's overall strategy must fit its environment (external fit), organization structures and management processes must align with strategy (internal fit) and the entire organization must continually adapt in order to maintain fit over time (dynamic fit). The three strategy types are described as follows:

> *Prospectors* are firms that continually develop new products, services, technologies and markets. They achieve success by moving first relative to their competitors, either by anticipating the market based on their research and development efforts or by building a market through their customer-relating capabilities.
>
> *Defenders* are firms with stable product or service lines that leverage their competence in developing process efficiencies. They search for economies of scale in markets that are predictable and expandable.
>
> *Analyzers* are firms that use their applied engineering and manufacturing skills to make a new product better and cheaper, and they use their marketing resources to improve product sales. They use proven

technologies with significant potential for generating new products and services.

Viewed from the perspective of the industry as a whole, innovation occurs because all three strategy types are present (Miles et al., 1993). That is, Prospectors create opportunities in the industry by developing new technologies. Analyzers follow Prospectors into new markets but tend to focus on those markets in which they already have products that can be enhanced or in which they have a particular process advantage. The unique capability of Analyzers lies in their ability to envision the market potential for a new product or technology and their skill in rapidly commercializing innovations. While Prospectors seek returns based on their ability to invent, Analyzers seek returns based on their ability to perform product modifications and enhancements using established technologies. For their part, Defenders focus on standardizing the technologies and products developed by other firms while lowering overall costs by becoming increasingly efficient.

Over the past three decades, management and marketing scholars have examined the Miles–Snow typology's validity and reliability (Shortell and Zajac, 1990); the research value of the typology compared to other prominent strategy typologies (Doty et al., 1993); the functional attributes and performance of the strategy types in different industries and countries (DeSarbo et al., 2005; Hambrick, 1983); how the strategy types can be changed and redirected (Zajac and Shortell, 1989); the relationship of each strategy type to the firm's marketing orientation (Olson et al., 2005; Slater et al., 2006); and the extent of the typology's use (Zahra and Pearce, 1990). Almost all of this research has been done on private sector firms which begs the question of the typology's applicability to public organizations. This is why the book by Rhys Andrews, George Boyne, Jennifer Law and Richard Walker is so important. More than any other group of researchers, they have used the Miles–Snow strategy typology to study the impact of strategic management on the performance of public service organizations. What they report in this book is most illuminating. First, strategic management makes a difference in how public organizations perform, just as it does in the private sector. Second, as might be expected, there are similarities in the behaviour of Prospectors and Defenders across both the sectors. Third, unlike our finding that Reactors are ineffective, this study finds that in some limited circumstances local government service agencies perform quite well using the Reactor approach. Beyond these broad findings, the book has many specific results, examples and implications that strategic management researchers will find valuable. Managers of public service agencies will appreciate the book because it confirms that their efforts to develop strategies and organizations specifically suited to the public sector are paying off.

References

DeSarbo, W. S., Di Benedetto, C. A., Song, M. and Sinha, I. 2005. 'Revisiting the Miles and Snow strategic framework: Uncovering interrelationships between strategic types, capabilities, environmental uncertainty, and firm performance', *Strategic Management Journal*, 26, 47–74.

Doty, D. H., Glick, W. H., and Huber, G. P. 1993. 'Fit, equifinality, and organizational effectiveness: A test of two configurational theories', *Academy of Management Journal*, 36, 1196–250.

Hambrick, D. C. 1983. 'Some tests of the effectiveness and functional attributes of Miles and Snow's strategic types', *Academy of Management Journal*, 26, 5–26.

Miles, G., Snow, C. C., and Sharfman, M. P. 1993. 'Industry variety and performance', *Strategic Management Journal*, 14, 163–77.

Miles, R. E. and Snow, C. C. 1978. *Organizational Strategy, Structure, and Process*. New York: McGraw-Hill.

Miles, R. E. and Snow, C. C. 1984. 'Fit, failure, and the hall of fame', *California Management Review* 26, 10–28.

Olson, E. M., Slater, S. F. and Hult, G. T. M. 2005. 'The performance implications of fit among business strategy, marketing orientation structure, and strategic behavior', *Journal of Marketing*, 69, 49–65.

Shortell, S. M. and Zajac, E. J. 1990. 'Perceptual and archival measures of Miles and Snow's strategic types: A comprehensive assessment of reliability and validity', *Academy of Management Journal*, 33, 817–32.

Slater, S. F., Olson, E. M. and Hult, G. T. M. 2006. 'The moderating influence of strategic orientation on the strategy formation capability-performance relationship', *Strategic Management Journal*, 27, 1221–31.

Zahra, S. A. and Pearce, J. A. 1990. 'Research evidence on the Miles-Snow typology', *Journal of Management*, 16, 751–68.

Zajac, E. J. and Shortell, S. M. 1989. 'Changing generic strategies – likelihood, direction, and performance implications', *Strategic Management Journal*, 10, 413–30.

Preface and Acknowledgements

This book brings together the authors' research interests over many years. Boyne, Law and Walker worked on a research project for the fledgling National Assembly for Wales from 1998 until 2000. This project examined the feasibility of implementing the 'Best Value' regime in Welsh local government. At the centre of this policy regime was a system of strategic management. This project on Best Value was the foundation for the first of a number of ESRC grants. The data reported in this book were collected on the first of these projects, and the study was entitled 'Strategy and Service Improvement in Local Government' which Andrews, Boyne, Law and Walker worked on from 2001 to 2006 (grant R000239249). Boyne and Walker secured Advanced Institute for Management Research Public Service Research Fellowships (ESRC/EPSRC funded) that drove forward this agenda (grant 331-25-0004 and 331-25-0006). Boyne's work focused on failure and turnaround in public agencies and Walker's on innovation. Both continued the agenda outlined in this book by asking questions about, and providing empirical evidence on, the performance of public agencies. Most recently Andrews, Boyne and Walker worked on 'How Public Management Matters: Strategy, Networking and Local Service Performance' (grant RES-062-23-00389) between 2006 and 2010. This project was undertaken in association with Kenneth J. Meier (Texas A&M University and Cardiff University) and Laurence J. O'Toole Jr. (University of Georgia), and the authors acknowledge the helpful thoughts and comments they have offered on the study of strategy in public agencies.

Many of the discussions associated with our research projects, teaching programmes and writing during this time took place in the Staff Common Room in Aberdare Hall at Cardiff University, and were fuelled by salads and copious amounts of tea and coffee. Beyond this, many people have contributed to the contents of this book. Portions of this agenda have been presented at conferences including the *American Academy of Management Meeting*, *British Academy of Management Conference*, *International Society for Public Management Research Conference* and *Public Management Research Association*. We are grateful for the range of comments and helpful feedback received at these events. Some readers may be familiar with components of the agenda laid out in this book, and have seen aspects of this work in *Administration & Society, Journal of Public Administration Research and Theory, Public Administration* and *Public Management Review*, and reviewers have assisted us in thinking through the various parts of the strategy–performance hypothesis. In this book, we have been able to empirically test large swaths of the Miles and Snow (1978) research framework, a task not possible in a single journal article. In doing this, we have substantially extended our prior work by re-analysing all our data and include considerable new evidence, particularly in the numerous joint effects models where we seek to tease out the contingent relationships that sit at the heart of the Miles and Snow's strategic management agenda. To this end, we would also like to acknowledge Raymond Miles and Charles Snow who attended a conference organized at Cardiff University in December 2008 titled *Organizational Strategy, Structure, and Process: A Reflection on the Research Perspective of Miles and Snow*. This event reflected the contributions made by Miles and Snow to the field of strategic management, and during it they generously shared their thoughts on the evolution of their research agenda from the 1970s through into the twenty-first century.

In sum, we see this book as the culmination and synthesis of our joint efforts to understand organizational strategy and performance in the public sector. We hope that others find it useful as a platform for further work in this important field.

Rhys Andrews
George A. Boyne
Jennifer Law
Richard M. Walker
Cardiff and Hong Kong, February 2011.

About the Authors

Rhys Andrews is Reader in Public Management at Cardiff Business School. Rhys' work has been published in *Human Relations, Journal of Public Administration Research and Theory, Public Administration, Public Administration Review* and *Public Management Review*. His research interests are in the determinants of performance in public organizations, organizational environments and social capital.

George A. Boyne is Professor of Public Sector Management and Dean at Cardiff Business School, Cardiff University, UK. He is Program Chair of the Public and Non-Profit Division of the Academy of Management. He has published regularly in journals such as *Public Administration, Journal of Public Administration Research and Theory, Public Administration Review* and the *Journal of Management Studies*. His previous books include *Constraints Choices and Public Policies, Public Choice Theory and Local Government, Evaluating Public Management Reforms, Public Service Performance: Perspectives on Measurement and Management, Public Service Improvement* and *Public Management and Performance: Research Directions*. His current research interests include executive succession, structural change and administrative intensity in public organizations.

Jennifer Law is a principal lecturer in the Department of Social Sciences at the University of Glamorgan. Jennifer's work has been published in *Public Administration, Journal of Public Administration Research and Theory, Administration and Society* and *Public Administration Review*. Her research interests are strategy implementation, accountability and outcome measurement.

Richard M. Walker is Professor of Public Management and policy in the Department of Public and Social Administration at the City University of Hong Kong. He has held professorships at Cardiff University and the University of Hong Kong and is currently Senior Research Associate, Centre for Performance Management, Xi'an Jiaotong University. Recent books include *Public Management and Performance: Research Directions* (with George A. Boyne and Gene A. Brewer), *Public Service Performance: Perspectives on Measurement and Management* (with George

A. Boyne, Kenneth J. Meier and Laurence J. O'Toole Jr.) and *The New Managerialism and Public Service Professions* (with Ian Kirkpatrick and Stephen Ackroyd). Richard's work has been published in *American Review of Public Administration, Journal of Management Studies, Journal of Policy Analysis and Management, Journal of Public Administration Research and Theory, Public Administration, Public Administration Review* and *Public Management Review.* His research interests are in the determinants of performance in public organizations, strategic management, innovation, red tape and sustainable development.

1 Introduction

In recent years it has become increasingly evident that the performance of public organizations is highly variable. Marked differences are present, for example, in the exam passes achieved by schools, death rates across hospitals, levels of crime successfully prevented and detected by police forces, rents collected by public housing authorities and the quality of care provided for elderly people in residential homes. The flood of performance indicators associated with 'new public management' reforms has produced much more comprehensive information on the successes and failures of different organizations, and revealed evidence of substantial inequality and ineffectiveness in service standards. These indicators of performance are, of course, open to interpretation and debate. Nevertheless, the evidence is overwhelming that, on specific criteria and measures of performance, some organizations are better than others at delivering effective public services. Taxpayers and service consumers cannot simply assume that they 'get what they pay for'; instead, service quantity and quality depends partly on where they live and whether local public organizations are performing well or poorly.

Our aim in this book is to contribute to the rapidly growing body of research that seeks to explain why such variations in performance exist. In particular, we focus on the impact of strategic management on the effectiveness of public services. Strategic management is traditionally associated with the behaviour of private firms in markets. To this end, strategy in the private sector is often viewed as a way of defeating rivals in competitive markets. Attention has been increasingly focused on the strategy of public organizations (Bryson et al., 2010; Lane and Wallis, 2009; Moore, 1995; Poister et al., 2010). In the public sector, strategy is more appropriately conceptualized as a means by which organizations can improve their performance and provide better services. It has been widely argued that strategic discretion is more limited in the public than in the private sector (Boyne, 2002; Perry and Rainey, 1988; Ring and Perry, 1985). For example, public organizations cannot easily switch into new markets, or quit a geographical location because it is inimical to good performance. Similarly, although public organizations often have monopoly powers and may be subject to only weak market pressures, their discretion is limited by political, legal and regulatory constraints. Nevertheless, a range of strategic options is available in the public sector, including product and process innovations such as the provision of new services, coverage of new client groups and delivery of services 'in house' or in collaboration with others (Boyne and Walker, 2004). Thus the concept of strategy is applicable in the public as well as in the private sector.

A long and rich tradition of research has examined the links between strategy and the commercial success of private firms (Mintzberg et al., 1998). By contrast, far less attention has been paid to the impact of strategy on performance in the public sector. Our work on this topic is motivated by a quest to discover whether strategy matters for public as well as private organizations. Does it make any difference if an organization seeks to achieve its objectives by continually searching for new arrangements for service delivery, by sticking with its tried and tested arrangements, or by waiting for instructions from higher levels of government? Should strategies be developed rationally and analytically through a formal planning process, or developed informally, iteratively and incrementally? And is it better to implement strategies through formal planning, incrementalism or some combination of the two? In this book we explore the theoretical basis of these questions, and provide empirical evidence on whether strategic management has an influence, positive or negative, on public service performance.

In this introductory chapter we discuss the meanings of the terms 'strategy' and 'performance', and set out the theoretical logic of potential links between them. Why should we expect public organizations with different strategies to achieve different service standards? We place these issues in the context of other theoretical perspectives on public service performance. We then summarize the sequence of the main chapters in the book, in which we consider the performance effects of the organizational environment, the content of strategies, how they are formulated and how they are implemented, and organizational structures. Taken together, our theoretical discussion and empirical evidence offer the most extensive analysis to date of whether strategy matters in the public sector, and adds significantly to existing perspectives on the determinants of public service performance.

What is organizational strategy?

Academic models of organizational strategy often conflate two or more of the following three concepts: (1) the strategic aim or 'mission' that is being pursued, (2) the means of achieving that aim (usually described as 'strategy content') and (3) the strategy processes that are used to determine the content of the strategy. For example, Whittington (2001) identifies four models of strategy for private firms: (1) classical ('analyse, plan and command'), (2) evolutionary ('keep your costs low and your options open'), (3) systemic ('play by the local rules') and (4) processual ('stay close to the ground and go with the flow'). He describes each of these as comprising one of two strategic aims (maximize profit or pursue plural objectives) and one of two types of processes (deliberate or 'emergent'). Unusually, strategy content does not feature explicitly in any of the four models, although it is implicit in them (in the extent to which organizations should lead market change, seek new options or conform to current external expectations). Rather than defining strategy in this 'compound' way, we believe that it is important to distinguish between aims, strategy content and strategy processes, not least so that the theoretical and empirical connections between them can be explored. We see these three elements as inter-dependent, as shown in Figure 1.1.

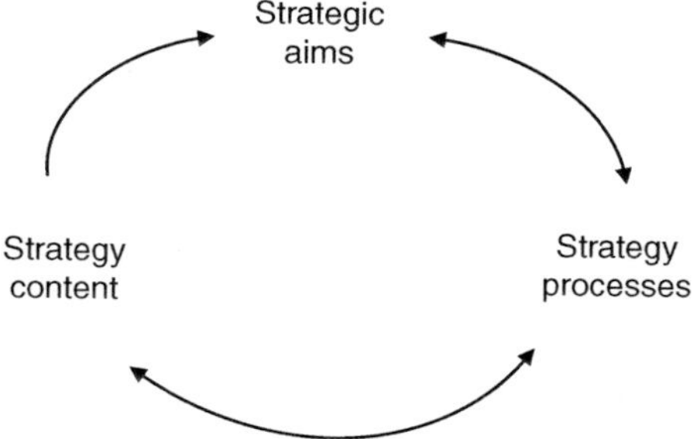

Figure 1.1 The elements of organizational strategy

In the private sector, organizations have substantial discretion to pursue their own strategic aims (e.g. to switch between product markets and geographical locations). By contrast, public organizations must usually live with objectives that have been set for them by political institutions that determine their powers and responsibilities and provide large parts of their funding. The nature of the strategic objectives is therefore subject to the political priorities of the government of the day, and any assessment of the impact of strategy content and processes must take account of this. For example, during the 1980s in the UK the emphasis was on the economy and efficiency of public services. Following the election of the Labour government in 1997, the focus switched to the improvement of service effectiveness. Managing fiscal austerity and cutback management became the focal point for strategy objectives for many Western nations following the global financial crisis of the early part of the twenty-first century. A consequence was that public service providers were expected to adopt strategy content and processes that would reduce their costs.

Strategy content is the way in which an organization seeks to achieve the objectives that have been selected (or selected for it). The major element of strategy content is how the organization relates to its environment, which is captured clearly in Miles and Snow's (1978) classic typology of strategies. Does an organization actively seek out new opportunities for providing existing services and opportunities for innovations in the types of service that are provided? Miles and Snow describe this type of organization as a 'prospector'. Does an organization instead concentrate its efforts on procedures rather than products, and seek to maintain a stable portfolio of services that are delivered reliably and at low cost? Miles and Snow characterize such organizations as 'defenders'. Or does an organization have no real strategy of its own, but instead take its cue from powerful actors in its environment, such as higher levels of government or regulatory agencies. Miles and Snow describe such organizations as 'reactors'. We draw upon the Miles and Snow framework in this book because it covers the three main options that are open to a public organization that seeks to meet the expectations of its external stakeholders: (1) search for something new, (2) stick with the existing pattern of services or (3) await instructions.

Strategy processes are the ways in which strategy content is formulated and implemented. As already noted, strategic objectives may be beyond the discretion of even senior managers in public organizations. Similarly, strategy content may be imposed on public organizations (e.g. in recent years central government in the UK has exhorted service providers to be more innovative, and to enter into partnerships with the private sector). Nevertheless, public managers have some autonomy with regard to strategy processes. For example, they may decide to undertake a lot of formal planning, by collecting and analysing large amounts of data on service needs, evaluating different options for meeting these needs and using sophisticated techniques to help them to weigh up the costs and benefits of each option. Alternatively, the preferred strategy process may comprise hunches, intuition and a reliance on the push and pull of organizational politics. Such 'rational' and 'incremental' approaches to the strategy process may apply not only to the formulation of strategies but also to how they are implemented. Despite the large literature on public policy implementation, little has been written on *strategy* implementation in the public sector. In this book, we seek to begin to redress this imbalance in the literature by analysing the links between public service performance and both the formulation and implementation of organizational strategies.

In sum, it is possible to differentiate between a number of elements of organizational strategy: aims, content and processes (and, within this last element, to distinguish between formulation and implementation). In this book, we treat strategic objectives as exogenous, because they are largely fixed for the organizations that we examine through the legislative requirements set by higher levels of government. We examine whether content and processes make a difference to the achievement of strategic objectives. Thus our basic model of the links between the various elements of strategy becomes, as shown in Figure 1.2.

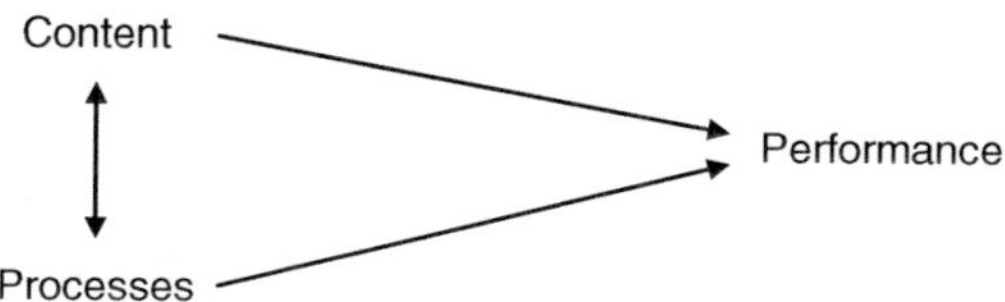

Figure 1.2 Strategy content, processes and performance

Contingency theory

The notion that the best way to organize is dependent upon the environment within which an organization is located, and that this fit in turn is a major influence on organizational performance, sits at the heart of contingency theory (Lawrence and Lorsch, 1969; Scott, 2001; Thompson, 1967). Contingency theory, predicated on the view that there is no one best way to organize, strikes at the heart of the approaches often adopted by governments to improve public services. It is not unusual for governments to roll out programmes of reform that apply to a variety of different types of public agencies – those charged with technical goals and those with human or social welfare-orientated objectives – and not to differentiate between the contexts within which they are located – rural, suburban or urban, complex or simple, munificent or miserly. For example, the Blair Labour government in the UK launched a programme of public service improvement in its second term in office (Blair, 2002; OPSR, 2002, 2003) – aspects of which were initially applied to Welsh local governments. This public service improvement strategy focused upon developing minimum standards (through performance management and target setting), devolution of responsibility, enhancing the flexibility of public organizations through leadership and improvement, offering incentives and increasing choice through contestability and user choice. Empirical analysis of this programme in English local government suggested that only some aspects assisted in performance improvement and that many organizations were required to implement reforms that had no consequence for their achievements (Walker and Boyne, 2006). Such one-size-fits-all approaches to the political management of public service organizations is a frequently cited criticism of government programmes of management reform (Walker and Enticott, 2004).

Contingency theory has been applied to the study of public organizations for some time. In the 1970s, Greenwood, Hinings and Ranson (1975a, 1975b) mounted a series of studies that examined organizational structure and argued that this was contingent on the organizational environment and the internal characteristics of goals, size and political control. The work has been extended to examine the relationship between organizational context and decision-making and the environment and budgets (Greenwood, 1987). While evidence that the organizational context affects the performance of public agencies is longstanding (see, e.g. Andrews et al., 2005a), other research has shown how organizational environments affect strategy (Pettigrew et al., 1988). The spotlight has also been turned to organizational processes, including strategic and corporate planning, and a number of important contingencies that lead to success, or otherwise, have been noted (Boyne, 2001; Clapham, 1984).

The strategy–environment fit is an important element in the Miles and Snow model. However, it receives comparatively less attention than the alignment of strategy with internal structures and processes. Nevertheless, it is clear that Miles and Snow believe that organizations have the discretion to adopt the strategy that is best suited to the circumstances that they face. For example, they follow Burns and Stalker (1961) in claiming that an organic structure is required in an uncertain environment, whereas a mechanistic structure is better in a predictable and stable environment. This implies that a strategy of prospecting should work best in an uncertain environment. Defending, by contrast, should be an especially effective strategy in the presence of environmental stability. Miles and Snow's arguments suggest that reacting will not be consistently linked to any set of external circumstances. However, while reactors 'do not possess a set of mechanisms which allows them to respond consistently to their environments over time' (Miles and Snow, 1978, 93), a dynamic and unpredictable environment may lead such organizations to seek cues from other external actors about the best way to respond to these circumstances.

While organizational environments are readily associated with contingency theory, it is traditionally and more strongly associated with the study of the technical environment. Miles and Snow's conceptualization of organizations and their environments fits this tradition, as does Dess and Beard's (1984) classic set of environmental dimensions of munificence, complexity and dynamism. However, as Scott (2003, xxii) notes, institutional perspectives '... call attention to the ways in which legal systems, widely shared belief systems, and norms define the environments of organizations and shape the response repertory available to any given organization'. Therefore, a systematic understanding of the contingent impact of the environment on organizational performance should include an examination of ways in which internal characteristics (in this case strategy) are affected by both the technical and the institutional environment. In this book, we take both types of external contingency into account when assessing the links between strategy and performance.

Theoretical perspectives on public service performance

Potential influences on organizational performance in the public sector can be categorized into three broad sets of variables: (1) the external environment, (2) internal organizational characteristics and (3) managerial strategies (Boyne, 2003b, 2004). In this section, we outline theories and evidence on the first two of these. We deal with the nature and theoretical effects of managerial strategies in the subsequent section.

External environment

Public organizations are 'open systems' (Easton, 1953) that are subject to influence by a number of aspects of their external environment, not least because they are accountable to a range of stakeholders and depend on other organizations (especially higher levels of government) for political and financial resources. As noted above, the external environment of any organization has two major components. First, the 'technical' environment that comprises characteristics such as the level of need for services, the financial resources available to purchase inputs to service production and market pressures towards efficiency and effectiveness. Prior research on these dimensions of the environment suggests that the complexity of service needs and the level of financial munificence are significant constraints on public service performance. For example, studies of Texas school districts and English local governments have shown that organizations in areas with a higher quantity and diversity of need (as measured, e.g. by the percentage of households with low incomes and the extent of social heterogeneity) are likely to be poorer performers. Similarly, if these organizations are blessed with more money (either from their own revenues or inter-governmental transfers), then they are likely to be able to achieve higher effectiveness in public service provision (Andrews et al., 2005a; Meier and O'Toole, 2006). Recent studies also find that higher dynamism in the external environment leads to lower performance (Andrews and Boyne, 2008; Boyne and Meier, 2009). By contrast, although the impact of market pressures has been studied widely (especially the extent of contracting-out to private suppliers), evidence on the impact on performance is mixed and inconclusive (Boyne, 2003a; Hodge, 2000). Accordingly in this book, we concentrate on the constraints imposed by munificence, complexity and dynamism, and seek to isolate the net effect of strategic management when these external influences on performance are incorporated in our empirical analyses.

The second component of the external circumstances in which public organizations operate is the institutional environment (Ashworth et al., 2009). Institutional theorists argue that organizational behaviour and performance are constrained by a set of external forces that bestow (or withhold) 'legitimacy'. An organization is perceived as legitimate by powerful stakeholders if its internal arrangements are consistent with prevailing norms (in other words, if it is managed in a way that is 'modern' or 'fashionable'). DiMaggio and Powell (1983) argue that organizations are subject to three types of pressures that shape their characteristics: (1) 'normative' (stemming from prevailing professional beliefs about appropriate management structures and processes), (2) 'mimetic' (arising from the ways in which organizations seek to copy and emulate their apparently more successful peers) and (3) 'coercive' (as a result of laws, regulations and accountability requirements imposed by the state). As public organizations are themselves part of the state, it is likely that coercive pressures upon them are particularly strong. This view is consistent with the findings of a range of studies of institutional pressures in the public sector, which have examined organizational strategies, structures and human resource practices (Frumkin and Galaskiewicz, 2004; Meyer et al., 1987; Rowan, 1982; Tolbert and Zucker, 1983). None of these studies, however, has examined the impact of coercive pressures on performance. During the era of new public management, public organizations have been subject to an 'audit explosion' (Hood et al., 1999; Power, 1997) that has unleashed a new range of regulation and inspection. We therefore seek to extend previous work on the institutional environment by examining whether such coercive pressures have positive or negative effects on public service performance.

Internal organizational characteristics

Public service performance is likely to be influenced not only by the external constraints that organizations face but also by their internal characteristics. A large literature on contingency theory suggests that organizations are not simply prisoners of their technical and institutional environments, but can adapt their internal arrangements in order to fit better with this environment and to boost their performance (Donaldson, 1996). The organizational attributes that have been included in studies of performance in the public sector include strategy processes, structures, culture and leadership (Boyne, 2004). The nature and impact of strategy processes are central elements of this book, and we further explore the theoretical rationale for this in the next section of this chapter. In addition, we focus on the impact of internal organizational structure on public service performance for a number of reasons.

First, structure is a core component of the Miles and Snow (1978) model of strategic management, both as a separate influence on performance and in combination with strategy content and processes. Other classic works in the strategic management field also emphasize the close connections between strategy and structure (e.g. Chandler, 1962). Thus there are strong theoretical reasons to expect that structure is part of the explanation for variations in organizational performance. Second, organizational structures in the public sector are often changed by policy makers and senior managers, perhaps because this appears to be an easier option than implementing other reforms such as changing the culture or composition of the workforce. In effect, structural change becomes the 'default strategy' that is frequently employed in the quest for public service improvement (Boyne, 2006). Finally, and perhaps reflecting the prominence of structural change on the policy agenda, structure is the internal organizational variable that has been tested most often in empirical studies of public service performance (Boyne, 2004). Prior work has considered the impact of organizational structure (and especially centralization) on a range of performance measures, but has not analysed whether structural effects are contingent on strategy content and processes. Accordingly, we seek to extend work in this area by applying the Miles and Snow (1978) model of strategy and structure to the performance of public organizations.

Why does strategic management make a difference to public service performance?

Strategic management is generally viewed as essential if organizations are to perform well. The generic management literature on strategy contains a large number of claims concerning the beneficial impact of strategic management on organizational functioning and effectiveness (Mintzberg et al., 1998). Strategy is believed to set a direction for collective effort, to help focus that effort towards desired goals and to promote consistency in managerial actions over time and across parts of the organization. The assumption here is that the presence of a clear and coherent strategy is better than the *absence* of identifiable content and processes (Inkpen and Chowdhury, 1995). This positive view of organizational strategy is also present in the public management literature. For example, Joyce (1999, 1) argues that 'strategic management has emerged as a multi-purpose tool which public services management must have to ensure that their organizations survive in the short and medium term and build for a long term future'. Similarly, according to Poister and Streib (1999, 308) 'effective public administration in the age of results-oriented management requires public agencies to develop a capacity for strategic management, the central management process that integrates all major activities and functions and directs them towards advancing an organization's strategic agenda'.

Yet, although an identifiable strategy may be regarded as necessary for good performance, it is clearly not sufficient. Strategy content and strategy processes may be perfectly clear but perfectly useless (or worse). Our aim in this book is to explore the styles of strategic management that are associated with high (or low) performance. Which strategy content and processes are most likely to lead to better public service performance?

This question is based on a number of assumptions, and it is important to make these explicit.

The first assumption that underpins the argument that 'strategy matters' is that performance is not completely determined by the technical and institutional environments and by organizational characteristics such as structure. Many studies in the private sector have shown that scope is left for the strategies that are adopted by organizations to influence their achievements (Bowman and Helfat, 2001). The impact of strategy may either sit alongside environmental and organizational variables as a separate contributor to performance, or it may moderate external and internal variables by strengthening or weakening their effects. In either case, even after environmental and organizational constraints are taken into account, sufficient space remains for strategy content and processes to leave an imprint on organizational effectiveness. The low-to-moderate levels of statistical explanation in studies of performance that include only environmental and organizational variables provide indirect support for this assumption (Boyne, 2003a).

A second assumption concerns the existence of causal mechanisms that link strategy to performance. One such mechanism may be the pure symbolism of a strategy that is recognizable to internal and external stakeholders. A strategy that is linked to identifiable goals for performance improvement may help to generate support from managers and front-line staff (Chun and Rainey, 2005). Beyond this, strategies that are viewed as legitimate by powerful groups in the institutional environment are likely to lead to greater financial and political support for an organization, and thereby lead to better service performance. Thus internal and external political forces are likely to explain part of the link between strategy and performance. In addition, strategies have technical characteristics that can help to deliver better results. For example, organizations with explicit strategies may spend more time researching client needs and evaluating different ways to meet these needs effectively. They may also be benchmarking their internal procedures against those used by other organizations, and seeking to align their strategy content, structures and processes in ways that boost performance. Thus the adoption of a specific strategy is likely to have a range of primary and secondary effects that have consequences for performance.

A final important assumption is that strategic management actually varies across public organizations. Performance differences cannot be attributable to strategy differences if all organizations have the same content and processes. Evidence of variations in strategy is provided by several studies of public organizations. For example, Greenwood (1987) finds differences in the extent of prospecting, defending and reacting across English local governments. Similar strategy variations are present across US local governments (Stevens and McGowan, 1983) and public agencies in Ohio (Wechsler and Backoff, 1986). Such evidence implies that, at some juncture, organizations may have made *choices* to pursue strategies of prospecting, defending or reacting, and to use rational or incremental processes. As Bourgeois (1984, 591) argues, 'the top management or dominant coalition always retains a certain amount of discretion to choose courses of action that serve to co-align the organization's resources with its environmental opportunities, and to serve the values and preferences of management'. Of course, even the same strategy may have different effects in different organizational environments or in combination with different organizational characteristics, but the source of performance variations would be these latter variables rather than strategic management *per se*.

In sum, we assume that strategic management is important because it varies across public organizations, and is not simply a trivial or redundant category once the impact of environmental and organizational variables is taken into account. Indeed, strategy itself shapes the impact of external and internal constraints on performance, and is thereby both directly and indirectly linked to performance. Taken together, these assumptions imply that strategy matters in principle; in the remainder of this book, we investigate to what extent, and in what ways, it matters in practice.

Plan of the book

Chapter 2 considers the relationship between the organizational environment and the performance of public services. Organizational environments are a key issue in management research. However, despite widespread acknowledgement of the unique circumstances that public organizations confront and a wide evidence base on spatial variations in the broader context that they face, a surprisingly small number of studies have systematically conceptualized organizational environments in the public sector and investigated their relationship with performance. The chapter explores the impact of key aspects of the external technical and institutional environment on the performance of public organizations. In doing so, we build on and develop existing theories of the organizational environment. We also outline our approach to conceptualizing and measuring public service performance, paying particular attention to concepts and measures of organizational effectiveness. The chapter also provides details on the controls variables used in all of the multivariate statistical models in later chapters.

Chapter 3 focuses on strategy content. The Miles and Snow typology of strategy content is introduced prior to a review of the existing literature on content and performance. The literature focusing on the Miles and Snow (1978) framework, and the strategic stances of prospecting, defending and reacting is burgeoning, though we note that the majority of this evidence has been collected on private organizations and that the contribution to this knowledge base is somewhat limited. While Miles and Snow's original conception was that prospectors and defenders achieve equal levels of performance, and both outperform reactors, we move on to the hypotheses that there is a hierarchy of strategic stances which descend from prospectors to defenders and finally to reactors. The former two have positive associations with performance; however, a reactor stance is likely to damage the performance of a public agency. In Chapter 3, we also introduce our approach to the measurement of strategy. We build upon Boyne and Walker's (2004) argument and operationalize strategy as a continuous rather than categorical variable, thereby allowing organizations to display a mix of strategic stances. We then move on to present statistical evidence on the validity of our hypotheses on strategy content and performance.

Chapter 4 examines the effects of strategy formulation processes on performance. It also probes questions about the combined effects of content and formulation processes on performance, and examines their joint and interactive effects. To this end, we further elaborate on the relationships between strategy, process and performance outlined by Miles and Snow. The chapter commences with a review of the existing literature on formulation and performance. We examine the dominant approaches to formulation – rational planning and logical incrementalism together with strategy process absence. The review leads us to hypothesize that there will be positive effects arising from strategy-making processes associated with rational planning but that logical incrementalism and strategy absence will be harmful to public service performance. These independent effects are empirically examined prior to moving on to joint and interactive effects. In this part of the chapter, we draw explicitly on the contingency theory outlined by Miles and Snow over three decades ago. This leads us to propose that incrementalism is likely to have a positive relationship with performance when combined with prospecting and that rational planning is positively related to performance in an organization with a defender stance. We address these issues with statistical evidence and qualitative interview material from our sample of Welsh local governments.

In Chapter 5, the focus is upon strategy implementation and its relationship with strategy content and public service performance. Questions central to this book are again present here when we ask: How does implementation style affect performance? Is the impact of implementation style contingent on strategy content? Whereas in other chapters we were able to draw upon the burgeoning private sector literature, our starting point in this chapter is to note the lack of existing evidence on implementation styles, strategy content and performance. Given this, we identify implementation approaches associated with the rational and incremental processes discussed in Chapter 4, and examine independent and joint effects parallel to the hypotheses developed there – for example, that incremental implementation processes are likely to be associated with successful performance in prospectors. We empirically model these and discuss the statistical results and our qualitative interview findings.

Chapter 6 evaluates the relationship between organizational structure, strategy and performance. Contingency theories have long devoted considerable attention to structural fit within organizations, especially in relation to the relative degree of centralization. We focus on the independent and combined effects of two key aspects of centralization on performance: (1) participation in decision-making and (2) hierarchy of authority. Existing evidence on the relationship between centralization and performance is inconclusive: neither centralized nor decentralized decision-making is consistently associated with service improvement. We argue that the relationship between structure and performance is likely to be contingent on other salient organizational characteristics, especially strategy content and process. In particular, Miles and Snow (1978) claim that prospecting organizations will perform better if decision-making is decentralized and if processes are fluid and informal, as this will permit middle managers the leeway required to identify and adopt innovative service delivery solutions. By contrast, defending organizations thrive when decisions are centralized and processes formal and planned, as this will enable senior managers to exert greater control over service delivery decisions and their costs. We explore these arguments using multivariate statistical techniques and qualitative interview material.

In Chapter 7, we delve more deeply into understanding organizational environments and examine their relationship with strategy and performance. We do this in two parts. Initially, we examine the technical environment focusing in particular on munificence, complexity and dynamism as well as the ways in which strategy content, strategy formulation and strategy implementation moderate the beneficial or detrimental effects of the organizational context. Hypotheses are developed for these various interactions thus: munificence is argued to strengthen all the positive relationships between content, formulation and implementation developed thus far in the book. Complexity and dynamism are argued to strengthen positive relationships between prospecting and performance, weaken the relationship for defending and have no impact for organizations with a reactor stance. Similar hypotheses are developed for incremental, rational and strategy absence processes and implementation approaches.

The second part of Chapter 7 examines the institutional environment, with a focus upon processes of regulation and inspection. Regulation has grown apace in the delivery of public services in the UK over recent decades (Hood et al., 2000; Power, 1997), and is a standard feature in the operating environment of all public agencies. While regulation is developed to ensure that there are checks and balances in the system, it represents an additional cost and burden to all public agencies as they deliver services. Regulation is a broad area of activity that includes audit, plans, budgetary controls and performance indicators. One of the more prevalent practices has been the use of inspection to regulate services, and we focus upon this regulatory mechanism. We argue that an inspection event will be disruptive for an organization on two counts: (1) the visit has to be prepared for within existing resources and (2) the recommendations of inspectors have to be followed up to comply with their requirements. Hypotheses are developed which suggest that inspection weakens the relationship between strategy content, processes and performance. If regulation is seen to be supportive, these effects will not be seen; rather, the relationship will be shifted in a positive direction.

The Appendices deal with the research context and methods. Appendix 1 provides more details for readers who are unfamiliar with Welsh local government. Appendix 2 provides details on our data and more technical aspects of our methods for researching strategy and performance, which draw upon quantitative and qualitative methodologies. Our approach to researching this topic takes a departure from much of the strategy and public management literature. We adopt a multiple informant survey approach to collect data on strategy and other aspects of management. This deviates from the typical approach in that much of the literature relies upon single informants; often elites who may be somewhat removed from many of the questions we examine.

In Chapter 8, we return to questions central to the book: Does strategic management matter? Does strategy content make a difference to organizational achievements? Do processes of formulation and implementation affect performance? Do content and processes interact to affect performance? Is the impact of strategic management contingent on the external environment and internal organizational structure? We offer answers to these questions by summarizing our empirical findings. Conclusions are drawn for theories of the relationship between strategy processes, strategy content and public service performance. We identify research questions for further work on strategy and organizational performance in the public sector, and the practical implications of our study are summarized.

2
Organizational Environments and Performance

The organizational environment is a key issue in management and organization studies (Boyd and Gove, 2006). Contingency theorists, in particular, posit a direct link between the relative 'task difficulty' that the environment poses and organizational outcomes (see Donaldson, 2001). In this chapter, we theorize the nature of the organizational environment in the public sector, distinguishing between its technical and institutional aspects; survey the existing quantitative evidence on the environment–performance relationship in public organizations; and empirically assess the effects of the technical and institutional environment on the achievements of local government service departments in Wales. Drawing on the Miles and Snow model, we then go on to examine the combined effects of the environment and strategic management on public service performance in subsequent chapters.

Miles and Snow emphasize that managers make strategic choices about their organization's relationship with the environment. Actively shaping the organization and its structures and processes to meet contextual challenges is therefore a key goal of strategic management – and one with serious implications for organizational outcomes. Indeed, Miles and Snow (1978) suggest that performance is ultimately dependent on the adoption of strategies, structures and processes that are aligned with an organization's environment. To explore the impact of the organizational environment on performance, this chapter draws on the model of the task environment developed by Dess and Beard (1984) to conceptualize the technical operating circumstances faced by public organizations. It then examines recent theories of the institutional environment in the public sector. Existing evidence on the impact of the technical and institutional environment on public service performance is reviewed, and hypotheses on the environment–performance relationship are developed. The measures of performance that we use for our empirical analyses are also described, along with measures of the technical and institutional environment. Finally, the results of our empirical analysis are presented and discussed.

Organizational environments

The conceptualization and measurement of organizational environments is a key theme within organization theory. Boulding (1978) reminds us that, broadly speaking, environments are 'everything else' beyond the immediate boundary of the organization. First and foremost, this comprises the technical constraints that are placed on how an organization delivers goods and services, such as the sheer quantity and diversity of clients' needs and demands. But it also encompasses the institutional constraints that legitimize certain forms of organizational activity and proscribe others, such as the formal and informal regulations through which powerful external stakeholders restrict an organization's behaviour.

Organizational theorists have developed a variety of methods for conceptualizing an organization's environment. Some of these, such as Michael Porter's (1980) well-known 'Five Forces' model focus on features of the environment faced by private firms, such as market structure and competition. Others, such as the popular Political, Economic, Social, Technological, Environmental and Legal (PESTEL) analysis (Johnson and Scholes, 2002), are basic classification schema rather than theoretically coherent accounts of the antecedents and effects of organizational environments. In this chapter, two key theoretical perspectives on the environment shape the empirical analysis that follows: Dess and Beard's (1984) model of organizational task environments, and the insights of institutional theory (Scott, 2001).

Drawing on contingency theories, Dess and Beard (1984) identify three dimensions of the organizational environment that influence the behaviour of organizations: (1) *munificence* (resource capacity), (2) *complexity* (client homogeneity–heterogeneity, concentration–dispersion) and (3) *dynamism* (environmental stability–instability, turbulence). These analytical categories are arguably as applicable in the public as they are in the private sector, since issues of capacity, client characteristics and environmental change are all key to strategic management in public and private organizations. Moreover, the openness of these categories means that they are able to incorporate the insights of other theoretical perspectives on the organizational environment, such as those found in institutional theory.

In this chapter, we do not seek to examine in full the many varieties of institutional theory. Rather, for the sake of clarity and brevity, we focus on one key aspect of institutional theory: the regulative aspect of the institutional environment. By this we mean those 'explicit regulatory processes' within an organizational field that encompass 'rule-setting, monitoring, and sanctioning activities' (Scott, 2001, 52). These processes often operate through more or less formal social and political structures which exert isomorphic pressures towards legitimacy on organizations (DiMaggio and Powell, 1983). Such pressures are sometimes regarded as a defining characteristic of the 'publicness' of public organizations (Boyne, 2002). Beyond the legal constraints placed upon public organizations, perhaps the most pervasive regulatory process that they now experience is the audit and inspection of their service provision (Martin, 2010). In fact, some commentators have argued that the public sector has experienced an 'audit explosion' in recent times (Power, 1997). The three dimensions of the environment identified by Dess and Beard (1984) are now described in more detail, and adapted to a public sector context, before the place of audit and inspection within the institutional environment is examined.

The technical environment: The Dess and Beard (1984) model

Munificence within the technical environment is constituted by 'the scarcity or abundance of critical resources' for operational activities (Castrogiovanni, 1991, 452). A high level of resource munificence can facilitate 'organizational growth and stability' (Dess and Beard, 1984, 55). It can also buffer organizations from environmental pressures by generating financial slack (Cyert and March, 1963). Although budgetary processes in the public sector work against the accrual of slack, there are several ways in which public organizations might experience a munificent environment. For instance, where there are more community-based organizations present within an area, public organizations can generate increased capacity for the delivery of services. A further important aspect of munificence is the political support organizations are able to mobilize, especially in times of crisis (Hirschman, 1970). Critically, the 'resource publicness' of public organizations makes them especially sensitive to changes in such levels of munificence, as their finances and institutional legitimacy are largely dependent on non-market sources (Bozeman, 1987).

Environmental complexity reflects the heterogeneity and the dispersion of an organization's clients. In a heterogeneous environment, organizations grapple with a wide range of markets, services and stakeholders (Dess and Beard, 1984), leading to greater strain on the existing resources of an organization (Dutton et al., 1983). Environmental dispersion is present where organizations provide services to widely dispersed clients (Dess and Beard, 1984). This generates additional costs because it increases the need for regional and local service production and supply arrangements. By contrast, where clients are narrowly concentrated, scope economies are likely to accrue (Starbuck, 1976). The environment faced by public organizations is usually a complex one because they often serve a heterogeneous and widely dispersed population.

Environmental dynamism comprises the rate of change in external circumstances (instability), and the unpredictability (or turbulence) of that change (Emery and Trist, 1965). Like environmental complexity, dynamism adds costs to service delivery because it increases the resources burden required to plan service production effectively (Dess and Beard, 1984). Unlike private firms operating in a competitive economic market, major shifts in the technical environment of public organizations are often known in advance (e.g. demographic change) and play a central role in central and local government planning and decision-making (Nutt and Backoff, 1993). Nevertheless, deviations from expected environmental changes may be especially likely to affect public service providers because they have less scope for entering new markets or changing service provision (Ginter et al., 2002). We turn now to the institutional environment in the public sector.

The institutional environment: Public services audit and inspection

The institutional environment comprises those constraints imposed on organizations by key external stakeholders. Rather than reflecting the needs of service users that compose the technical environment, the institutional environment is a product of the demands made by suppliers of organizational funding and legitimacy. A defining characteristic of the institutional environment of the public sector is the scale, scope and extent of the regulatory constraints imposed by government upon service delivery organizations (Bozeman, 1987). Unlike their private sector counterparts, public organizations are largely subject to political principals who seek to circumscribe their activities in line with some predefined set of goals (James, 2000). Such constraints have conventionally been associated with accountability requirements in the public sector, especially the need to ensure probity and equity. In the UK in recent years, however, regulation not only expanded significantly (Hood et al., 1999, 2000) but also shifted in a new direction. In particular, the audit and inspection of public bodies became an instrument for promoting service improvement. The main novelty here was the growth in the number of agencies and instruments for enhancing service performance, especially in health care and local government.

Traditionally, inspection was seen as solely an accountability mechanism, focused on providing assurance to central government that minimum service standards were being met (Rhodes, 1981). It was restricted to a small number of local services, including policing, fire and schools. During the past decade, all local services, councils, prisons and National Health Service (NHS) trusts became subject to formal inspection procedures that assessed and classified their performance. This expansion of regulatory pressure emerged in response to high-profile failures, especially in the NHS, and mirrored the wider growth of an 'audit society' (Power, 1997). At the heart of these developments was the notion that the performance of public organizations should be measured, monitored and made public. Thus, the exertion of ever-greater regulatory pressure was anticipated to drive service standards upwards through a variety of more or less overt coercive processes, including the use of naming and shaming or sanction threats.

Beyond providing public assurance that minimum quality thresholds are being met, audit and inspection are also regarded as compensating for the absence of competitive pressures in the public sector. The introduction of public processes of benchmark or yardstick competition, in the shape of performance classification, encourages organizations to do better in the contest for residentially mobile clients. Clear and comparable performance information is hypothesized to lead to better services by enhancing the 'voice' of service users and their awareness of 'exit' options (Hirschman, 1970). If service users are unhappy with the quality of service that they receive from a particular organization, then they can simply 'vote with their feet' in search of a better deal (Tiebout, 1956). This, in turn, is hypothesized to generate efficiencies as competition for clients becomes more intense (Salmon, 1987).

In addition to being a quasi-market mechanism, the actual process of audit and inspection itself is hypothesized to lead to better service provision. By working with and helping public services to understand their own achievements more clearly, auditors and inspectors can play a vital role in stimulating improvement. This is largely thought to be accomplished through the promotion of 'best practice' models of management and service delivery (see Office for Public Service Reform, 2003). While such isomorphic pressure may have dysfunctional consequences on organizational behaviour in the public sector (Hargreaves, 1995), it is claimed by the supporters of public service audit and inspection that local flexibility and knowledge creation can be incorporated within the inspector–inspectee relationship (Grace, 2005; Office for Public Service Reform, 2003). Indeed, inspectorates may come to regard themselves 'primarily as an improvement agency... [that] aspires to work hand-in-hand with senior managers to the benefit of all stakeholders' (Humphrey, 2002, 470). This indicates that there are two key dimensions of the regulatory environment confronted by public services: the first is the pressure exerted by the sheer quantity and intensity of audit and inspection events; while the second is the degree to which oversight is perceived to be supportive of the efforts of organizations to improve services.

Prior evidence on organizational environments and public service performance

This section reviews empirical evidence from research which has focused explicitly on isolating the independent impact of the technical and institutional environment on public service performance. The objective of the review is to furnish a preliminary assessment of the likely nature of the environment–performance relationship, which can guide the formulation of testable hypotheses. The review begins with an assessment of the quantitative research examining the effects of each dimension of the technical environment identified by Dess and Beard, before considering the available evidence on the relationship between regulation and performance.

Studies of the technical environment and performance

A wide range of studies assess the effects of the technical environment in the public sector at the individual level, especially for health (e.g. Shah and Cook, 2008; Wilkinson, 1997), and educational outcomes (e.g. Jasinski, 2000; Tam and Bassett, 2004). However, to date, far less research has examined the relationship between the technical environment and organizational performance in the public sector. To identify published studies which analyse the impact of the technical environment on public service performance, a thorough review of the available evidence requires the adaptation of search terms for each of the environmental dimensions identified by Dess and Beard. For environmental munificence, terms such as 'deprivation', 'poverty' and 'resources' were used; for complexity, 'diversity', 'heterogeneity' and 'sparsity'; and, for dynamism, 'change', 'growth' and 'instability'. At the same time, it was necessary to supplement searches using the term 'performance', with other relevant terms (e.g. achievement, effectiveness). This extensive search revealed only 12 studies that quantitatively analyse the relationship between some feature of the technical environment and organizational performance in the public sector. The selected studies were all undertaken in single countries, with most being conducted in England (7), with the US represented on three occasions, and Norway and Scotland once each. The content of the relevant studies examining the technical environment is summarized in Table 2.1.

Table 2.1 Impact of technical environment on public service performance

Study	Organizations and sample size	Dimension of technical environment	Measure of performance	Net effect on performance
Andrews (2004)	144 English local governments, 2000–01	Munificence	Best Value performance indicators	Low munificence associated with worse performance
Andrews and Boyne (2008)	148 English local government areas, 2002–04	Munificence Complexity Dynamism	Failure judgements made by regulatory agencies	High munificence associated with less failure, high complexity and dynamism with more failure
Andrews et al. (2005a)	147 English local governments, 2002	Munificence Complexity	Comprehensive performance assessments	High munificence associated with better performance, high complexity with worse
Croll (2002)	40 English primary schools, 1997	Munificence	Standard assessment tests	Low munificence associated with worse performance
Gordon and Monastiriotis (2006)	779 English secondary schools, 1999	Munificence	5 GCSEs A* – C	Low munificence associated with worse performance

Table 2.1 (Continued)

Study	Organizations and sample size	Dimension of technical environment	Measure of performance	Net effect on performance
Hall and Leeson (2010)	607 Ohio school districts, 1999	Complexity	Maths test scores	High munificence associated with better performance, high complexity with worse
Gutiérrez-Romero et al. (2008)	148 English local governments, 2002–04	Munificence Complexity	Comprehensive performance assessments	High munificence associated with better performance, high complexity with worse
Lynch (1995)	208 Scottish general practices, 1991–92	Munificence	Child immunizations	Low munificence associated with worse performance
Meier and Bohte (2003)	1043 Texas School districts, 1995–98	Complexity	Absenteeism, student retention, class dropout	High complexity associated with more failure
Odeck and Alkadi (2004)	47 Norwegian bus operators, 1994	Complexity	Efficiency	Low dispersion associated with scale efficiency
West et al. (2001)	96 English local service departments, 1996	Munificence	KS1 target met 5 GCSEs A*–G 5 GCSEs A*–C	Low munificence associated with poor performance
Xu (2006)	50 US state governments, 2001	Munificence Complexity	Health achievement index	High munificence associated with better performance, high complexity with worse

The studies exploring organizational environments and public service performance rarely draw upon a comprehensive theoretical model of the environment. Rather, they tend to focus on the relationship between one or more specific features of the technical environment in the public sector, such as deprivation (e.g. Croll, 2002) or neighbourhood segregation (e.g. Gordon and Monastiriotis, 2006), and investigate the links between these features and public service outcomes. Nevertheless, the studies do provide an initial platform for developing an understanding of the relationship between the technical environment and performance. The evidence covers a wide range of public services ranging from single-purpose organizations, such as schools, to multipurpose organizations, such as local governments. Each of the studies typically draws on a large sample of organizations and utilizes different dependent variables, including measures of organizational failure. They all use formal tests of statistical significance, and most implement multivariate techniques to control for the potential effects of other relevant contextual variables.

Four studies examine the effects of technical *munificence* alone on performance. West et al. (2001) focus on levels of poverty and educational attainment in 96 English local government education departments. In this study, indicators gauging the proportion of children experiencing socio-economic disadvantage are used to measure munificence, and three measures of education performance in 1996 are adopted: (1) the proportion of six-year-olds attaining the expected level of achievement; (2) the percentage of pupils of school-leaving age attaining one or more General Certificates in Secondary Education (GCSE) grades A–G; and (3) the percentage attaining five or more GCSE grades A–C. All of the measures of poverty were found to have separate and combined negative effects on each measure of performance.

Croll (2002) considers the extent to which the academic achievement of pupils in 40 English primary schools is influenced by levels of socio-economic munificence. The percentage of pupils eligible for free school meals is used as a measure of the relative level of poverty within each school. The proportion of key stage 2 pupils (11-year-olds) attaining level 4 or above in the 1997 Standard Assessment Tests (SATs) served as a measure of academic performance. Croll finds a very strong negative correlation (−0. 70) between free school meal eligibility and achievement in the SATs.

Andrews (2004) examines the impact of socio-economic munificence on 144 English local governments. The Average Ward Score on the Index of Multiple Deprivation (Department of Environment, Transport and Regions, 2000) serves as a measure of low munificence. This is the standard population-weighted measure of deprivation used by UK central government, which gauges the extent of disadvantage in different domains (e.g. income, employment and health). Measures of local government performance are drawn from the statutory Best Value Performance Indicators (BVPIs) for 2000. Bivariate correlations reveal that three-quarters of the education indicators, half of the housing and waste management indicators and a third of those for benefits administration were negatively correlated with deprivation.

Lynch (1995) assesses differences between child immunization rates in 208 general practices in deprived and prosperous areas in Greater Glasgow. Deprivation was measured using the Jarman index, which comprises items of particular relevance for health-care provision: elderly living alone; single-parent households; under-fives; overcrowded households; unskilled workers; house-movers; unemployed; and residents in ethnic minorities. Performance was measured as the achievement of high-target payments for childhood immunization uptake rates of 90 per cent or more during the four-quarters of 1991–92. Lynch finds a statistically significant relationship between deprivation and non-achievement of the performance target.

Public organizations arguably face a more complex technical environment than their private sector counterparts, due to the contested nature of the public sphere and the mandated role of public service providers in responding to multiple dimensions of market failure (Hoggett, 2006). However, only one study focuses exclusively on the effects of heterogeneity on public service performance, and only one other on the impact of dispersion.

Meier and Bohte (2003) examine the impact of various measures of task *heterogeneity* on organizational 'micro-failures' in over 1000 Texas school districts during a four-year period (1995–98). Three measures are used to gauge relative complexity: (1) the percentage of black students; (2) the percentage of Latino students; and (3) the percentage of low-income students. Failure within school districts is measured in terms of absenteeism rates, class retentions and student dropouts. Meier and Bohte find that school districts in Texas are more likely to have high absenteeism if they have a higher percentage of black and Latino students. The class dropout rate is also influenced by numbers of low-income students, with retention better in districts with a low percentage of such students, as well as a lower percentage of black students.

Odeck and Alkadi (2004) assess whether the performance of 47 Norwegian public transport services is harmed by the presence of scale and scope diseconomies in rural areas. The effects of *dispersion* are gauged by using urban/regional dummies. Transport performance is evaluated by deriving efficiency scores, measured as outputs (seat and passenger kilometres) divided by inputs (number of seats, driving hours, staff, fuel consumption and equipment) for 1994. Odeck and Alkadi show that the provision of services in rural areas is significantly associated with scale diseconomies, but not scope diseconomies. They go on to speculate that geographical aspects of rural areas, such as the terrain, may be responsible for their findings, but do not test for this.

Five studies have explored the impact of both environmental *munificence and complexity* taken together. Andrews et al. (2005a) assess the performance of 147 English local governments. Four measures of munificence are used. First, the needs-based grant distributed by central government to local governments in 2001. Second, the proportion of lone-parent households. Third, population growth in each area in 2001, and finally, population size in the same year. Environmental heterogeneity was measured as age diversity, ethnic diversity and social class diversity, while population density served as a proxy for the relative 'concentration–dispersion' of clients. Comprehensive Performance Assessments (CPAs) undertaken by the Audit Commission in 2002, which categorize local governments on the basis of performance indicators and inspection results (Audit Commission, 2002), were used to gauge performance. The authors find that socio-economic munificence is conducive to better service performance, but that socio-economic heterogeneity makes high standards more difficult to achieve.

The findings of Andrews et al. (2005a) are corroborated and extended in a subsequent analysis of the performance of English local governments carried out by Gutiérrez-Romero et al. (2008). Based on panel data analysis, they find that different dimensions of multiple deprivation have varying effects on CPAs, with poor skills, high crime and poor living environment having a statistically significant negative effect, but poor housing and low income no significant effect.

The impact of socio-economic munificence and complexity on educational outcomes is considered in Gordon and Monastiriotis' (2006) study of 779 secondary schools in Greater London. Munificence is measured as the proportion of lone-parent families and unemployed adults within the school catchment area. Complexity is gauged as the percentage of population that is Asian, black, other non-white, and the percentage of the population that is professional social class and manual social class. School performance is measured as the percentage of pupils attaining 5 or more GCSE grades A–C in 1999. The statistical results suggest that low munificence is associated with worse school examination performance. Schools serving larger middle class and Asian feeder populations performed better, indicating that some dimensions of heterogeneity may have a positive relationship with public service performance.

Hall and Leeson (2010) examine the impact of poverty and racial fractionalization on the performance of 607 Ohio school districts, when controlling for other relevant contextual features. Munificence is measured as the rate of free school lunches within a district, while complexity is gauged as the relative ethnic diversity of school district's population. The percentage of students passing their 9th Grade maths tests serves as a measure of performance. Hall and Leeson find that both poverty and ethnic diversity have a statistically significant negative effect on performance.

Xu (2006) assesses the impact of demographic and economic characteristics on health achievement across the 50 US states. Munificence is gauged as the percentage of individuals below the poverty line and the unemployment rate. Environmental heterogeneity is measured using indicators of percentage of females; percentage of population aged 65 or over; and the percentage of minorities. Percentage urban population represents a proxy for dispersion. The Health Achievement Index (HAI) for 2001 is used as a measure of state health performance. The HAI gauges the level and distribution of self-rated health. High levels of poverty and unemployment were associated with poorer health achievement. Higher proportions of females, older individuals and minorities in the population were also associated with lower health achievement, while a large urban population was associated with better achievement.

Although dynamism is arguably characteristic of technical environments in the public sector (Boyne, 2002; Ginter et al., 2002), there is currently little research investigating its independent influence on public service performance. Nevertheless, Andrews and Boyne (2008) furnish evidence on its impact when controlling for munificence and complexity. Indeed, their study provides a comprehensive analysis of the Dess and Beard model of the organizational task environment.

Andrews and Boyne (2008) examine the effects of technical *munificence, complexity* and *dynamism* on the likelihood of public organizations operating within 148 English local government administrative areas being classified as failing by regulatory agencies. Socio-economic munificence is measured as the average ward score on the index of multiple deprivation in each local area and the population size and growth in each area. Environmental heterogeneity is measured as ethnic and social class diversity, and diversity in the proportions of the population that are young and elderly. Population density is used to gauge 'concentration–dispersion'. Dynamism measures were created by multiplying the extent and the unpredictability of change between 1991 and 2001 for each of the munificence and complexity measures. Public service failure between 2002 and 2004 was measured as the number of health trusts scoring 0 stars; councils attaining 'poor' CPA scores; 'poor' local education authorities; 'poor' social services departments; schools 'subject to special measures'; other local authority services classified as 'poor'; 'poor' police authority services; fire authorities 'making no progress on the modernisation agenda'; and 'poor' performing prisons. The statistical results suggest that organizations are more likely to fail if they confront an environment low in munificence, complex (in both the diversity and distribution of client groups) and dynamic (especially if changes in munificence are unpredictable).

The evidence reviewed above illustrates that variations in public service performance are, as expected, influenced by measures of the environmental munificence, complexity and dynamism confronted by organizations. This highlights that it is important to take the potential impact of the technical environment into account when studying strategic management and performance.

Studies of the institutional environment and performance

To date, little research has systematically investigated the effects of the institutional environment faced by public service providers at either the organizational or individual level. There is a fast-growing literature on the impact of self-regulation programmes on the environmental performance of industrial firms (e.g. Darnell and Sides, 2008; Enander et al., 2007; Potoski and Prakash, 2005), and on regional variations in public service outcomes that may be attributable to alternative regulatory regimes (e.g. Andrews and Martin, 2007, 2010). In addition, several studies examine the perceptions of inspection amongst public servants (e.g. Chapman, 2001) and its effects on their practice (e.g. Case et al., 2000; Kelley et al., 2003). However, far less attention has been paid to modelling the direct effects of the quantity and quality of inspection on organizational performance in the public sector. Of those studies that have explored inspection and public service performance, none draw upon a comprehensive theoretical model of inspection. Typically, they focus on the effects of a single intervention on achievements in the subsequent period (e.g. Cullingford and Daniels, 1999; Shaw et al., 2003) – though one study assesses the link between inspection recommendations and performance (McCrone et al., 2007).

To identify published studies which analyse the impact of the institutional environment on public service performance, several additional search terms were adapted for audit, inspection and regulation (e.g. accountability, intervention and oversight). This extensive search revealed a mere five studies that sought to quantitatively analyse the relationship between the institutional environment and organizational performance in the public sector. The selected empirical studies were nearly all undertaken in England (4), with one being conducted in the Netherlands. The content of the studies examining the institutional environment and public service performance is presented in Table 2.2.

Evidence on the impact of inspection on public service performance is exclusively from the education sector, especially on the relationship between the incidence of inspection and pupils' examination results on graduating from secondary schools. The narrowness of this evidence base may in part be due to the long history of formal inspection in

Table 2.2 Impact of institutional environment on public service performance

Study	**Organizations and sample size**	**Dimension of institutional environment**	**Measure of performance**	**Net effect on performance**
Cullingford and Daniels (1999)	426 English secondary schools 1994–97	Inspection event	% pupils attaining 5 A*–C grades in GCSE exams	Worse performance in year of inspection
Luginbuhl et al. (2009)	6,164 Dutch primary schools 1999–2003	Inspection event	Test scores for reading, maths, language and information	Improvements, especially for more intensive inspections and in schools with more disadvantaged pupils
McCrone et al. (2007)	1,597 English primary and secondary schools 2005–06	Inspection quality Inspection event	Exam results for 11- and 16-year-olds Perceptions of teaching effectiveness	Recommendations lead to improvement Improvement

Rosenthal (2004)	2,362 English secondary schools 1992–97	Inspection event	% pupils attaining 5 A*–C grades in GCSE exams	Worse performance in year of inspection
Shaw et al. (2003)	3,000 English secondary schools 1992–97	Inspection event	% pupils attaining 5 A*–C grades in GCSE exams	Improvements in high and low performers, no changes in average performers

schools, the availability of suitable data for statistical modelling or to scholars' greater interest in studying these issues than regulation in social care or other public services. Each of the studies identified utilizes a large sample of organizations and includes formal tests of statistical significance, with most seeking to control for other relevant contextual variables using multivariate techniques.

All of the studies seek to explore the impact of an inspection event on performance. Cullingford and Daniels (1999) analyse GCSE results in a sample of English secondary schools in the wake of inspections over a four-year period, finding that the rate of improvement in pupil achievement is significantly lower in inspected schools than those that were not inspected. Rosenthal (2004) too uncovers a negative relationship between inspection and performance. He models the effects of inspection on GCSE results in the population of English secondary schools over a six-year period, revealing a small but strong statistically significant negative effect of inspection during the year of the inspection. However, this negative relationship is not borne out in other studies.

Luginbuhl et al. (2009) explore the impact of inspections on the average test scores achieved in the population of Dutch primary schools and a randomly selected sample of those schools. They discover that more intensive inspections result in better performance in the organizational population, and that this effect was also observed for schools in the randomly selected sample with more disadvantaged pupils. Shaw et al. (2003) furnish evidence of a statistically significant positive connection between inspection and subsequent GCSE examination results in selective English secondary schools (about 5 per cent of the population). Mixed comprehensive schools, though, experienced neither improvement nor decline in their standards during the six-year study period. In McCrone et al.'s (2007) study of over 1000 primary and secondary schools in England, they present evidence suggesting that on average headteachers perceived the quality of teaching within their schools to have improved following inspection. They also uncover a link between specific recommendations for subject development and improved examination results in primary schools and in high-performing secondary schools. This indicates that the quality of the inspection and how it is perceived by regulatees may have an especially important part to play in determining its overall effects.

The, albeit limited, evidence on the relationship between the institutional environment and public service performance suggests that inspection may have divergent effects on organizational outcomes depending on the timing of the inspection event and the prior achievements of the inspectee. This highlights that it is important to take these potentially divergent institutional influences on organizational outcomes into account when studying strategic management and performance.

Limitations of the existing evidence on organizational environments and public service performance

Prior research suggests that organizational environments influence public service performance. Nevertheless, the existing evidence is problematic in at least three ways. First, existing studies rarely adopt a comprehensive model of the environment. The available evidence on technical environments invariably focuses on only one (e.g. munificence in Croll, 2002) or two (e.g. munificence and complexity in Hall and Leeson, 2010) dimensions, with only one study providing evidence on the impact of dynamism (Andrews and Boyne, 2008). To develop and fully test theoretical models of organizational environments, it is important to investigate the effects of all three dimensions of the technical environment.

Second, the meagre evidence on the institutional environment is almost exclusively focused on the impact of inspection events, rather than the quality of those interventions and the accompanying support that is provided by inspectors and inspectorates (e.g. Shaw et al., 2003). Although McCrone et al. (2007) offer a deeper analysis of the inspection process, to date there has been no consideration of how the extent of regulatory support may influence performance. At the same time, the existing evidence is entirely restricted to the performance of schools.

Third, there has been little consideration of the impact of technical and institutional environments on performance within the same study. Research tends to focus on either the technical environment (e.g. Andrews et al., 2005a) or the institutional environment (e.g. Rosenthal,

2004). To get a complete picture of the environment–performance link, it is necessary to include measures of the technical and institutional environment within the same model. We now develop hypotheses on the likely effects of the organizational environment on public service performance.

Hypotheses on the impact of organizational environments

Variations in performance are likely where some public organizations have more economic resources than others. Prosperous organizations can afford to provide more and better services. Beyond central government compensation to equalize levels of funding (Bennett, 1982), the economic resources available to public organizations is likely to be influenced by the relative prosperity of local inhabitants. Prosperous individuals and families are better able to 'co-produce' services (Williams, 2003). For example, wealthier families can subsidize state schools (e.g. through donations or unpaid help) or pay for home tuition to raise the level of their children's school exam performance. They may also reduce resource pressures by substituting public with private services. The first hypothesis on the impact of the technical environment is then:

H2.1 Environmental munificence is positively related to organizational performance.

The environmental complexity faced by public organizations is likely to reflect the demographic characteristics of their clients. In particular, if the public is relatively homogeneous (e.g. mostly white middle class), it may be much easier to provide a 'standardized' service that meets their needs. By contrast, for a heterogeneous population (e.g. many different ethnic and economic groups), it may be necessary to provide a wider range of services to meet their requirements (Boaden and Alford, 1969). At any given population level, complexity will also increase when inhabitants are dispersed across a wide geographical area. For example, it may be necessary to provide additional schools, day-care centres and supplementary 'outreach' programmes. By contrast, providing services within a narrow geographical area could generate economies of scope through multi-output production and shared services (Panzar and Willig, 1977). All of which suggests:

H2.2 Environmental complexity is negatively related to organizational performance.

Organizational decision-makers require a certain degree of environmental stability to plan effectively, which, in turn, necessitates the accumulation of knowledge in order to respond to environmental challenges (Dutton et al., 1983). Large or unexpected shifts in the circumstances that they face may lead public managers to be cautious about developing new services. As a result, they can become less willing or able to adapt to environmental change, potentially leading to the problems of 'threat-rigidity' (Staw et al., 1981). Instability and unpredictability are therefore likely to hamper public managers' efforts to coordinate effective responses to existing and future service needs. Thus:

H2.3 Environmental dynamism is negatively related to organizational performance.

A theoretical model of the efficacy of the regulatory element of the institutional environment has been developed by Boyne et al. (2002). They argue that the net effect of inspection events will hinge on the expertise of the inspectors. More specifically, an inspection event can be expected to have a positive impact if the expertise of inspectors is greater than that of local service managers. By contrast, if inspectors have lower expertise than those whom they are inspecting, then their impact on services will be negative. In this case, inspectors may be providing 'bad' advice that service providers feel constrained to heed, at least in part. Thus the potential relationship between inspection events and service improvement is complex. The relative expertise of inspection teams and service managers is likely to vary across organizations, and the positive and negative effects may cancel out at the aggregate level. We therefore state a null hypothesis for the impact of inspection:

H2.4 Inspection has no significant net effect on organizational performance.

Although the impact of an inspection event in itself is difficult to call, the effect of the broader characteristics of a regulatory regime may be more predictable. A large literature suggests that regulation is more likely to have positive outcomes when it is viewed as *supportive* by those who are regulated (Day and Klein, 1987; Hawkins, 1984; Hughes et al., 1997). In particular, it can increase the probability that the affected parties will overcome collective action problems associated with enforcement and compliance (Scholz and Gray, 1997). Regulators who are perceived as supportive are more likely to engage in a mutualistic and collaborative process with regulatees, and to develop a better understanding of the local context for service improvement. By contrast, if regulators are not viewed as supportive, then their relationship with regulatees is likely to be antagonistic, and may lead to displacement of management effort towards resistance and game playing (Ashworth et al., 2002). Thus, we expect that:

H2.5 Supportive regulation has a positive effect on organizational performance.

Measuring performance and the environment

Public service performance

The performance of public services is complex and multidimensional. Public organizations are typically required to meet multiple and potentially conflicting organizational goals (Rainey, 2010). Moreover, their achievements are judged by a diverse array of constituencies, such as taxpayers, citizens, staff and politicians (Brewer and Selden, 2000). The different interests of various stakeholder groups therefore influence the conceptualization and measurement of performance at every point. Furthermore, evidence of the achievement of public agencies comes from alternative sources. Government-authenticated performance indicators are important (though contestable benchmarks for assessing public service performance (Boyne, 2003a)), as are survey data gauging the perceptions of citizens and users about the nature of the services that they receive. Below, we outline some of the issues surrounding the use of differing measures of organizational performance in public agencies before discussing the way in which performance is operationalized in this book.

The best measures of public sector performance are often thought to be drawn directly from government sources. Information from such sources is often regarded as the 'gold standard' because it is believed to reflect the 'real' world more accurately and to 'minimize discretion' on the part of those collecting the data (Meier and Brudney, 2002, 19). In the literature, these data are sometimes referred to as objective, though in this book we prefer to use the term 'administrative data' (see Andrews et al. (2006b) for a discussion).

Broadly speaking, performance indicators should be impartial, independent and detached from the unit of analysis. To reduce discretion and be as objective as possible, a measure of performance must involve the precise assessment of a dimension of performance, and an external process to verify its accuracy. Furthermore, this information should ideally be publicly available and open to scrutiny by citizens. Many measures meet these criteria. School examination results, in particular, are a good example of objective measures – they gauge the effectiveness of schools, and students' achievements are validated through the marking of their work by external examiners (see the extensive use of such measures in studies of management and performance drawn from the Texan schools' data set (Meier and O'Toole, 2002; O'Toole and Meier, 2004)). Other such indicators include crime statistics and mortality rates within hospitals.

Survey-based performance measures, like objective ones, should also refer to a dimension of performance that is relevant to the organization and be susceptible to verification. Good examples of such data are the judgements on the various achievements of organizations that can be obtained from surveys of citizens, service users and managers. However, survey measures are often criticized because they suffer from methodological biases, of which common-method bias is believed to be the most serious (Wall et al., 2004). Common-method bias is caused by informants' general predilection towards giving similar responses to separate survey questions (i.e. using only the higher or all lower points on a response scale). This is an especially acute problem when survey respondents' judgements on both management and performance are used within the same statistical model. In addition, reliance upon recall together with uncertainty about informants' knowledge of actual performance may problematize the use of survey data (Golden, 1992).

Validity is not, however, a problem only for subjective measures. Serious questions have also been posed about the accuracy of archival measures following major accounting scandals in private firms such as Exxon or WorldCom and evidence of 'cheating' on indicators in the public sector (Bohte and Meier, 2000). Furthermore, the administrative measures often used in management research are financial, and can be questioned because organizations may make decisions about capital and revenue expenditure subject to anticipated profit – in short, financial measures are also socially constructed. This problem is also witnessed in relation to external administrative measures of performance in the public sector because scorecards are collated by officials of regulatory agencies through field visits: for example, Programme Assessment and Rating Tool scores in the USA and the Comprehensive Performance Assessment used in English local government in the first decade of the twentieth century.

Although the distinction between administrative and survey measures is clear in principle, some cross-contamination is bound to occur in practice. For example, the content of administrative performance indicators is determined by the views of external stakeholders on what matters most. At the same time, survey respondents' perceptions of performance are likely to be influenced by an organization's performance indicators. External stakeholders make the decisions about what gets measured in the public sector and how. These external stakeholders are usually politicians or their agents, so what is being measured inevitably reflects what political principals value most. Thus, government-sponsored performance indicators (though contestable) are often the primary means for assessing the achievements of public organizations. For public management researchers and practitioners, it may therefore be best to use measures of performance which reflect the values of political principals, and are least likely to be contaminated by methodological limitations such as common source bias.

In the context of our study, the National Assembly for Wales Performance Indicators (NAWPIs) met these criteria. The performance of all major Welsh local government services was gauged during the period in which our study was conducted through performance indicators set by the regional government to whom they are accountable: the National Assembly for Wales, which provides over 80 per cent of their funding. The NAWPIs were based on common definitions and data which are obtained by councils for the same time period with uniform collection procedures. The figures were then independently verified by the Audit Commission, a UK central government regulatory agency.

For our study, 29 of the NAWPIs available for the financial year 2002/03 were used. These were those measures that focused most closely on service effectiveness, including: the average General Certificate in Secondary Education (GCSE) score achieved in each education department and the percentage of welfare benefit renewal claims processed on time by benefits departments (see Table 2.3). To compare the NAWPIs across different service areas, they were first divided by the mean score for all Welsh local governments, inverting some (e.g. number of car users killed or seriously injured in road accidents per 100,000 population) so scores above the mean always denote high performance. We then combined different indicators within a service, weighting each indicator equally by taking z-scores to ensure that our analysis was not influenced by particular indicators. These procedures allow the data for all different services in Wales to be pooled, because the measurement process removes service effects from the scores on the

Table 2.3 Objective performance measures 2002–03

Service area	Effectiveness measure
Education	% Unqualified school leavers (inverted) Average General Certificate in Secondary Education (GCSE) score % 5+ GCSEs A*–C % 1+ GCSEs A*–G % KS2 Maths level 4 % KS2 English level 4 % KS2 Science level 4 % KS3 Maths level 5 % KS3 English level 5 % KS3 Science level 5 % GCSE C+ in English/Welsh, Maths/Science
Social services	% Care leavers 1+ GCSE A*–G
Housing	% Rent collection[1] % Rent arrears (inverted) % Write-offs (inverted)
Highways	Pedestrians killed or seriously injured (inverted) Cyclists killed or seriously injured (inverted) Motorcyclists killed or seriously injured (inverted) Car users killed or seriously injured (inverted) Others killed or seriously injured (inverted) Pedestrians slight injury (inverted) Cyclists slight injury (inverted) Motorcyclists slight injury (inverted) Car users slight injury (inverted) Others slight injury (inverted)
Public protection	Burglaries (inverted) Vehicle crimes (inverted)
Benefits and revenues	% Renewal claims on time % Cases processed correctly

[1]This performance indicator was not collected in 2003. Thus the effectiveness measure for that year is made up of only two housing PIs.

indicators. Factor analysis was not used because the number of cases per service area was too small to create reliable factors. Similar statistical results were obtained when the analysis was repeated using a performance measure which gave one 'key' indicator for each service area a weight equal to the total number of indicators in that area.

This combined service score provides a measure of performance across six service areas (education, social services, housing, highways, public

Table 2.4 Descriptive statistics for service performance

	Mean	Minimum	Maximum	SD
Service performance 2001/02	.07	−1.51	1.92	.72
Service performance 2002/03	.08	−1.56	1.92	.64

protection and benefits). Table 2.4 lists descriptive data for our measures of organizational performance.

Technical environment

Environmental munificence was measured using a proxy gauging the relative prosperity of the population served by each local government department: the average ward score on the index of multiple deprivation for 2000. This is the standard population-weighted measure of deprivation used by UK central government, which captures the level of deprivation across multiple domains (e.g. income, employment and health). The presence of scale economies attributable to the size of the client base was measured using population figures from the UK National Census in 2001. An overall munificence index was then created by first reversing the deprivation measure and adding a standardized version of this variable and a standardized version of the size measure together.

Environmental complexity was measured by capturing three aspects of client heterogeneity: (1) age diversity, (2) ethnic diversity and (3) social class diversity. To measure these aspects of heterogeneity the proportion of each age, ethnic and social group found in the national census of 2001 within a local government area was squared and the sum of these squares subtracted from 10,000, with a high score representing greater heterogeneity. Population density, measured using population per square kilometre figures for 2001, serves as a proxy for relative environmental dispersion. An overall objective complexity index was constructed by creating a mean standardized score for the three heterogeneity measures and adding this to a standardized version of the dispersion measure.

Environmental dynamism is a product of change (or instability) in munificence and complexity, and the unpredictability (or turbulence) of that change. A dynamism measure was therefore created by combining measures of instability and turbulence. Munificence instability was measured by summing z-scores of the percentage change in the lone-parent households in each local area from 1991 to 2001 and the percentage population change between these years. The lone-parent measure is used as the Indices of Multiple Deprivation were unavailable in 1991. It represents a useful proxy for deprivation as there is a strong positive correlation (0.67) between lone-parent households in Wales recorded in the 2001 national census and levels of multiple deprivation in 2000.

Complexity instability was measured using z-scores of the percentage change in age diversity, ethnic diversity and social class diversity in a local area between 1991 and 2001 and the percentage change in population density for the same years. These two instability variables were added together to give a measure of the overall extent of change in the organizational task environment. Measures of unpredictability were then constructed by summing the standardized residuals from autoregressive models of the instability variables (the standard method for assessing environmental unpredictability, see Boyd and Gove (2006)). These aggregate measures of instability and unpredictability were multiplied together to form an index of environmental dynamism. The characteristics of an environment that is changing rapidly in unpredictable ways alter at a faster pace than one that is simply unstable or turbulent. The rationale for multiplying rather than summing instability and turbulence is therefore that a large change may not affect organizational performance unless it is also unexpected.

Institutional environment

To gauge the impact of the institutional environment on performance, we measured the presence and supportiveness of external regulation. The extent of regulatory intervention in Welsh local government was measured using a dummy variable coded 1 for those service departments that had been subject to Best Value inspection between 2000 and 2002, and 0 for those that had not. Education departments were not subject to Best Value inspection. To create a proxy for the extent of inspection in education departments, the percentage of primary and secondary school inspections carried out by the school inspections body *Estyn* between 2000 and 2002 was therefore calculated. Education departments with an above school inspection rate were coded 1 for our extent of inspection variable, and those with a below-average school inspection rate were coded 0. The level of regulatory support was measured using a survey item that evaluated the degree to which respondents felt regulatory agencies were supportive of their service department. We assessed this by asking respondents to indicate their level of agreement with the statement 'Regulatory agencies (e.g. External inspectorates such as the Audit Commission, Estyn, Social Services Inspectorate for Wales, and so on) are supportive of the service'.

Control variables: Past performance and service expenditure

Public organizations are best understood as autoregressive systems which change incrementally over time (O'Toole and Meier, 1999). This implies that performance in one period is strongly influenced by performance in the past. It is therefore important to include prior achievements in statistical models of performance, to ensure that the coefficients for the other independent variables are not biased. Effectiveness in the previous year was therefore entered in the analysis of service standards in 2002/03. By including the autoregressive term, the coefficients for the environmental measures show what these variables added (or subtracted from) the performance baseline. Thus, in effect, our findings show the impact of the external environment on the improvement (or deterioration) in service effectiveness during the study period.

Performance may vary not only because of the characteristics of the technical and institutional environment but also because of the financial resources expended on services. Differences in spending across services may arise for a variety of reasons (the level of central government support, the size of the local tax base and departmental shares of an authority's total budget). At the extreme, a prosperous service in one authority may be able to buy success while a poor one in another area can afford only mediocrity. Prior research supports the contention that public expenditure levels have a significant effect on performance (Boyne, 2003b).

We controlled for potential expenditure effects by using figures drawn from only the 2000/01 NAWPIs, because coverage of service expenditure data was less comprehensive in the NAWPIs following this year. Nonetheless, research has shown that relative levels of spending in local authority departments vary little year on year (Danziger, 1978; Sharpe and Newton, 1984). To make them suitable for analysis, the service expenditure indicators were standardized by taking z-scores for groups of relevant indicators of expenditure in each service department. So, for instance, we standardized four indicators of education expenditure (expenditure per nursery and primary pupil under 5, expenditure per primary pupil over 5, expenditure per secondary pupil under 16 and expenditure per secondary pupil over 16). We then repeated this method for expenditure indicators in social services, housing, highways, public protection and benefits and revenues, thereby deriving a single measure of expenditure that is comparable across the six service areas. The indicators used for our expenditure measure are shown in Table 2.5. The descriptive statistics and data sources for all the measures are listed in Table 2.6.

Table 2.5 Service expenditure measures 2001–03

Service area	Expenditure NAWPI
Education	Net expenditure per nursery and primary pupil under 5 Net expenditure per primary pupil aged 5 and over Net expenditure per secondary pupil under 16 Net expenditure per pupil secondary pupil aged 16 and over
Social services	Cost of children's services per child looked after
Housing	Average weekly management costs Average weekly repair costs
Highways	Cost of highway maintenance per 100 km travelled by a vehicle on principal roads Cost per passenger journey of subsidized bus services Average cost of maintaining street lights
Public protection	Total net spending per capita*
Benefits and revenues	Cost per benefit claim

Note: *Spending per capita for the local government as a whole is used as expenditure data for this service area are not available.

Table 2.6 Descriptive statistics

	Mean	Min	Max	s.d
Dependent variable				
Service performance 2002/03	.10	−1.56	1.92	.68
Objective environmental measures				
Deprivation 2000	23.56	12.31	40.02	7.25
Population	123069	66829	172842	28343
Age diversity 2001	8764.81	8716.58	8827.84	24.76
Ethnic diversity 2001	579.04	353.27	1326.01	214.73
Social class diversity 2001	8696.31	8550.70	8782.11	66.41
Population density 2001	344.92	24.25	726.32	246.46
Socio-economic instability 91–01	−.79	−2.95	1.67	1.27
Socio-economic turbulence 91–01	−.33	−2.84	2.66	1.59
Institutional environment				
Inspection	.43	.00	1.00	.50
Supportive regulation	4.22	1.00	6.33	1.21
Control variables				
Service performance 2001/02	.08	−1.51	1.92	.74
Service expenditure 2000/01	−.01	−1.43	2.40	.87

Data Sources:	
Service performance 2001–03	National Assembly for Wales. 2003. *National Assembly for Wales Performance Indicators 2001–2002*; National Assembly for Wales. 2004. *National Assembly for Wales Performance Indicators 2002–2003*.
Deprivation	Department of Environment, Transport and Regions (2000) *Indices of Multiple Deprivation*, London: DETR.
Age diversity, ethnic diversity, population, population density, social class diversity	Office for National Statistics. (2003). *Census 2001: Key Statistics for Local Authorities*. London: TSO. Age diversity comprised 12 groups: 0–4, 5–9, 10–14, 15–19, 20–24, 25–29, 30–44, 45–59, 60–64, 65–74, 75–84, 85+. Ethnic diversity comprised 16 groups: White British, Irish, Other White, White and Black Caribbean, White and Black African, White and Asian, Other Mixed, Indian, Pakistani, Bangladeshi, Other Asian, Caribbean, African, Other Black, Chinese and Other Ethnic Group. Social class diversity comprised 7 groups: Managerial and Administration; Professional and Technical; Clerical and Secretarial; Craft and Related; Personal and Protective; Sales; Plant and Machine Operators.
Environmental dynamism (including lone-parent households)	Office for National Statistics. *1991 Census: Key Statistics for Local Authorities*. London: HMSO, 1994; and Office for National Statistics. *Census 2001: Key Statistics for Local Authorities*. London: TSO, 2003. The dynamism measure included: 12 age groups (0–4, 5–9, 10–14, 15–19, 20–24, 25–29, 30–44, 45–59, 60–64, 65–74, 75–84, 85+); 9 ethnic groups (White; Black Caribbean; Black African; Black Other Non-Mixed; Black Other Mixed; Indian; Pakistani; Bangladeshi; Chinese); and 7 social groups (Managerial and Administration; Professional and Technical; Clerical and Secretarial; Craft and Related; Personal and Protective; Sales; Plant and Machine Operators).

Statistical results

The results of the statistical model of organizational environments and public service performance are shown in Table 2.7. Environmental variables, past performance and service expenditure explain about two-thirds of the variation in the performance of Welsh local government service departments. The model therefore provides a sound foundation for assessing the influence of organizational environments. Indeed, the evidence suggests that the environment may be an important determinant of the performance of public organizations.

Table 2.7 Organizational environment and performance

	Slope	t-score	VIF
Constant	.0681	.37	
Technical environment			
Munificence	.1283	2.14*	1.74
Complexity	−.1328	−1.73+	1.76
Dynamism	−.0383	−2.14*	1.15
Institutional environment			
Inspection	−.1443	−1.38	1.14
Supportive regulation	.0363	.87	1.19
Control variables			
Service performance 01/02	.7020	9.62**	1.08
Service expenditure 00/01	.0336	.55	1.09
R^2	.66**		
Adjusted R^2	.61**		
$N = 58$			

Note: Significance levels: $+p \leq 0.10$; $^*p \leq 0.05$; $^{**}p \leq 0.01$ (two-tailed tests).

The technical environment

Hypothesis 2.1 is supported by our statistical analysis: the coefficient for munificence is positive and statistically significant. Even when controlling for other dimensions and measures of the environment, areas with a high level of munificence seem to benefit from better public service provision. This mirrors prior research suggesting that the low munificence associated with providing services in disadvantaged areas has an especially persistent negative statistical association with local government performance (Andrews, 2004). Indeed, performance may be particularly adversely affected by the lack of local neighbourhood support needed to assist vulnerable or needy people in such areas (Wilson, 1991). In addition, munificence may reflect economies of scale accrued by serving large client populations.

Hypothesis 2.2 is also supported by our statistical analysis. The coefficient for complexity has a negative sign and is statistically significant. Delivering services in sparsely populated, socially heterogeneous areas is associated with worse performance, even when controlling for environmental munificence and dynamism. The results for complexity thereby corroborate evidence which suggests that community heterogeneity makes good performance more difficult. Public organizations operating in ethnically diverse areas often devote substantial resources of time and money to building, developing and maintaining good community relations (Office of the Deputy Prime Minister, 2004). At the same time, areas with a wider spread of age groups also have more complex housing (Withers, 1997) and health-care (Birch and Maynard, 1986) needs. Dealing with these 'wicked issues' seems to be having a negative influence on the performance of our sample service departments. At the same time, service departments in more densely populated or urban areas appear to be reaping the benefits of more opportunities for sharing production inputs, such as computing facilities and administrative staff and offices (Grosskopf and Yaisawamg, 1990).

Hypothesis 2.3 is supported by the results: the coefficient for objective environmental dynamism is statistically significant and negative. This finding suggests that service achievements are constrained by both recorded levels of munificence and complexity, and changes in these variables, at least over the decade covered by the data. Dynamism thus seems to be adding significantly to the constraining effects of munificence and complexity *per se*. To cope with rapid demographic change, public organizations may have to devote increased resources to maintaining a consistent level of performance, which, in turn, could add significantly to the fiscal burden levied on taxpayers. As a result, in a dynamic environment, it is possible that public organizations might allow service quality to deteriorate in the short-run to protect their long-term financial plans (Ladd, 1992).

The institutional environment

Table 2.5 shows that inspection has no statistically significant effect on service performance, and Hypothesis 2.4 is therefore rejected. There is no support for Hypothesis 2.5 either, on the benefits of supportive regulation: while the coefficient for that measure is positive, it does not achieve statistical significance.

The results indicate that inspection appears to have no independent effect on public service performance. It is conceivable that this is because inspections targeted low-performing services that were yet to show signs of improvement. Moreover, the impact of service inspection in Wales may have been especially weak because of councils' hostility to the Best Value Inspectorate, which led to the abolition of the regime late in 2002 (Andrews et al., 2003). An alternative explanation is that our results are a consequence of the positive and negative effects of inspection on service outcomes cancelling each other out. Systematic investigation of Boyne et al.'s (2002) arguments on the moderating effects of inspectors' expertise, in particular, would require data on the qualifications and experience of each inspection team.

Another broader interpretation of the insignificant impact of this explanatory variable is that the 'service improvement' approach to inspection is simply unable to deliver significant changes in performance. Best Value inspections were intended to gauge existing performance and corporate capacity for delivering gains in performance. However, the inspectors were perceived by Welsh local authorities as paying too much attention to processes rather than outputs (Welsh Local Government Association, 2001). One of our interviewees who had experienced formal inspection suggested that in practice it was 'a paper exercise' that entailed 'spending too much time on corporate issues'. Indeed, it became apparent that the unpopularity of Best Value inspection in Wales was attributable to the perceived determination of the Audit Commission to judge Welsh services against a predetermined model of managerial modernization (Andrews et al., 2003).

Regulation may be inherently more suited to enhancing the accountability of public organizations rather than driving service improvement. Alternatively, it is possible that formal inspection is the least effective tool available to public sector regulators attempting to elicit positive changes in public service delivery. Regulators also play an advisory role by seeking to promote good practice and supporting the home-grown improvement strategies of service providers. Evidence from the US suggests that this 'educative' approach can actually lead to increased levels of self-regulation within organizations (Scholz and Gray, 1997). The positive impact of such regulatory behaviour receives some support in the sign of the coefficient for the measure of regulatory support. Furthermore, a manager who had 'built up a rapport with District Audit' felt that this had been critical to the improvement of the service. Nevertheless, the absence of a statistically significant relationship indicates that the benefits of supportive regulation may be contingent on other organizational characteristics. We explore the moderating effects of strategy, structure and process on the relationship between the technical and institutional environment and performance in Chapter 7.

Conclusion

This chapter has explored the relationship between organizational environments on performance. Building on prior theoretical and empirical work in the field of management and public administration, hypotheses were developed around the likely effects of technical and institutional dimensions of the organizational environment on public service performance. These hypotheses were tested by using multivariate statistical techniques to analyse variations in the performance of local government service departments in Wales. Our empirical findings provide support for the argument that the technical environment is an important determinant of organizational performance. However, no support was uncovered for the tenets of improvement-led regulation.

Despite the divergent independent effects of the technical and institutional environments observed here, it is still important, as prior theory and evidence highlight, to include both aspects of the environment in studies of strategic management and performance. In particular, within the context of the Miles and Snow model, it is especially important that both the independent effects of environments on performance are taken into account as well as their effects in combination with internal organizational characteristics. To gain a fuller picture of how and in what ways public organizations can be best aligned with their environments, we develop hypotheses about the potential interactive effects of each environmental dimension and organizational strategies, structures and processes based on the Miles and Snow model in Chapter 7. These hypotheses are then tested by including interactions between the environment and internal organizational characteristics within our statistical models. This enables us to draw conclusions about the likely environment–organization contingencies that influence public service performance. Before turning to those complex contingent relationships, we examine the independent effects of strategic management on performance in detail in Chapters 3–6.

3
Strategy Content and Performance

Public management research has long been concerned with the service public agencies provide and the way it is provided (Rainey, 2010). However, only in more recent years has attention been turned to the strategy content of public organizations (Joyce, 1999; Moore, 1995). This may have arisen because of the 'traditional' view that public organizations are controlled by higher levels of political authority, giving managers limited discretion to manage, or because public agencies have multiple goals, many stakeholders and decisions are rule-bounded. As such only a limited number of authors sought to develop strategy models for public organizations. For example, Stevens and McGowan (1983) examined strategy during times of fiscal austerity in US local governments, and Wechsler and Backoff (1986) sought to derive four models of strategy in four agencies in Ohio. The focus on strategy content has, however, increased over recent years (Joldersma and Winter, 2002; Joyce, 1999; Lane and Wallis, 2009). This is in part because stakeholders (including users, regulators and often higher levels of government) have become interested in and have greater expectations about the performance of public agencies. Simultaneously, the emphasis of many reform efforts has been to increase managerial discretion while changes in the environment have required organizations to rethink their approaches, be these changes in the technical environment which have increased uncertainty, or be technological changes which make information on the behaviour of other organizations available. These changes have led to growing interest in the ways in which services are delivered and the strategies that organizations have put in place. This has also been accompanied by the growing availability of data on the performance of public organizations (see Walker, Boyne and Brewer, 2010), making questions of strategy content and performance an important and topical research issue.

Strategy content is the central variable in the Miles and Snow (1978) framework. Miles and Snow argue that there are key relationships between the strategic stances of analyzers, defenders, prospectors and reactors and their performance. Questions about the most appropriate strategy content approach and organizational performance are central to this chapter. As such, we commence with an exploration of the existing literature on strategy content, and develop hypotheses on strategy and performance. This discussion is followed by the results of the statistical analysis, and discussion thereof prior to conclusions being drawn.

The Miles and Snow model

In order to examine the link between strategy and performance in public organizations, we use a classic model of strategy: the Miles and Snow framework (1978). It has a venerable status in the field of strategic management. Hambrick (2003, 115) for example, argues that it 'has had a profound effect on the fields of strategic management and organization theory'. Further evidence of its significance is demonstrated by the number of citations it has had. A search of the Business Source Premier database indicated that it had been cited 11,179 times and a study by Ramos-Rodriguez and Ruiz-Navarro (2004) showed that Miles and Snow was the 8th most cited work in the *Strategic Management Journal* between 1980 and 2000. It has been tested empirically many times and in fields as diverse as retail (Moore, 2005), banking (James and Hatten, 1994), small- and medium-sized enterprises (Aragon-Sanchez and Sanchez-Marin, 2005) and hospitals (Shortell and Zajac, 1990). Although studies of public and non-profit organizations have begun to explore strategy and links with other organizational characteristics, research using the Miles and Snow framework in this sector is still relatively limited (for exceptions see Greenwood, 1987; Lane and Wallis, 2009).

Miles and Snow (1978) developed a typology of organizational strategies from detailed case studies. The framework was argued to be generic and would apply to any type of organization; indeed their empirical work included hospitals in the USA, which in part have a public purpose. They derived four strategy 'ideal types'. *Prospectors* are organizations that 'almost continually search for market opportunities, and... regularly experiment with potential responses to emerging environmental trends' (Miles and Snow, 1978, 29). In public organizations a prospector is likely to be a leader in their field, a 'first mover', or winner of innovation awards. A prospecting public agency may be seeking to expand its budget, may invade the 'policy space' of other agencies

(Downs, 1967) or may be innovative within its pre-existing budget where organizational slack permits (Bourgeois, 1981). Strategic priorities in a public sector prospector would revolve around being more proactive than other agencies, innovating and risk taking (Boschken, 1988).

Defenders are organizations that take a conservative view of innovation, and are not leaders in the field but instead are late adopters of innovations once they have been tried and tested. They typically compete on price and quality rather than on new products or markets and 'devote primary attention to improving the efficiency of their existing operations' (Miles and Snow, 1978, 29); in short, they seek better performance by focusing on core services to retain their existing activities and protect their share of the public budget. *Analyzers* represent an intermediate category, sharing elements of both prospector and defender. Analyzers are rarely 'first movers' but, instead, 'watch their competitors closely for new ideas, and... rapidly adopt those which appear to be most promising' (Miles and Snow, 1978, 29). *Reactors* are organizations in which top managers frequently perceive change and uncertainty in their organizational environments but lack a consistent and stable strategy. A reactor 'seldom makes adjustment of any sort until forced to do so by environmental pressures' (Miles and Snow, 1978, 29). A reactor stance is equivalent to strategy absence, because an organization largely responds to external forces, and has no consistent or coherent strategy of its own (Inkpen and Chaudhury, 1995). Boschken (1988, 18) argues that the lack of positive direction is likely result in a reactor 'fail[ing] at the "invisible hands" of shifting environmental forces'.

Theoretical arguments and empirical evidence have been presented for the applicability of the Miles and Snow framework to public organizations. Some evidence on the likelihood of public agencies adopting the four strategic styles was provided by Greenwood (1987), who noted that local authorities were likely to describe themselves as reactors (half his sample of 208 English local authorities). The balance categorized themselves thus: analyzers (29 per cent), prospectors (11 per cent) and defenders (10 per cent). Greenwood (1987, 300) argues that the large per cent of reactors '... may indicate that several authorities are in a transitional stage, moving from one coherent approach to another'. The concern of the Greenwood study was with the relationship between strategy content and structure. Analysis bore out the hypothesis that content influences structure, in that the choice of strategy led to an alignment with structure as predicted in the wider framework developed by Miles and Snow (see Chapter 6): prospectors were externally focused, decentralized with high complexity of integration.

Boyne and Walker (2004) argued for the adoption of the Miles and Snow framework as a model of strategy content for public organizations because it captures the main responses organizations are likely to make in the face of changes in the organizational environment. A prospector would be proactive, scan the external environment and be innovative. A defender, by contrast, would maintain its current focus and consolidate its existing position in response to changes in circumstances and adopt innovations when they have been tried and tested elsewhere. A reactor, with no consistent strategy of its own, would await instructions from the external environment.

Miles and Snow argue that performance is contingent on internal characteristics, of which strategy content is one, and environmental circumstances (which we reviewed in Chapter 2). We explore these contingent issues of strategy, structure, internal processes and environment in relation to Miles and Snows' strategic types in subsequent chapters. Here we trace out one example of the relationships across these variables for defenders, to offer an illustration of the wider argument developed by Miles and Snow on these contingent relationships. Defenders align themselves with centralized organizational structures because they need to both control operations centrally and vest power in top-level managers who can take an overview of the organization as a whole (Miles and Snow, 1978, 41–44). Defenders adopt high levels of planning in their organizational processes because they need to undertake detailed analysis on how to achieve their goals. This emphasis on mechanistic structures and processes suggests that defenders are more likely to achieve optimal levels of performance in predictable and stable environments. In this chapter, our attention focuses upon the separate relationship between strategy content and organizational performance.

Strategy content and performance

The central contention of Miles and Snow's (1978) model of strategy is that prospectors, analyzers and defenders perform better than reactors, which is supported by studies of private firms (Conant et al., 1990; Hawes and Crittenden, 1984; Shortell and Zajac, 1990; Slater and Olson, 2001). However, a reactor stance is not always associated with poor performance. Snow and Hrebiniak's (1980) study of four industries confirmed Miles and Snow's primary hypothesis, except in the case of highly regulated industries where reactors outperformed prospectors and defenders. This finding may have implications for the relative effectiveness of different strategies in the public sector. A reactor stance may be a deliberate and positive choice in a public sector environment that values responsiveness to the shifting demands of external stakeholders, especially if strategy content is routinely imposed by regulatory agencies (Bozeman and Straussman, 1990; Nutt and Backoff, 1993; Rainey, 2010). Prospectors may be perceived as excessively eager to take risks, and defenders may be seen as reluctant to respond to pressures for change. Reactors, unconstrained by a fixed strategic posture, may be more pliable and more ready to please their political superiors (Boyne and Walker, 2004). Thus, in principle, a reactor stance can be seen as the best fit with the political circumstances that shape perceptions of organizational performance in the public sector (Rainey and Steinbauer, 1999).

Miles and Snow (1978) maintain that there are no performance differences between prospectors, analyzers and defenders, a view supported by the findings of Slater and Olson (2001). However, the evidence on the relative performance of prospectors and defenders is neither comprehensive nor conclusive. Evans and Green's (2000) study of Chapter 11 bankruptcy firms in the US notes that business turnaround is more likely to be achieved by prospectors than defenders. Hambrick (1983) concludes that prospectors outperform defenders on market share changes, but that this pattern is reversed for return on investment. Zajac and Shortell's (1989) analysis of US hospitals found that the performance of defenders fell behind other generic strategy types when the environment called for a more proactive approach. Woodside et al.'s (1999) analysis concludes that prospectors outperform defenders, who in turn outperform reactors.

Private sector evidence on the proposition from the writings of Miles and Snow that the performance of prospectors, defenders and analyzers is higher than that of reactors receives broad but mixed support. The application of the Miles and Snow framework to the public sector has led to a slight variation on these propositions, which was initially derived from the private sector evidence. The evidence derived from public sector studies differs slightly from the propositions of Miles and Snow, and is that a prospector stance is positively related to organizational performance, prospectors and defenders outperform reactors and defenders outperform reactors. Finally, a reactor stance is negatively related to organizational performance (Andrews et al., 2006a). The evidence that leads us to this conclusion, and the hypotheses we propose below, are derived from the relatively limited number of public sector studies of strategy content. This evidence is summarized in Table 3.1 and now elaborated upon.

Table 3.1 Impact of strategy content on public service performance

Study	Organizations and sample size	Strategy type	Dimension of performance	Net effect on performance
Boschken (1988)	6 pacific coast seaports	Prospector Analyzer Defender Reactor	Composite of: market share, land-use efficiency, operating revenues, liquidity	+ + – –
Andrews et al. (2005b)	80 English local governments	Prospector Defender Reactor	Consumer satisfaction	+ NS –
		Prospector Defender Reactor	Aggregate organizational performance	+ NS NS
Andrews et al. (2006a)	119 English local governments	Prospector Defender Reactor	Aggregate organizational performance	+ NS –
Meier et al. (2007)	3,024 Texan school districts	Prospector Defender Reactor	Student exam pass rates	NS + NS
		Prospector Defender Reactor	Pass rates for ethnic groups	– + NS
		Prospector Defender Reactor	High-end pass rates	+ NS +
		Prospector Defender Reactor	Low-end pass rates	NS NS NS
Enticott and Walker (2008)	72 English local governments	Prospector Defender Reactor	Aggregate organizational performance	+ NS NS
		Prospector Defender Reactor	Sustainability performance	+ NS NS
Andrews et al. (2008)	396 English local governments	Prospector Defender Reactor	Aggregate organizational performance	NS NS NS
Walker and Brewer (2009)	135 English local governments	Prospector Defender Reactor	Aggregate organizational performance	+ NS –
Meier et al. (2010)	3041 Texan school districts	Prospector Defender Reactor	Student exam pass rates	NS + NS
		Prospector Defender Reactor	High-end pass rates	+ NS +
Walker et al. (2010)	101 English local governments	Prospector Defender Reactor	Aggregate organizational performance	+ – NS

Boyne and Walker's (2004) application of the Miles and Snow (1978) model of strategy content to public organizations resulted in some modifications that primarily arose from their argument that organizations simultaneously pursue a variety of strategies, and that this in turn requires a different approach to the operationalization of strategy. (This is discussed in detail below in the section on 'measuring strategy'.) Suffice to stay at this stage that Boyne and Walker (2004) argued that the analyzer stance should be dropped because it captures aspects of both defenders and prospectors. Boyne and Walker's (2004) modified version of the framework has subsequently been tested in England and the USA using the following data sets. In the studies of English local government, the measures of strategy are derived from responses by managers to survey questions that tap the central components of the Miles and Snow typology. For example, Andrews et al. (2006a, 56) use single items to capture prospecting ('the service is at the forefront of innovative approaches'), defending ('focusing on core business is a major part of our approach') and reacting ('pressures from auditors and inspectors are important in driving performance improvement'). The English studies draw on a panel of data collected between 2000 and 2008 and report on a survey of just under 140 major local governments providing data on managers' perceptions and behaviours in relation to a variety of measures of management and organization. This is supplemented with a measure of organizational performance taken from the Audit Commission (2002) and background variables, typically based on UK Census data.

The Texas school district studies constitute a large-scale data set pooling data from 2000 to 2005 and include performance data (typically exam pass rates, drop-out rates and equity measured by pass rates by ethic group) and a variety of socio-economic controls from the Texas Education Authority. It is supplemented by a bi-annual survey of school district superintendents. In total, just over 3000 cases from this data set have been used for research on strategy content.

It is important to note that the organizations in these studies are not assigned exclusively to a single strategic category (see the Section 'Measuring Strategy' for further details). Rather, following the arguments of Boyne and Walker (2004) that all organizations are likely to pursue a mix of strategies, the strategy measures reflect the extent to which survey respondents agree that their organization can be characterized as prospecting, defending and reacting. Finally, in this review of prior public sector evidence, we include one study that is not an empirical quantitative analysis of Miles and Snow. Boshken's (1988) study of American west coast seaports adopts a case study approach examining six ports between the 1960s and the 1980s.

The first published empirical study on strategy content and organizational performance in the public sector was undertaken by Andrews et al. (2006a) in English local government. The measures of prospecting, defending and reacting in their study are based on Likert-scale survey responses from senior and middle managers in a sample of 120 organizations. The empirical results reveal a hierarchy of strategy types: the impact of prospecting is positive, defending neutral and reacting negative. Thus, controlling for the presence of other strategic stances in an organization and a range of environmental conditions, prospecting is the best option and reacting is the worst. This evidence is consistent with the view that strategy matters not only in the private but also in the public sector.

Similar findings are presented in a study of sustainable management and organizational strategy (Enticott and Walker, 2008). Drawing on a sub-sample of the English panel in 2003, these authors primarily focus on the effect of sustainable management on organizational performance and sustainable performance. Sustainable management is concerned with attitudes and behaviours towards social, economic and environmental factors, and the study measured the importance of this in systems of internal management. Sustainable performance was measured by one item that asked respondents to assess achievements on a four-point scale in terms of 'promoting the social, economic and environmental well-being of local people'. The study notes that sustainable management only has an effect on sustainable performance and not on a wider measure of organizational performance. In their models they control for prospecting, defending and reacting. They also find that prospecting trumps other strategy stances, but do not find that reacting has a detrimental effect on sustainable performance. Thus, controlling for a range of variables that includes sustainable management and environmental controls this leads to a further subtle change away from the hierarchical set of propositions developed and supported by Andrews et al. (2006a). These variations may arise because of different control variables and different time periods, and also a different sample.

In a similar vein, Walker and Brewer (2009) examine the relationship between strategy content, red tape and organizational performance in English local governments drawing upon a segment of the panel data.

They demonstrate that a strategy of prospecting can offset the detrimental impacts of red tape, but that in organizations with a reacting stance the presence of red tape worsens performance. The interaction between red tape and defending neither assists nor detracts from performance outcomes. In their study of representative bureaucracy Andrews et al. (2005b) note in their independent effects model that prospecting increases performance while reacting has a harmful effect, reflecting the findings of Andrews et al. (2006a). Their modelling shows that local authorities with high percentages of senior managers from ethnic minorities are viewed to have lower performance, when performance is measured by citizen's satisfaction with their local government. This negative finding, is not, however, uncovered in organizations that have a high propensity towards prospecting. While these studies do not address the central propositions of the strategy literature, they show that a strategy of prospecting can have a number of beneficial effects on variables of particular importance to public management. Boschken's (1988) case study of six ports also noted a hierarchy of achievement with prospectors the highest performers followed by defenders and reactors. However, Boschken was more circumspect about the achievements of defenders, often casting them as considerably poorer performers than prospectors.

Drawing upon a sample of the English data, Walker et al. (2010) examine the relationship between strategy content, strategy formulation and networking. Their findings for strategy are somewhat at odds with prior evidence from this data set. When controlling for strategy formulation and networking (as an aggregate measure and disaggregated into its constituent parts), they find that prospecting has the anticipated positive effect on organizational outcomes but that defending is harmful (with a negative statistically significant sign). In one of their statistical models, they include an autoregressive term for prior performance, as in the analysis in this book. The argument for the inclusion of a control of prior performance is that public organizations are relatively inert systems, and what matters for performance in the current year is largely a function of prior behaviour and achievements (O'Toole and Meier, 1999; Staw and Epstein, 2000). An autoregressive term also shows how variables in the model have added to (or subtracted from) the performance baseline, permitting observations to be made about the effect of strategy on performance at different points in time. When this term is included reacting remains statistically insignificant, prospecting falls from significance and defending remains negative and statistically significant. The authors interpret these findings thus: prospecting has a long-term positive effect on governmental performance, but defending is harmful in both the short and long term.

In stark contrast to the findings reported by Walker et al. (2010), defending is shown to be the strategy most likely to result in higher levels of organizational performance in Texas school districts when the dependent variable is measured as the student exam pass rate. In these models, Meier et al. (2007) control for a number of facets of management (networking, school board contact, quality, experience and personnel stability) and a variety of socio-economic and school-based external constraints. By examining differing aspects of organizational performance, Meier et al. uncover an interesting set of relationships, suggesting that the impact of strategic stance is contingent upon the organizational goal being measured. For example, evidence on the exam pass rates for different ethnic groups suggests that prospecting can harm the achievements of black students while reacting assists white students. When focusing upon performance measures that examine the number of university-bound students, an important but not core measure of organizational performance, reacting and prospecting have positive effects, while defending no longer matters. For low-achieving students (and using measure of attendance and dropout), strategy content is shown not to matter, rather other facets of management are more important.

This brief review, of an admittedly small number of studies, points towards the contingent nature of strategy in public organizations. As we moved through these articles, the range of additional variables included in the models increased. While controlling for other variables is an important aspect of model specification, what is crucial in the context of this chapter is that strategy content remains a significant variable that explains the performance of public agencies. Clearly, there are questions of external validity in stating this: the theories are tested in three different contexts. The English context placed emphasis on new approaches to management and service delivery during the period of the research (Walker and Boyne, 2006). Alternatively, in Texas the dimension of performance of greatest importance to school superintendents was basic examination passes, or a focus on core business, but beyond this a number of dimensions of performance could be tapped suggesting that different aspects of the production function of education were dependent upon different strategic stances and other facets of management.

Taking the public and private sector evidence together, we conclude that there is broad but mixed support for Miles and Snow's model of strategy and performance. The application of this model to the public sector leads to the following hypotheses:

H3.1 A prospector stance is positively related to organizational performance
H3.2 Prospectors outperform defenders and reactors
H3.3 A defender stance is positively related to organizational performance
H3.4 A reactor stance is negatively related to organizational performance.

Measuring strategy

Miles and Snow's framework was developed from case study research in a number of industries. Measurement of the typology has moved from unidimensional classification based upon categorical variables to multi-item dimensional scales, which in part reflects changes in the wider social sciences. This shift and the approach of Boyne and Walker (2004) is outlined in this section.

The dominant approach to the operationalization of the typology assumed that an organization can be placed into one of the strategic types, that is a prospector, a defender, an analyzer or a reactor. Managers, when completing questionnaires on this typology, were asked to read a series of competing paragraphs that categorized an organization and to indicate which approximated to their organization. This approach, referred to as self-typing was widely adopted (for private sector studies, see Hambrick, 1983; Segev, 1987; Snow and Hrehiniak, 1980; Zahra and Pearce, 1990). Table 3.2 provides an illustration of this approach and shows the survey items used in Greenwood's (1987) study of English local authorities. Boyne and Walker (2004, 237) note that this approach does not result in the complete, mutually exclusive and internally homogeneous categories necessary to achieve a good typology, and concluded that this work takes the '...form of asking private managers to identify whether their company is, for example, a "cat", "dog", or "fish" '. To overcome these difficulties, they proposed that organizations are not likely to display a single dominant strategy, but rather a mix of strategic stances in relation to different spheres of their activities. Thus strategy variables should be treated as 'continuous, not categorical' (Boyne and Walker 2004, 236).

Scholars in the generic management community were also engaged in debate about the best way to operationalize the framework

Table 3.2 The paragraphing approach to strategy content: defenders, analyzers, prospectors and reactors

The style of the local authority

Which one of the following descriptions most closely fits your local authority compared to other local authorities? There may be elements of each description in the authority – in fact, there probably are – but we would like you to indicate which description is more typical of your local authority. Please tick the appropriate box.

☐ TYPE A. This type of local authority prefers stability to experimentation and innovation. It concentrates resources upon statutorily prescribed services and makes a deliberate effort to provide stability in their provision. Established and understood ways of working are preferred. A central concern is to make the local authority more efficient.

☐ TYPE B. This type of local authority consciously and systematically seeks to learn how other local authorities and other types of organizations perform similar functions. There is a desire to know what new services are being developed, and what new ways of delivering services are to be found elsewhere. But there is a preference not to try out unproven ideas or develop new, untested services. Nevertheless new patterns of services and new ways of working are systematically identified and appraised, and adopted quickly when their efficacy has been demonstrated.

☐ TYPE C. This type of local authority actively seeks new opportunities and challenges. New kinds of services and new ways of working are vigorously sought and implemented. The local authority values being 'first in' on service developments and ways of working, even though some experiments will be unsuccessful. Continual innovation and experimentation are preferred to stability.

☐ TYPE D. This type of local authority values stability but introduces change as circumstances require. Knowledge of new ideas and practices is not systematically sought but acquired through the informal local government grapevine. Existing practices are made as effective as possible and change occurs largely in response to external events.

Source: Greenwood (1987, 310–11).

(see, e.g. Snow and Hambrick, 1983). The major change came when Conant et al. (1990) criticized prior research for adopting the paragraphing or self-typing approach because it only captures one or two aspects of the contingent relationships between strategy, process, structure and environment. To this end they developed 11 multi-item scales to measure the overall Miles and Snow framework, that is both the strategic types and the adaptive cycle of components: entrepreneurial (organizational goals and which strategy to adopt), engineering (technological goals and approach) and administrative (the selection of structures and process). Table 3.3 provides an illustration of

Table 3.3 Conant et al.'s multi-item scale to operationalize Miles and Snow

Administrative – structure
In comparison to other HMOs, the structure of my organization is

(a) Functional in nature (i.e. organized by department – marketing, accounting, personnel, etc.) (D)
(b) Service or market orientated (i.e. departments like pediatrics or Ob/Gyn have marketing or accountability responsibilities) (P)
(c) Primarily functional (departmental) in nature; however, a service- or market-orientated structure does exist in newer or larger service offering areas (A)
(d) Continually changing to enable us to meet opportunities and solve problems as they arise (R).

Engineering – technological goal
One of the most important goals in the HMO, in comparison to other HMOs, is our dedication and commitment to

(a) Keeping costs under control (R)
(b) Analyze our costs and revenues carefully, to keep costs under control and to selectively generate new services or enter new markets (A)
(c) Insure that the people, resources and equipment required to develop new services and new markets are available and accessible (P)
(d) Make sure that we guard against critical threats by taking whatever action is necessary (R).

Entrepreneurial – product market domain
In comparison to other HMOs, the services which we provide to our members are best characterized as

(e) Services which are more innovative, continually changing and broader in nature throughout the organization and marketplace (P)
(f) Services which are fairly stable in certain units/departments and markets while innovative in other units/departments and markets (A)
(g) Services which are well focused, relatively stable and consistently defined throughout the marketplace (D)
(h) Services which are in a state of transition, and largely based on responding to opportunities or threats from the marketplace or environment (R).

Note: (P) = prospector, (D) = defender, (A) = analyzer, (R) = reactor.
Source: Conant et al. (1990, 381–82).

the types of questions posed; in this example, they are associated with the entrepreneurial problem or product and market domain. However, Conant et al.'s analysis moves back from allowing organizations to vary by strategic stance, as argued by Boyne and Walker (2004), and they categorize organizations on a majority-rule decision structure: '... organizations were classified as defenders, prospectors, analyzers, or reactors, depending on the archetypal response option that was selected most often' (Conant et al. 1990, 373). Desarbo and colleagues (2005, 56), in an extensive exploration of the Miles and Snow framework, implement the Conant et al. questionnaire and adopt more stringent decision rules requiring '...at least seven "correct" answers out of the 11 items' to be classified as a prospector or defender. Thus while a more sophisticated and nuanced approach has been developed to operationalize strategy across the entrepreneurial, engineering and administrative components, management researcher preference is to use categorical variables to measure the effect of strategy on performance.

The arguments presented for viewing strategy as a continuous variable do not just relate to questions of measurement. Public organizations, in particular, are likely to pursue a mix of strategies at the same time because they are expected to satisfy a range of conflicting and competing goals, which are judged by an array of diverse stakeholders (including citizens, service users, the media, regulators and politicians) (see Boyne, 2003a). It is therefore inappropriate to categorize organizations in the public sector as belonging solely to a single type. This logic implies that the 'analyzer' category is redundant because it is 'essentially an intermediate type between the prospector strategy at one extreme and the defender strategies at the other' (Ruekert and Walker, 1987, 17). All organizations are likely to be prospecting and defending to some extent (although the balance will vary with the priority attached to these stances, and that attached to a reactor strategy). Consequently, although evidence on the degree of prospecting and defending provides some indication of an analyzer-like stance, 'analysing' is not treated as a discrete strategy in our test of the Miles and Snow model. Given these arguments, research operationalizing the Miles and Snow framework in public organizations has predominantly focused on strategy content, allowed for strategy to vary within agencies and has thus recorded strategy content as a continuous variable (Andrews et al., 2006a; Meier et al., 2007).

Two competing views emerge from this discussion on the most appropriate way to operationalize strategy content: from the generic management literature, a view that strategy is a categorical variable, and from the public management literature that it is a continuous variable. Our position is that strategy is continuous and can vary. The implication of this is important for the measurement of strategy and associated variables. As we noted above, the approach adopted by Conant et al. (1990) and subsequently developed by DeSarbo and colleagues (2005) conflates strategy with structures and processes by designing questions that juxtapose strategy content with engineering and administrative problems. As we treat strategy content as conceptually distinct and empirically continuous, so it is necessary to separately measure strategy content, strategy formulation and implementation, and other measures of organization and the environment.

The full descriptions of our measures of organizational strategy are listed in Table 3.4. A prospector strategy was operationalized through four measures of innovation and market exploration, as these are central to Miles and Snow's (1978) definition of this orientation. The specific

Table 3.4 Measures of organizational strategy and factor analysis

Measures	*X*	SD	Factor 1	Factor 2	Factor 3
We continually redefine our service priorities (P)	4.98	1.31	−.31	**.71**	.07
We seek to be first to identify new modes of delivery (P)	4.59	1.38	−.20	**.86**	.01
Searching for new opportunities is a major part of our overall strategy (P)	5.05	1.20	−.38	**.74**	.20
We often change our focus to new areas of service provision (P)	4.38	1.22	.11	**.82**	−.16
We seek to maintain stable service priorities (D)	5.12	1.17	−.09	.07	**.79**
The service emphasizes efficiency of provision (D)	5.36	0.93	−.34	.31	**.62**
We focus on our core activities (D)	5.17	1.03	.00	−.19	**.79**
We have no definite service priorities (R)	2.27	1.04	**.77**	−.21	−.07
We change provision only when under pressure from external agencies (R)	1.87	0.87	**.89**	−.04	−.12
We give little attention to new opportunities for service delivery (R)	2.08	0.87	**.70**	−.41	−.10
The service explores new opportunities only when under pressure from external agencies (R)	2.00	0.87	**.90**	−.05	−.07
We have no consistent response to external pressure (R)	3.03	1.23	**.47**	−.35	−.23
Eigenvalues			3.31	2.95	1.79
Cumulative variance			27.60	52.21	67.10

N = 90 Rotated Factor loadings; P = prospecting; D = defending; R = reacting.

measures are derived from Snow and Hrebiniak (1980) and Stevens and McGowan (1983). The Intra-class Correlation Coefficient (ICC) for the prospecting measures was 0.53 ($p > .001$), signifying a statistically significant level of perceptual agreement amongst individuals within the same service departments. To explore the extent to which Welsh local authorities displayed defender characteristics, informants were asked three questions assessing whether their approach to service delivery was focused on core activities and achieving efficiency (Miller, 1986; Snow and Hrebiniak, 1980; Stevens and McGowan, 1983). The ICC for the defending measures was 0.34 ($p > .001$). Reactors are expected to lack a consistent strategy and to await guidance on how to respond to environmental change. We therefore asked our informants five questions about the existence of definite priorities in their service and the extent to which their behaviour was determined by external pressures. We again based these measures on prior work (Snow and Hrebiniak, 1980), taking particular care to avoid leading questions by excluding the term 'react' from the relevant items. The ICC for the reacting measures was 0.41 ($p > .001$). To determine if there are distinct underlying strategic stances amongst services in Welsh local government, the survey items were factor analysed (Table 3.4). This produced three statistically significant and clear factors explaining 67.1 per cent of the variance in the data.

The measures of prospecting, defending and reacting load on one common factor each. The eigenvalues for all three factors are high, suggesting that the services sampled in this study display distinctive strategies. The rotated factor loadings for each strategic orientation are highlighted in the table and are all above 0.4, indicating that they are important determinants of the variance explained by the factors (Hair et al., 1998). The prospecting and reacting factors have excellent Cronbach's Alpha internal reliability scores of 0.82 and 0.84, respectively (Nunnally, 1978). Although the defending factor has a comparatively low Cronbach's Alpha score of 0.60, it is nevertheless suitable for exploratory analysis (Loewenthal, 1996). To test the argument that organizations display a range of strategic stances, a single factor score was created for each group of items (i.e. prospecting, defending and reacting), and the correlations between these un-rotated factors were analysed.

Table 3.5 highlights that there is a small positive correlation between prospecting and defending (0.17), suggesting the presence of some overlap between the two strategic stances, which, in turn, may mean that some services pursue both strategies. By contrast, negative correlations between reacting and the other strategic stances (−0.47 for prospecting, and −0.33 for defending) imply that reactors are far less likely to engage

Table 3.5 Correlations between strategy archetypes

	Prospecting	Defending	Reacting
Prospecting			
Defending	0.17+		
Reacting	−0.47**	−0.33**	

$N = 90$ + $p \leq 0.10$;** $p \leq 0.01$ (one-tailed tests).

in prospecting or defending. This implies that (at least for this data set) reacting is the most distinctive of Miles and Snow's strategic archetypes in the public sector.

Statistical results

The results for the statistical tests of strategy content on service performance are presented in Table 3.6. The model explains over two-thirds of the variation in the service performance measure and is highly statistically significant. We find strong but not overwhelming support for Hypotheses 3.1–3.4 on strategy content. The results are consistent with Hypotheses 3.1 and 3.3 on strategy content and performance. The coefficients for prospecting and defending are statistically significant and have a positive sign. Hypothesis 3.2 is not supported: while prospecting out-performs reacting, the coefficient for defending is also statistically significant and positive, thus prospectors do not out-perform defenders. As we noted, the coefficient for defending was positive, and statistically significant, giving support to Hypothesis 3.3.

Table 3.6 Strategy content and public service performance

Independent variable	Slope	t-score
Prospecting	.1367	2.78*
Defending	.1537	2.93**
Reacting	.0610	1.26
R^2	0.70**	
Adjusted R^2	0.67**	
N = 47		

Note: Significance levels: +$p \leq 0.10$;* $p \leq 0.05$;** $p \leq 0.01$ (two-tailed tests).
All equations include control variables entered in the models shown in Table 2.7.

The results for reacting do not support Hypothesis 3.4 because the coefficient on the reactor variable is statistically insignificant in this model.

Discussion and implications

The results presented in this chapter indicate that strategy content is important for the performance of public organizations. In particular, strategies of prospecting and defending are associated with higher levels of performance. These results reflect the propositions of Miles and Snow (1978) who argued that prospectors and defenders would out-perform reactors. The positive association between prospecting and performance reflects the findings of a variety of other studies (Andrews et al., 2005b, 2006a). This evidence indicates that there is reward to be found for public agencies that pursue a strategy that includes indentifying new priorities, searching out new opportunities for, and modes of, service delivery and where there is a willingness to change service provision. In short, this finding suggests that public agencies can purse strategies that are associated with innovation – that is developing new service delivery mechanisms and thereby achieve higher performance.

The findings presented here vary slightly from findings reported in other quantitative studies of public agencies in the UK that have typically reported a statistically significant and negative coefficient for reacting (Andrews et al., 2005b; Andrews et al., 2006a). Nonetheless our model in this chapter once again indicates that reacting is not likely to be a successful route to higher levels of service performance. These results have confirmed one of the central propositions of Miles and Snow – that prospecting and defending have a positive relationship with organizational performance – which has also been supported in private sector studies (Zahra and Pearce, 1990).

Other public sector studies have also identified a positive relationship between defending and organizational performance, and have a common element with this study of Welsh local government services. Meier et al. (2007) undertake a study of strategy content in school education districts in the US – where defending is predominantly the strategy stance associated with success (also see Meier et al., 2010). Both US school districts and service departments in local government, the unit of analysis in this study, are single-purpose organizations, with a mission to deliver services in one policy domain. The complexity of the different policy areas is likely to vary widely: contrast garbage collection which typically involves technological problems of collection and disposal and the management of the workforce with, say, social services to children, families and the elderly which requires complex decisions about levels of risk and the appropriate action to take to prevent, and if necessary, alleviate problems. A single service department, even if a complex area of public service production, is likely to be more clearly focused on a limited number of goals (Chun and Rainey, 2005). This is particularly likely when a single service department is contrasted with large multipurpose organizations, such as a local authority. Evidence to date suggesting that defending has a neutral impact on organizational performance has come from this more complex setting of multipurpose organizations. It is possible to speculate that this result arises from the different unit of analysis, single-purpose organizations versus multipurpose. Findings from health services suggest that when a hospital changes to a defender strategy (from any other strategic stance) rather than a prospector or analyzer, there are no differences in performance between these three strategic stances (Zajec and Shortell, 1989). More research is clearly needed to corroborate this argument, but it goes some way towards explaining variations in research results from different settings and points towards the significance of organizational goals as a factor influencing the strategy content adopted by an organization and its likely relationship with organizational effectiveness.

Positive coefficients for both prospecting and defending suggest that Miles and Snow's (1978) composite typology, an analyzer, might also be a strategy to achieve higher levels of organizational performance. Miles and Snow (1978, 29) argue that an analyzer is rarely a first mover but instead 'watch their competitors closely for new ideas, and ... rapidly adopt those which appear to be the most promising'. In our work we have not used the analyzer typology because it shares its characteristics with both defenders and prospectors. Rather we have argued that strategy varies across an organization and as such needs to be measured as a continuous and not a categorical variable (Boyne and Walker, 2004). We take the findings in this study as evidence to confirm our view that organizations have multiple strategies: an analyzer is a balanced approach to strategy content. A further area for additional research is to examine to what extent single-purpose organizations simultaneously seek to innovate and take risk (prospecting) while focusing upon their core business (defending) and what the relative weight of each strategic stance is in different settings.

Conclusion

This chapter has explored the relationship between strategy content and performance. The chapter outlined the Miles and Snow strategy content ideal types, and then subjected these to an empirical test in a multivariate statistical regression with a measure of organizational performance as the dependent variable. The findings provide some support for the hypotheses that were developed in the public management literature on the likely impact of different strategic stances on organizational performance. In particular, the statistical results offered strong support for the arguments initially developed by Miles and Snow that prospectors and defenders would out-perform reactors.

The Miles and Snow strategies of prospecting, defending and reacting are the most widely known aspects of the framework. But as we have noted here and in the Introduction, strategy content, and its likely relationship with organizational performance, is predicated on processes, structure and the organizational environment. Given the importance of these contingent relationships, we proceed to examine each in turn. In the next Chapter, we examine strategic formulation processes, and their independent effect on performance and the joint effect of this variable and strategy content. Chapter 5 also asks questions about process, but focuses upon implementation processes and their relationship with strategy content. Structure is explored in Chapter 6 and the technical and institutional environment in Chapter 7. In each of these chapters, we examine if the propositions raised by Miles and Snow about the relationship between strategy content and the other variables are upheld in our empirical study of Welsh local government.

4
Strategy Formulation, Content and Performance

In this chapter, we explore the effects of strategy formulation on performance, and whether these effects are moderated by strategy content. This discussion attends to two of the central facets of the wider strategic management literature examining the ways in which strategy is formed, referred to as strategy formulation, and the substance of those decisions, or strategy content (which was explored in Chapter 3) (Boyne and Walker, 2004; Hart, 1992; Ketchen et al., 1996). By focusing upon content and formulation, we contribute towards the literature on strategic management in a number of ways. To date, research in the public sector has typically focused on either formulation or content (Andrews et al., 2006a; Boyne and Gould-Williams, 2003, for an exception see Walker et al., 2010). Furthermore, when such studies are undertaken on public agencies they typically focus on either a single approach to formulation or a limited range of alternative strategy content options (Elbanna, 2006; Zahra and Pearce, 1990). This is perhaps one of the central weaknesses in much of the prior literature. Over a decade ago, Ketchen et al. (1996, 231) passed similar remarks: 'The traditional distinction between strategy process and strategy content has perhaps limited the ability of strategic management research to explain the determinants of organizational performance.' Therefore, in this chapter, we take a small but important step on this journey and examine multiple formulation and content approaches and assess their independent and joint impact on organizational performance.

At the heart of the Miles and Snow (1978) framework are questions about relationships between strategy content, processes, structure and organizational environments and performance. In this chapter we delve into one of these areas and examine the effects of strategy formulation on performance and the ways in which strategy content moderates this relationship. Miles and Snow (1978) were quite explicit in their strategic stance typologies about anticipated relationships between these variables and pointed towards wide-ranging, provisional and exploratory approaches to strategy formulation in prospectors and more planned approaches in defenders. By contrast the managerial behaviours of reactors are argued to be shaped more by the environment than by the action of managers and as such Miles and Snow contend that organizations displaying this type of strategy content are not likely to have a steady approach to strategy formulation processes.

We initially explore the existing literature on strategy formulation and performance, and then develop hypotheses on the combined effects of formulation processes and strategy content. This is followed by a discussion of the measurement of strategy formulation. The results of our statistical analysis are then presented and subsequently interpreted before we conclude by considering if the evidence we present supports the notions advanced by Miles and Snow.

Strategy formulation and performance

Attention to strategy formulation by public administration scholars extends substantially beyond that for strategy content (see Bryson, 1995; Joyce, 1999; Moore, 1995). While a range of strategy formulation models have been developed (see Mintzberg et al., 1998), rational planning and logical incrementalism are the two main models of strategy formulation in the management literature (Elbanna, 2006). Where neither of these approaches is present, organizations are likely to lack clearly discernable processes, thereby exhibiting 'strategy absence' (Inkpen and Chaudhury, 1995).

Rational planning is characterized by analytical, formal and logical processes through which organizations scan the internal and external environment, and develop policy options which differ from the status quo. The options that are generated by this process are evaluated prior to the setting of organizational targets, which are then regularly reviewed and monitored (Dror, 1973; Mintzberg, 1994). Planning operates within a framework of bounded rationality because of the cognitive limits of decision-makers and the iterative way in which they move between the various planning phases (Elbanna, 2006). There have been large-scale experiments in rational planning in the public sector. A notable example of this has been the widespread use of corporate planning in UK local government during the 1970s. Interestingly, assessments of this experiment have not been positive and it was generally adjudged to have been unsuccessful (Boyne, 2001; Clapham, 1984).

Rational or strategic planning runs deep in public management, and is presented in a variety of ways. For example Johanson (2009) posits three models of formulation. Strategic design, the first, draws heavily upon the strategic planning and rational planning literature. Internal strategic scanning, the second, draws its conceptual framework from the resource-based view of the firm (Barney, 1991), and strategic governance, the third, relates the strategy formulation process to models of partnership, networking and collaborative management. Moore's (1995) discussion of strategic management deals with key concerns about managing the internal and external organizational environment. Moore (1995, 280) draws heavily upon strategic planning in his discussion: 'Strategic planning... is deliberately selective. It does not try to give an account of everything that happens in the organization. It focuses only on the key problems and opportunities facing the organization, and the adaptations the organization must make to deal with the problems and exploit the opportunities.' Moore's work builds upon a long tradition of research on strategic planning in the USA. This stream of research is most clearly associated with the work of John Bryson (see, e.g. 1995; 2010; Bryson et al., 2010). Bryson (2010, 255) contends that: '... strategic planning typically "works" and often works extremely well'. He points to benefits that include promoting strategic thinking, acting and learning, improved decision-making, enhanced organizational effectiveness, responsiveness and resilience, enhanced effectiveness of broader societal systems and direct benefits for the people involved in the process.

Difficulties in implementing rational planning, such as in the case of corporate planning in the UK in the 1970s, are usually attributed to technical and political problems. Recent evidence on planning amongst local authorities in Wales suggests that technical problems are more difficult to overcome than political factors (Boyne et al., 2004). Despite these challenges, rational planning processes can provide a valuable framework for the formulation of objectives and actions.

The alternative strategy process framework developed in the public management literature commenced with Lindblom's (1959) widely cited article 'The Science of Muddling Through' which posited that decision-making in the public sector is an incremental process. This was developed by Quinn (1980) into 'incrementalism with a purpose' or logical incrementalism which emphasizes the importance of setting broad organizational goals (Boyne et al., 2004). It suggests that strategy formulation is a political process – actors within organizations may have conflicting views on the most appropriate ways to meet organizational goals. How these are reconciled is reflected in the strategy-making process. Political conflicts may be over resource allocation, policy goals or organizational power, inside or outside the organization (Elbanna, 2006). Internal politics may therefore be counterproductive for the attainment of higher levels of organizational performance, as conflict can result in inopportune decision-making, drift in seeking goal attainment, a lack of transparency by decision-makers and a poor interpretation of the external organizational environment (Dean and Sharfman, 1996; Eisenhardt and Bourgeois, 1988; Elbanna, 2006). All of this suggests that logical incrementalism will have adverse effects on organizational performance.

Not all public organizations will have clear strategy formulation processes. Inkpen and Choudhury (1995) argue that strategy absence occurs when an organization is undergoing a substantial change or a deliberate decision has been made to avoid developing a clear and coherent strategy process. They claim that it is conceivable that strategy absence can have benefits, but these are argued to mainly accrue to younger firms, those experimenting or in the process of forced strategic transition. The limited empirical tests support arguments made by authors such as Segev (1989, 499) that strategy absence is 'ill-conceived' and inimical for performance. For example, Spanos et al. (2004) find that firms with no strategy perform more poorly than those who adopt hybrid strategies. This evidence taken together with the arguments made by Miles and Snow (1978) for the performance of reactors, the strategy content version of absence of strategy processes, would suggest that an avoidance of strategic management is typically associated with lower levels of organizational performance.

Empirical studies of strategy formulation in the public sector are notable by their absence. In relation to strategic planning, Bryson (2010) notes that the evidence for the contention that strategic planning works comes largely from case study work, with few large-N studies. Prior evidence on the consequences of rational planning for organizational performance drawing largely on studies of private organizations is, however, mixed (Boyne, 2001; Elbanna, 2006). While the balance of the international research from the public, private and nonprofit sectors leans towards a positive relationship between planning and performance (Boyne and Gould-Williams, 2003; Crittenden et al., 1998; Odom and Boxx, 1988; Siciliano, 1997), 'planning is neither a necessary nor a sufficient condition for performance improvement' (Boyne et al. 2004, 200).

Table 4.1 presents the prior evidence on strategy formulation and performance. The sources for these studies include the English local government and Texas School District data sets referred to above. However, other data have been brought to bear on the question of strategy

Table 4.1 Impact of strategy formulation on public service performance

Study	Organizations and sample size	Formulation approach	Dimension of performance	Net effect on performance
Hyndman and Eden (2001)	9 Northern Ireland central government executive agencies	Rational planning: mission statements, objectives and targets	Broad outcomes to clients, customers and stakeholders	+
Boyne and Gould Williams (2003)	71 Welsh local government departments	Targets Internal External Perceptions of the process Action Plans	Service quality	– NS NS + NS
		Targets Internal External Perceptions of the process Action Plans	Efficiency	– NS NS + NS
		Targets Internal External Perceptions of the process Action Plans	Cost-effectiveness	NS – + + NS
Hendrick (2003)	14 Departments of the City of Milwaukee	Strategic planning process	Strategic and manager capacity	NS
Walker and Boyne (2006)	117 English local governments	Target setting Target ownership	Aggregate organizational performance	NS +

		Target setting Target ownership	Perception of output and efficiency	NS +
		Target setting Target ownership	Perception of responsiveness	– +
		Target setting Target ownership	Perception of outcomes	NS +
Boyne and Chen (2007)	147 English local governments	Targets Stretch Number of targets	School exam pass rates	+ + +
Yang and Hsieh (2007)	684 employees of local governments in Taipei		Performance management effectiveness	
Walker et al. (2010)	101 English local governments	Rational planning Logical incrementalism	Aggregate organizational performance	+ NS

formulation and includes a US city government, employees of local governments in the capital of Taiwan, Taipei and chief executive officers of central government executive agencies in Northern Ireland. One study also draws upon the units of analysis in this book, an earlier data set on Welsh local government departments.

The first point to note from this table is the lack of tests conducted on strategy absence and the single statistical study that examines the relationship between logical incrementalism and performance. The Walker et al. (2010) study develops an index measure of logical incrementalism drawing on survey statements including: 'the strategy with the greatest level of political support is usually adopted as policy'; 'the extent to which policy options are similar to present ones'; 'when we make strategy we produce policy options which are very similar to those we already have'; 'strategy develops through a process of adjustment'; and 'strategy develops through a process of bargaining and negotiation between groups and individuals'. They conclude that the relationship is not statistically significant, which does not offer support for their hypothesis that incremental processes have adverse effects on performance.

Hyndman and Eden's (2001) qualitative study examines rational planning amongst the chief executives of nine Executive Agencies in

Northern Ireland. They focused their efforts on exploring the development, use and impact of mission statements, objectives and targets, and adopt a qualitative approach using semi-structured interviews. They find that organizations rated high on managerial effectiveness are also more likely to adopt performance management and rational planning approaches. Many of those they interviewed associated a rational approach to planning and management with improved performance. They quote an agency chief executive who said: 'It gives people inside the organization a greater sense of direction and therefore achievement. It also ensures a better service to the clients/customers/stakeholders' (Hyndman and Eden, 2001, 592). However, their conclusion on this is somewhat tempered by their assertion that the processes adopted by these agencies were akin to logical incrementalism: '... decisions emerge through a constant process of analysis, re-analysis, and modification throughout the development and implementation of a strategy in order to keep in line with the environment' (Hyndman and Eden, 2001, 595). Another drawback of this study is that performance is not crisply operationalized and is discussed as a broad measure of the services received by clients, customers and stakeholders.

A number of studies have been conducted that examine rational planning. It is noteworthy that many of the studies on rational planning only examine an aspect of planning – target setting. These studies reflect the growth of performance management and managing for results under the new public management rubric (Moynihan, 2006; Organization for Economic Cooperation and Development, 2005). The one study that includes a broader measure of rational planning is that by Walker, Boyne and Brewer (2010). Rational planning is measured by variables that capture the detailed nature of the planning process, the appraisal of alternative options and working with stakeholders. They posit a positive relationship between rational planning and performance and provide evidence to support this in the long term. Hendrick (2003) examines rational planning, this time amongst 14 departments in Milwaukee City government in the late 1990s. This study conceptualizes strategic planning processes as consisting of index measures of comprehensive planning, extent of monitoring, broad participation in planning, external/internal participants, internal centralization and commitment to planning. Hendrick correlates these six variables with 'strategic and manager capacity' resulting in two statistically significant correlations. Given the expectation in the study that all measures of planning would be correlated with strategic and manager capacity, these results can be judged as weak. One further issue arises in this study: the measure of performance captures aspects of the process of planning and management rather than measures of organizational outputs and outcomes (as in a measure of effectiveness, etc.).

The studies that drill down into the performance management aspects of rational planning typically offer a positive assessment of its effectiveness in achieving higher levels of organizational performance. For example, Yang and Hseih (2007) examine the extent of adoption of targets, that is indicators of inputs, outputs, outcomes, efficiency and satisfaction on 'managerial effectiveness' in city governments in Taiwan. While their results are supportive of the positive impact of these elements on performance, their dependent variable was somewhat clouded by the inclusion of measures of performance management itself as a component of managerial effectiveness.

A number of the studies listed in Table 4.1 examine the issue of target setting, a key aspect of rational planning. These studies offer more concrete evidence on the rational planning–performance hypothesis. Boyne and Gould-Williams (2003) undertook an analysis of the impact of the number of targets on the achievements of local authority service departments in Wales (the same unit of analysis as in this study). They found that a higher number of targets was associated with lower managerial perceptions of performance on two measures of service quality and one of efficiency, and found insignificant relationships with performance for the process of producing a formal planning document that specified a programme of activities for the achievement of targets. Boyne and Gould-Williams (2003) did, however, uncover positive associations between planning processes and service quality, efficiency and cost effectiveness, similar to the Yang and Hseih (2007) study.

Focusing on Welsh local government's near neighbour, English local government, Boyne and Chen (2007) examine the impact of a target setting regime called 'Local Public Service Agreements' (LPSAs). The LPSA regime offered a financial reward (2.5 per cent of revenue budget) based on achievements against 12 targets negotiated between each local government and central government. This presented Boyne and Chen (2007) with the opportunity to compare authorities with and without targets on particular performance indicators across time. Focusing upon education they find that authorities with a target performed better than those without a target, and also performed better than in the pre-target time period. Again focusing on English local government, Walker and Boyne (2006) examined the extent to which the ownership of targets was associated with performance by exploring whether targets were agreed by those responsible for meeting them and whether the targets were viewed as achievable. Target ownership was shown to have a statistically significant relationship with four measures of performance (one is an external measure of service performance devised by the regulator and three perceptual measures that examined service efficiency, responsiveness and effectiveness).

The range of empirical studies on the relationship between strategy formulation and the performance of public organizations is limited. The majority of the evidence focuses upon the rational planning and offers some support for the notion of a positive relationship between this strategy formulation approach and performance. The evidence in relation to logical incrementalism and strategy absence is incomplete, and here we largely draw upon inferences from theory to assist our hypothesis generation. The arguments for logical incrementalism presented above suggest a likely negative association with performance. No empirical tests have been undertaken on strategy formulation process absence in public organizations therefore, we fall back on the arguments presented by Miles and Snow (1978) and Segev (1989) and private sector evidence. In summary, the hypotheses developed suggest one positive and two negative relationships with organizational performance:

H4.1 Rational planning is positively related to organizational performance

H4.2 Logical incrementalism is negatively related to organizational performance

H4.3 Strategy process absence is negatively related to organizational performance.

The combined effects of strategy content and formulation

The central propositions of the strategic management literature go beyond strategy content alone, and argue that an organization needs to align its strategy with the organization's internal characteristics and the external environment. Only when this is achieved will organizational effectiveness be enhanced. This contingency framework is central to Miles and Snow's (1978) characterization of strategy, and from this perspective research that primarily examines strategy content can be seen to deal with somewhat underspecified relationships. Organizations have to find appropriate relationships between the 'entrepreneurial' problem (which strategy to adopt), the 'engineering' problem (which technologies to use) and the 'administrative' problem (which processes and structures to select). By their nature prospectors are more focused on entrepreneurial questions and examine the services they deliver with a view towards innovation, whereas defenders, by placing emphasis on core services and efficiency, focus upon engineering problems. Nevertheless, prospectors and defenders are also concerned with the questions and solutions to the administrative problem. Reactors respond to these issues in uncertain and inconsistent ways and are more likely to be influenced by the environment (Miles and Snow, 1978, and also see Conant et al., 1990).

Our interest in strategy formulation processes focuses our attention on the administrative problem. Miles and Snow (1978, 23) argue that administrative systems have both a 'lagging' and a 'leading' relationship with strategy:

> As a lagging variable, the administrative system must rationalise, through the development of appropriate structures and processes, the strategic decisions made at previous points in the adjustment process. As a leading variable ... the administrative system will facilitate or restrict the organization's future capacity to adapt.

Thus, over time strategy content and processes reinforce each other: organizations choose an administrative system that is consistent with their strategy and then find that this system continues to propel them in the same strategic direction. The result is a cycle of mutual cause and effect that tightens the relationship between a strategic stance and a set of organizational characteristics and performance. This leads to the view that prospectors and defenders have distinct processes. Reactors, lacking a coherent and stable strategy, have no consistent internal arrangements.

Miles and Snow (1978) distinguish between the extent of planning associated with different strategies. In a defender, 'the planning sequence proceeds through a series of steps which allows the organization to exploit current and foreseeable environmental conditions fully. These steps mainly involve the setting of output and cost objectives which are then translated into specific operating goals and budgets' (Miles and Snow, 1978, 43). The planning process in a prospector, by contrast, is broad and tentative. Prospectors are poised to expand or contract their activities, depending on the opportunities or threats that they face, so the planning cycle is seldom systematic or complete. Rather, planning is fluid and shifts with new organizational directions. In a prospector, '... organizational objectives are allowed to coalesce around current areas of prospecting and thus seldom achieve a stable equilibrium. Unlike the defender, whose planning process is usually finalised before implementation begins, the prospector must often directly engage a new problem or opportunity before detailed planning can be completed' (Miles and Snow, 1978, 61).

Thus, whereas the defender is a rational planner, the strategy process in a prospector is similar to 'logical incrementalism' (Quinn, 1980). Both defenders and prospectors plan, but the former do so formally and precisely, whereas the latter follow a more informal and iterative process. Finally, reactors again are predicted to exhibit a range of approaches to planning. In a reactor '... management does not fully shape the organization's structures and processes to fit a chosen strategy' (Miles and Snow, 1978, 93). Nevertheless, the absence of a clear vision about where the organization is headed, and the reliance on external pressures to shape strategy, makes it difficult if not impossible for reactors to plan. Any planning process would quickly become redundant as the organization shifts in unpredictable ways.

The achievement of high levels of performance in prospectors is proposed to be dependent upon an alignment of decentralized structures (see Chapter 6) and decision-making to permit staff at multiple levels to apply their expertise and implement fluid planning processes because they are in a state of flux, engaging in new opportunities prior to the completion of planning (Miles and Snow, 1978, 59–62). While theoretical arguments have been advanced by Miles and Snow, little if no attention has been focused on examining these moderated relationships between strategy formulation and strategy content in the public management literature. In public organizations, two attempts have been mounted to explore the relationship between formulation and content. However, these studies move beyond the two-way joint relationships we are discussing in this chapter and have sought to test in a more comprehensive manner the contingent nature of the strategy–performance hypothesis as advanced by Miles and Snow. Andrews et al. (2008), working with the English local government data set, tested the fully specified Miles and Snow model: that is, relationships between strategy content, strategy processes, structure and environment, using four years of data across 396 local governments. In the base model, they again note the hierarchical relationship between organizational performance and strategy content: prospecting is positively associated with performance, defending is statistically insignificant and reacting is negative when controlling for structure (decentralization), processes (incremental) and environmental uncertainty and environmental constraints. To model the complex relationships between these variables, the authors examine multiple interactions. They commence with two-way interactions (e.g. prospecting × decentralization, prospecting × incremental processes and prospecting × uncertainty) and then move to three- and finally four-way interactions (e.g. prospecting × decentralization × incremental processes × uncertainty). Only the inclusion of the two-way interactions offers additional explanatory power to the model. Overall these are lacklustre results, and the addition of further interactions leads to the effects of strategy content and strategy formulation on performance dissipating. In a second study, these authors (Meier et al., 2010) examine the interactive relationships between strategy, structure and the environment amongst school districts in Texas and again demonstrate that the anticipated contingencies are not uncovered.

The authors of these two studies speculate that this may be because of poor theory (strategic fit has no link with organizational effectiveness) or that the theory does not operate amongst public organizations as it does amongst private. They speculate that the non-significant results could arise because the scope for organizational adaptation to achieve fit may be lower in the public than in the private sector given the frequent external pressures to adopt new structures and processes. It is also possible that successful performance outcomes and alignment across internal and external characteristics could be linked to the goals of public organizations. In particular the multiple and sometimes competing objectives of public organizations may work to cloud these relationships. A further suggestion is that there are potential methodological challenges. These include those posed by data requirements to undertake complex statistical analysis, and as such it is possible that the statistical estimates influence the results because of the size of the data set (although the Texas tests include over 1000 organizations), or because of the ways in which strategy content is operationalized (as a continuous variable, whereas in the original Miles and Snow model it was treated as categorical) or by the use of single-item measures for some of the constructs rather than indexes which may better capture the range of behaviours associated with content and processes. This latter point once again raises questions about the most appropriate way to measure strategy.

Given the limited empirical evidence brought to bear on questions about the relationship between formulation, content and performance, we draw again on theory presented by Miles and Snow to assist in our hypothesis generation. Three hypotheses are offered:

H4.4 Rational planning is likely to be positively related to performance in an organization with a defender stance

H4.5 Logical incrementalism is likely to be positively related to performance in an organization with a prospector stance

H4.6 Strategy process absence is likely to be negatively related to performance in an organization with a reactor stance.

Measuring strategy formulation

To explore processes of strategy formulation, survey informants were asked five questions assessing the extent to which the approach to strategic decision-making in their service followed established formal procedures and two questions on logical incrementalism, all of which are drawn from prior studies (see Table 4.2). Single rational planning and logical incremental factors for these measures were then extracted using principal components analysis as shown in Table 4.2. Our measures of rational planning sought to capture the use of formal organizational processes to make strategy (Hart and Banbury, 1994), the assessment of alternative strategy options (Bailey et al., 2000) and the use of target-setting (Bailey et al., 2000). The ICC for the planning measures was 0.53 ($p > 0.001$), and the Cronbach Alpha score of 0.86 demonstrates their excellent scale reliability (Nunnally, 1978). The key characteristics of logical incrementalism are an ongoing process of adjustment to new circumstances and negotiation with key stakeholders (Hart and Banbury, 1994). These concepts were separately captured in the questions we posed on logical incrementalism. The ICC for the incrementalism measures was 0.39 ($p > 0.001$), with a satisfactory Cronbach Alpha scale

Table 4.2 Measures of strategy formulation

Variable definition	X	SD	F1	F2
Strategy making is a formal procedure in our service (R)	5.28	1.21	.78	
Strategy is based on formal analysis of the service's needs (R)	5.18	1.09	.87	.85
We assess alternative strategies (R)	4.84	1.30	.83	.85
We follow precise procedures to achieve targets (R)	4.68	1.42	.77	
Targets in the service are matched to specifically identified citizen needs (R)	4.71	1.22	.79	
Strategy is made on an on-going basis (LI)	5.46	0.95		
Strategy develops through negotiation with external stakeholders (e.g. voluntary/private sector groups) (LI)	5.06	1.22		
There is no discernible strategy process	2.18	1.14		
N	90			

Note: R = rational, LI = logical incrementalism.

reliability coefficient of 0.59 (Loewenthal, 1996). Finally, given that a reactor is expected to wait for signals in the external environment to shape its strategic stance, it is not expected to have a coherent approach to making decisions. To tap this likelihood we turned to Inkpen and Choudhury's (1995) work on strategy absence and posed the statement: 'There is no discernible strategy process'.

Statistical results

The statistical results in Table 4.3 provide little support for the hypotheses on strategy formulation and performance. The coefficient for the rational planning variable is not significant and Hypothesis 4.1 is therefore rejected. The coefficients for logical incremental and strategy absence variables are, as anticipated, negative, but only the measure of an absence of a clear strategy formulation process achieves statistical significance. These results reject Hypothesis 4.2. By contrast, they offer support to Hypothesis 4.3, indicating that strategy process absence is detrimental to the achievement of higher levels of organizational performance.

Hypotheses 4.4 through 4.6 are examined in Table 4.4. The model explains nearly 74 per cent of the variance and is statistically significant. The results offer only partial support for our hypotheses. The coefficient for 'rational planning × defending' is positive but not statistically significant and Hypothesis 4.4 is therefore rejected. A positive and statistically significant relationship is identified for the joint effect of logical incrementalism and prospecting on performance, thus Hypothesis 4.5 is supported. This is an important finding because it indicates that prospecting positively reinforces the relationship between logical

Table 4.3 Strategy formulation and public service performance

Independent variable	Slope	t-score
Rational planning	−.0204	−.32
Logical incremental	−.0974	−1.41
Strategy absence	−.1105	−1.85+
R^2	0.70**	
Adjusted R^2	0.67**	
N = 47		

Note: Significance levels: $+p \leq 0.10$; $^{*}p \leq 0.05$; $^{**}p \leq 0.01$ (two-tailed tests). All equations include control variables entered in the models shown in Table 2.7.

Table 4.4 Strategy formulation × content and performance

Independent variable	Slope	t-score
Rational planning × defending	.0089	1.25
Logical incremental × prospecting	.0027	4.08**
Strategy absence × reacting	.0012	.47
R^2	.79**	
Adjusted R^2	.74**	
$N = 47$		

Note: Significance levels: * $p \leq 0.05$; ** $p \leq 0.01$ (two-tailed tests).
All equations include control variables entered in the models shown in Table 2.7.

incrementalism and performance. Finally Hypothesis 4.6 is also rejected: the coefficient for the strategy 'absence × reacting' variable does not attain statistical significance.

Discussion and implications

The results of this research imply that strategy formulation in public organizations has the greatest consequences for service performance when considered alongside strategy content. This suggests that organizations may need to carefully consider the ways they make strategies as well as their content. The results show that (when we control for strategy content and the environment) an absence of clear strategy processes is harmful for organizational performance. Finally, the interactions between strategy content and formulation offer some evidence to support Miles and Snow's argument that the effects of content and formulation processes are indeed dependent upon one another. In this case, prospectors who adopt logical incremental processes were more likely to be high performers and move the neutral impact of logical incrementalism on performance to a positive effect.

The non-significant result for the rational planning variable is not as hypothesized. As we noted earlier (see Table 4.1), other studies have only on balance indicated that rational planning has a positive effect on organizational performance – a number of studies offer alternative findings. In the model presented in this chapter, we did not explicitly explore variations in different aspects of the external environment, but instead we controlled for it by the inclusion of our prior performance variable and service expenditure. It is, however, possible that the extent to which the environment is uncertain, changing or complex will have a bearing on the impact of planning: the majority of prior research found that rational planning was more effective when the external environment was unstable (Miller and Friesen, 1983; Priem et al.,

1995). However, other studies point towards a positive relationship between stable environments, planning and performance improvement (e.g. Frederickson, 1984; Capon et al., 1987). Further research is required to explore the effect of different aspects of the external environment on the relationship between rational planning and performance – we commence this line of research in Chapter 7 when we examine the interaction between the environment, strategy and performance.

It is also possible that the policy context may be influencing the findings in this chapter. Just prior to our research instrument being distributed to local authorities in Wales, a service improvement regime called Best Value had been abandoned. This was one of the first examples of policy divergence between England and Wales following devolution of responsibility for health and local government to the Welsh Assembly (Andrews et al., 2003). The Best Value regime focused heavily on many of the facets of rational planning: environmental scanning, collection of data on management arrangements in other organizations, systematic assessment of internal capacities, option appraisal and target setting. This planning regime also included an action plan which was laden with targets and required an annual process of monitoring and reporting against achievements (Boyne, Martin and Walker, 2004). Best Value was deeply unpopular in Welsh local government and many services had stopped implementing the regime some time prior to its formal abolition in 2002. The Wales Programme for Improvement replaced it – a regime that placed less emphasis on rational planning. It is possible that the services surveyed in this research had (or were in the process of) jettisoning rigorous planning processes. Limitations of research design and context mean that we are not able to explore these possible contextual reasons for the non-significant result for rational planning. Though we have run lagged models, longitudinal studies of the relationship between strategy and service performance will be able to examine the impacts of changing policy contexts more carefully. Such studies could combine quantitative and qualitative methodologies to tease out some of the more nuanced aspects of strategy in public agencies.

The findings on the impact of logical incrementalism on service performance were not as anticipated. Organizations which emphasize the political aspects of strategy making and continually review decisions are not likely to achieve higher or lower levels of organizational performance in comparison to those adopting rational planning. Research testing the impact of logical incrementalism on different types of performance measures, indicators and regimes would provide useful additional information on the consequences of this approach to strategy formulation.

A perceived absence of strategy processes is associated with lower levels of service performance. Inkpen and Chaudhury (1995) argue that strategy absence is a legitimate choice by an organization, but it is not a choice that will produce higher levels of organizational performance, according to our results. Much of the research literature identifies reacting as the 'lemon' of strategy content; similarly an absence of a clear approach to formulation would appear to be the lemon of strategy processes. The lack of positive findings here does, however, beg the question about the types of strategy formulation that may lead to better service performance. It may be that future studies should explore alternative and more nuanced approaches to strategy formulation – including, for example, the symbolic, command and generative types suggested by Hart (1992) or the cultural, political or enforced choice models proposed and validated by Bailey et al. (2000).

Turning to the interaction models between process and content, our evidence indicates that a combined approach of prospecting and logical incrementalism is beneficial to organizational performance. This would suggest that the selection of an administrative system that is consistent with an organization's strategy content does indeed lead to higher levels of organizational performance. In this case, prospectors plan in a fluid manner in response to the opportunities and threats they face. Research from hospitals in the USA also confirms a relationship between content and formulation. Ketchen et al. (1996, 239) note that process and content interactions have long been recognized in the literature on the management of firms and argue that: '... the interpretation of a firm's strategic options is a reflection of both its strategic processes and the content of its past strategic decisions'. Thus content and formulation build upon one another in a mutually reinforcing manner and '... the process/content interactions may impact performance by facilitating (or failing to facilitate) both internal coordination and fit with the demands of the environment'. This line of reasoning is clearly related to the arguments of Miles and Snow examining process and content independently is valuable because they can make their own contribution to performance, but that the synergistic effect that can emerge from them jointly is particularly important. However, our results do not provide such strong empirical support for these arguments.

Conclusion

In this chapter, we have examined the relationship between two central parts of strategic management – strategy formulation processes and strategy content – and public service performance. The empirical evidence presented has indicated that an absence of strategy is detrimental to the achievement of higher levels of performance and that processes associated with logical incrementalism when combined with prospecting assist organizational achievements. These results provide lacklustre support for the contentions of Miles and Snow because strategy formulation processes are only significantly related to performance in one of three cases for independent effects (strategy absence) and the same for joint effects (logical incrementalism and prospecting).

The questions we pose here are not just academic. Strategy content and formulation is at the heart of government attempts to achieve public service improvement in a variety of international settings (Pollitt and Bouchaert, 2004). In the UK, a range of processes have been promoted by central government over recent years to achieve service improvement. This includes reforms associated with increased rationality in strategy formulation (e.g. target-setting), and with aspects of decision-making (such as devolved management and flexibility) (Office of Public Service Reform, 2003; Walker and Boyne, 2006). A number of reforms have also attempted to stimulate changes in strategy content, by promoting innovation, partnership and a customer focus in public organizations (Boyne, Martin and Walker, 2004; Office of Public Service Reform, 2002; Walker and Boyne, 2006). Aspects of this agenda, as experienced by Welsh local governments in the early part of the twentieth century appear to have paid dividends. However, there remains some way to travel before the strategic management determinants of performance in public services organizations are fully understood.

As was noted in the introduction to this chapter, Miles and Snow argued that strategy content is linked to structure and environment in addition to processes. In Chapter 6, the links between strategy content and strategy formulation processes and structure are examined, and we test propositions about the configurational relationship amongst these variables. Chapter 7 similarly explores the association between content, process and the environment. Our analysis takes the Miles and Snow framework into new areas by examining not only these relationships with the technical environment, as discussed by Miles and Snow, but also seeks to advance knowledge by exploring the institutional environment. Prior to this, attention is turned to another stage of the strategy process: implementation.

5
Strategy Implementation, Content and Performance

The effective implementation of strategies has long been recognized as crucial to organizational success. Clearly, strategies may only contribute to organizational performance if they are actually implemented. However, many have argued that organizations are not very good at implementation; for example, Nutt (1999) suggests that as many as half of strategies are not implemented. This is a critical issue for all organizations, but it may be especially important for public organizations, as it has been argued that they are increasingly using strategic management models and techniques more traditionally associated with private corporations, but are failing to learn and are simply recycling 'techniques which have been shown to be badly flawed' (Ferlie, 2002, 287).

Within the field of strategic management there has been a significant amount of research on strategy processes which have been described as how 'a strategy decision is made and implemented and the factors which affect it' (Elbanna, 2006, 2). However, there is only a small amount of evidence on implementation as most attention has traditionally been paid to the formulation of strategy (see Chapter 4). The existing literature on strategy implementation in public organizations is limited in its extent, and also in the lack of a connection of implementation processes with subsequent performance. There is a long-standing literature on policy implementation (see, e.g. O'Toole, 2000) and a large literature on the management of change (e.g. Pettigrew et al., 2001), both of which provide some insights into strategy implementation. However, these are of limited value for this chapter: the policy implementation literature focuses typically on inter-organizational implementation, and both literatures lack empirical research linking processes to performance.

Strategy implementation is defined as 'the communication, interpretation, adoption and enactment of strategic plans' (Noble, 1999, 120), and it can be undertaken in a number of ways or styles. The style of implementation has been identified as especially important for performance: as Long and Franklin (2004, 311) state 'a key variable when studying implementation is the approach that each agency uses to implement policy'. The strategy process literature suggests that there is a range of possible styles of implementation (Bourgeois and Brodwin, 1984), with rational at one end of the spectrum and incremental at the other. However, what style leads to better performance? Internal processes of formulation and implementation are important elements of the Miles and Snow framework. One of the arguments that Miles and Snow put forward is that these processes should be aligned with the strategic stance of the organization. Does performance improve when an organization's strategy content and implementation style are closely matched? In this chapter, we examine the effects of strategy implementation on performance and the ways in which strategic stance moderates this relationship.

We seek to answer these questions in a number of stages. In the first part of this chapter, we focus on implementation style and performance. We review the existing empirical evidence and develop theoretical arguments and hypotheses on implementation style and public service performance. We go on to examine the possible role that strategic stance may play in moderating the relationship between implementation style and performance, and assess the limited empirical research on this issue. In the second part, we outline our research findings. We present and interpret our statistical results, and draw conclusions on the relationship between implementation style, strategic stance and public service performance.

Strategy implementation and performance

Implementation is a key stage of the strategy process, and one that is generally perceived as a highly significant determinant of performance. As Noble (1999, 119) states, 'well formulated strategies only produce superior performance for the firm when they are successfully implemented'. Similarly, Olson et al. (2005, 47) point out that: '...many executives argue that brilliant execution is more important than brilliant strategy. The reason is simple: doing is harder than dreaming, and a poorly executed strategy is merely a vision of what it could be'.

Despite this consensus on the importance of implementation, there are a number of gaps and problems with the existing literature. Although the literature on strategy implementation is growing, one criticism that has been made is that it is fairly fragmented. Noble (1999) suggests that in part this is because there are a number of different perspectives on strategy implementation. His review of the literature on definitions of implementation finds that some identify it as control, and that others perceive it to be the straightforward operationalization of a strategic plan. He argues that 'this view is limited as it fails to acknowledge the emergent nature of many implementation processes – initial plans are often adapted due to changing organizational or environmental conditions' (Noble, 1999, 120). There appears to be no widely accepted definition of strategy implementation and therefore in this chapter we will define it as the process by which policies, programmes and action plans are put into place across the organization (Harrington, 2004).

The fragmentation of the existing literature may also be because implementation is increasingly recognized as a complex and multifaceted phenomenon encompassing structural and interpersonal processes (Thorpe and Morgan, 2007). Noble (1999) recognizes that there are a number of studies which are relevant to implementation, as long as a broadened perspective is used, and he summarizes this 'implementation-related research' under the categories of structural views (the effects of organizational structure and control on implementation) and interpersonal views (the effects of different behaviours on implementation). However, many of the studies he cites are limited in that they only examine one element (e.g. participation). Although these shed some light on implementation, a framework or model that incorporates a number of elements and the relationship between them is needed. Okumus (2003, 871), for example indicates that 'a comprehensive implementation framework has yet to be developed in the strategic management field'.

In this chapter we focus on the implementation style of the organization. That is, the approach that organizations adopt when putting strategies into practice. One of the advantages of examining implementation style is that it overcomes some of the limitations identified above by providing a framework that incorporates and examines more than one element. An examination of the existing models of implementation style indicates that there are a number of core elements: the extent to which responsibility is centralized or decentralized, and whether formulation and implementation are distinct and sequential activities or are intertwined (Long and Franklin, 2004; Thompson, 2000). An organization's implementation style forms part of its administrative routine, which has long been recognized as crucial to understanding the dynamics of implementation (Hill and Hupe, 2002). Johnson (2000,

403) highlights the 'marked influence of the "taken for grantedness" of management practice and its effects on strategy development'. Pollitt and Bouckaert (2000, 40) also point to the importance of what they call the administrative culture in relation to implementation, stating that it 'refers to the expectations the staff of an organization have about what is "normal" and "acceptable" in that organization'. An organization's implementation style reflects the taken for granted routine of putting strategies into practice and can be described as 'the way we do things around here'. Thus, an organization's implementation style tends to become institutionalized and established over time. Nutt (1987) for example, shows that managers often develop a particular style of implementation and stick with it. Hence, we are interested in the general approach to implementation taken in the organization, rather than individual examples of the implementation of single policies or specific decisions.

There are a number of conceptual studies which attempt to categorize different approaches to strategy making and implementation (Bourgeois and Brodwin, 1984; Hart, 1992; Hickson et al., 2003). These models illustrate the range of implementation styles that may exist in organizations, but they differ both in the variables that they consider and the terms that they use. For example, Hickson et al. (2003) use the terms planned and prioritized. The planned option operates when the organization has experience and they can then 'plan and control implementation by assessing aims and performance critieria, specifying tasks, and resourcing them and this is likely to win the acceptance from all concerned that is essential to success' (Hickson et al, 2003, 1822–23). A prioritized approach involves concentrating on the strategy, pushing it forward and 'learning by doing'. Bourgeois and Brodwin's (1984) examples of implementation style are commander, change, collaborative, cultural and crescive. The commander model indicates a significant role for the chief executive who operates as a ' "rational actor" issuing directives from the seat of power' (Bourgeois and Brodwin, 1984, 243), and a much more limited role for others in the organization who become 'doers' rather than 'thinkers'. In the change model, the focus is still largely on the role of chief executive, but considers issues such as the changes to structure, staffing, incentive structures and culture that can be made. The collaborative model allows for more participation from middle managers, but still 'preserves the artificial wall separating thinkers and doers' (Bourgeois and Brodwin, 1984, 249). In the cultural model the chief executive sets the vision, but encourages individuals to be involved in decision-making and as a result there is more emphasis on adaptation of plans as they get implemented. In the final model – the crescive approach – the participation by staff is enhanced, power is decentralized and adaptation of plans increased.

Thompson (2000) overcomes this problem of different terminology by categorizing these models to produce a spectrum of approaches to implementation with rational/command at one end and incremental/generative at the other. A similar approach is also taken by Cespedes and Piercy (1996) in their classification of marketing implementation tactics and strategies. In our study, we examine two distinct styles of implementation at either end of the spectrum – rational and incremental.

We now go on to examine the theory and, where available, the evidence on implementation style and performance. Much of the literature on strategy processes focuses on a rational approach to implementation. For example, Joyce (1999, 80) argues that 'the main advice on implementation tends to be couched in terms of the rational steps to be taken'. A rational implementation style is characterized by centralized control, the use of formal means to secure compliance and the separation of formulation and implementation. A key aspect of this approach is that formulation and implementation are sequential activities. Strategy is first deliberately formulated and only then is it put into place. As part of its evaluation of appropriate strategies, an organization may even pilot the strategy before full implementation (Bryson, 1995; Hart, 1992). Fernandez and Rainey (2006) reiterate that one factor that contributes to the successful implementation of change is the provision of a plan which can act as an organizational roadmap. Rational implementers are likely to define activities clearly, through formal methods such as business or project plans, which identify tasks with targets (Bourgeois and Brodwin, 1984; Bryson, 1995; Hart, 1992). Control has also been identified as crucial to the implementation process and in rational approaches this is done centrally through techniques such as action plans and monitoring. A number of studies have claimed these activities are critical to successful implementation; for example, action plans can help implementers to translate strategy into a more short-term and focused plan (e.g. Chustz and Larson, 2006; Hrebriniak and Joyce, 1984; Pinto and Prescott, 1990). Centralized control can also facilitate coordination and integration of activities. One of the advantages of this style is that explicit strategies can be controlled and reviewed (Ansoff, 1991). However, does this lead to improved performance?

Despite the traditional prominence of the rational approach to strategy processes, a significant body of work has highlighted the value of an approach at the other end of the spectrum – that is an incremental approach to implementation. Organizations using this style decentralize responsibility and have a much looser distinction between formulation and implementation. A number of authors argue that the separation of formulation and implementation, as prescribed in the rational approach, was a key reason for implementation failure (Hambrick and Conella, 1989; Mintzberg, 2000). Connecting these processes means that organizations can learn more effectively and respond to changes in the environment (Montgomery, 2008). In an incremental style responsibility is decentralized: Bourgeois and Brodwin (1984, 257) argue, for example, that in the crescive model 'the chief executive must relax his expectations concerning the extent to which strategic plans can be developed centrally'. In addition, the role of the organization's members is enhanced as they are active participants in the process of developing and implementing strategies (Rajagopalan and Rasheed, 1995). This involvement of staff enables organizational learning as strategy can be fine tuned and adjusted, leading to the continual adaptation of strategies as they are being implemented. For example, Nutt (1999), Rainey (2003) and Woolridge and Floyd (1990) found that staff participation in decision-making is associated with improved implementation and organizational performance. Overall, does an incremental style enhance performance?

In addition, there may be organizations that do not have a discernible or consistent style of implementation. In these organizations there is no taken for granted routine for implementing strategies, which reflects Inkpen and Choudury's (1995) concept of 'strategy absence'. There is very little consideration in the literature of organizations that do not have a clear approach to implementation. A lack of a consistent approach to implementation may lead to poorer performance because those involved in implementation are confused and lack understanding of how they are expected to implement policies. An organizational routine provides coordination and control, stability, and is a mechanism for storing knowledge and reducing uncertainty (Becker, 2004). An organization that lacks such a routine therefore is likely to experience lower levels of performance.

It is important to note that the categories identified above are not mutually exclusive in practice. It is likely that an organization's implementation style is made up of a mixture of these approaches, with the balance of rational and incremental styles varying between organizations, and with greater or lesser clarity on the approach which is usually adopted.

Prior empirical evidence and hypotheses

Despite attempts to classify approaches to implementation, there has been very little empirical research which links these processes to performance. A number of authors have argued that this is a major problem. For example, Fernandez and Rainey (2006, 18) state 'researchers must confront the challenge of analysing the relationship of the content and process of change to organizational outcomes such as performance'. Similarly, Pettigrew et al. (2001, 701) highlight the need to measure the outcomes of change process and argue that this provides the exciting possibility of 'exploring how and why variations in context and process shape variability in the observed performance outcomes across a comparative investigation'. Poister et al. (2010, 522) add to these criticisms of existing research, stating that: 'although there is considerable literature on strategic planning and management in the public sector there has been little effort to synthesize what has been learned concerning the extent to which these tools are used in government, how they are implemented and the results that they generate'.

A significant concern with much of the research that is available is the variation in the definition and measurement of performance, which reflects the concerns we outlined in Chapter 2 when we discussed operationalizing public service performance. In some cases, success is identified as the adoption of the strategy, rather than higher performance (e.g. Nutt, 1989). This is problematic as a decision may be adopted but may still fail to be implemented effectively or indeed to make a difference to performance. Some studies of firms in the private sector have used financial measures of performance such as profit (Parsa, 1999), and this type of measure has been criticized for not necessarily being related to long-term success. Others have used managers' perceptions of the success of the policy (e.g. Hickson et al., 2003; Thorpe and Morgan, 2006) which raises issues of subjectivity.

Of the studies that have explored implementation style and performance, few draw on a comprehensive model of implementation style. The model most often employed in the empirical studies reviewed in this chapter was Bourgeois and Brodwin (1984) which was utilized by both Thorpe and Morgan (2006) and Parsa (1999). To identify published studies of the impact of implementation style and performance, a range of search terms were used, including 'planned', 'incremental', 'rational', 'emergent', 'centralized', 'decentralized', as well as terms such as 'commander', 'change', 'collaborative', 'cultural' and 'crescive'. Searches were supplemented by using the term 'performance', with other relevant terms (e.g. 'achievement' and 'success'). This search revealed seven studies which examined the relationship between implementation style and performance. The data sources for these studies are varied but are mainly focused on private organizations. Of the larger studies (Parsa, 1999; Thorpe and Morgan, 2006; Veliyath and Shortell, 1993), two focus exclusively on private organizations (Parsa, 1999; Thorpe and Morgan, 2006) and therefore existing evidence of implementation style in the public sector is based on a very small number of examples. Only Stewart and Kringas (2003) focus exclusively on public organizations and their number of cases is six. The studies are all undertaken in single countries with three conducted in the UK, three in the US and one in Australia. Overall, the studies provide some rather limited evidence on rational and incremental styles of implementation and only one study identifies the impact of no clear implementation style. Table 5.1 presents the available evidence.

Table 5.1 Impact of strategy implementation style on public service performance

Study	Organizations and sample size	Implementation approach	Dimension of performance	Net effect on performance
Thorpe and Morgan (2006)	115 medium or large, service-based organizations in telecommunications, transport and financial services	Change, collaborative and cultural models (Bourgeois and Brodwin, 1984)	Manager perception of effective strategy execution and strategy meeting targets	Change more positive than collaborative. Collaborative more positive than cultural
Hickson et al. (2003)	55 decisions in 14 organizations, 6 manufacturing, 5 services and 3 public organizations	Planned and prioritized	Manager perceptions of extent to which strategy achieved objectives	Planned approach and prioritized approach successful. Dual approach better. No approach least effective
Parsa (1999)	141 franchise organizations	Commander, Change, Collaborative, Cultural, Crescive	Sales per year	Collaborative model had best performance

Table 5.1 (Continued)

Study	Organizations and sample size	Implementation approach	Dimension of performance	Net effect on performance
Miller (1997)	11 decisions in 6 organizations: 2 public and 4 private organizations	Investigates range of factors including specificity, assessability and flexibility	Manager perceptions of completion, achievement and acceptability of strategy	Specificity and assessability were critical to success. Flexibility was not
Stewart and Kringas (2003)	6 Australian public agencies	Range of factors including negotiation and participation	Staff and manager perceptions, some PIs	Negotiation and participation important
Bantel (1997)	166 Technology companies in the US	Range of factors including employee empowerment Also examined stance – product leadership strategy × empowerment	Manager perceptions of future prospects, financial stability, growth rate and profitability	Empowerment linked to growth rate but not financial stability or profitability. Product leadership × empowerment is linked to higher growth rate
Veliyath and Shortell (1993)	406 hospitals in the US. Approximately one-third are for-profit, two-thirds are non-profits	A range of factors including the extent of planning implementation	Profitability	Planning implementation higher in prospectors than defenders. Highest performing prospectors did less planning implementation than other prospectors

One of the few studies to examine implementation style is Thorpe and Morgan (2006). They focus on marketing strategy, and attempt to assess the impact of implementation style on performance of service organizations in the private sector. They use Bourgeois and Brodwin's model of implementation styles but miss out the two styles at the extreme ends of the model (Commander and Crescive). These were originally included, but were later removed because of insufficient observations. Their sample is 115 middle-to large-sized organizations in the transport, telecommunications and financial industries in the UK. Bourgeois and Brodwin's model does not suggest that one style will lead to better performance than another, but Thorpe and Morgan (2006, 664) argue that the hierarchical structures that are evident in the change model 'are essential for creating the efficient and flexible co-ordination of marketing strategy implementation'. They hypothesize therefore that the change model will be better than the collaborative model, which in turn will be better than the cultural model in relation to strategic performance, strategic clarity, strategic efficiency, mid-level manager compliant behaviour and senior management executive team strategic direction. Their results show that the change model of implementation is associated with more compliant behaviour, greater strategic clarity and direction from the senior marketing executive team. Although results were not significant for strategic efficiency (the speed of executing the strategy), they were for strategic performance (the extent to which the strategy was a success, and is meeting its targets). The results indicate that the change model of implementation style was more effective than either the cultural or the collaborative models. They conclude that 'firms that emphasise the importance of a rigid organizational structure, visible control systems and other hierarchical factors, such as reward systems should implement their marketing strategies better than firms which try to foster consensus, and a team working culture with more decentralised and informal structures' (2006, 670). These results suggest that a style which is closer to the rational end of the spectrum is likely to lead to better performance.

Parsa (1999) also used the models of implementation suggested by Bourgeois and Brodwin – Command, Change, Collabrative, Cultural and Crescive, in his study of the performance of franchise organizations in the US. This model was chosen as it 'is comprehensive and is based on specific theoretical assumptions' (1999, 175). In this study the cultural model was eventually deleted from analysis as it had too few cases. In contrast to Thorpe and Morgan (2006), Parsa (1999) argues that there is not enough evidence to suggest which model may be better in terms of performance and hypothesizes simply that 'in franchise systems the performance levels of franchisees differs significantly when classified according to the type of implementation' (176). This is tested using two different measures of performance: sales per year and profit (measured by income before fixed charges). The results demonstrate that those franchisees that used a collaborative model performed better in relation to sales. However, the findings were not consistent in relation to performance as measured by profit. In this case, the change model had the highest mean value, but not significantly so. Parsa concludes that strategy implementation affects the financial performance of franchises and that 'different performance objectives (profit vs. sales) demand different implementation models. The "match" between the outcome objectives and the implementation model is essential to achieve desired performance objectives' (1999, 183). His evidence suggests that implementation style matters and that a contingency model is appropriate. However, both the change and the collaborative models contain some elements of a rational approach (to varying extents), and this evidence suggests that this has a positive effect on performance.

Hickson et al. (2003) also find that different styles of implementation (in this case planned and prioritized) can both lead to organizational success. They examine the implementation approach used in 55 decisions in 14 organizations in the UK. It is important to note that they assessed the style used in individual decisions, rather than that consistently adopted by the organization. They used a case approach and interviewed senior managers within the organization. The material was then coded into eight independent variables regarding process and the dependent variable (achievement). From the eight variables, Hickson et al. (2003) identify two approaches that were used in the decisions they studied. These are the experience-based approach and the readiness-based approach. The experience-based approach involves 'assessing the end goal clearly and operationally, that is, identifying the targets; specifying what has to be done beforehand, that is setting out the steps and tasks; and resourcing with the appropriate personnel, finance and time' (2006, 1809). This becomes what they describe as a 'planned option' available to managers. The readiness-based approach incorporates the extent to which the decision was a priority, and the climate is receptive. This is the 'prioritized option' which allows 'learning by doing'. Their evidence indicates that those decisions that used a single approach could succeed (both planned and prioritized approaches worked). In fact, those that used a prioritized approach had a slightly higher achievement score (3.8), compared to those using a planned approach (3.5). These findings should be treated with some caution as they involve only 6 and 8 cases, respectively. A style that incorporated both approaches was found to have the greatest likelihood of success. This study provides the only evidence of strategies which have no clear approach to implementation: these strategies scored only 2.9 in terms of achievement.

Miller (1997) also uses a case study approach in her investigation of 11 decisions in 6 organizations in the UK (2 from the public sector and 4 private). These decisions were examined in depth through interviews with 113 people as well as the scrutiny of company documents and reports. As she is undertaking exploratory research, she does not test a particular implementation style. However, she finds that there are ten potentially important factors that may influence implementation success. These are backing, assessability, specificity, cultural receptivity, good fortune, familiarity, priority, resource availability, structure and flexibility. A number of these factors are associated with the rational style (assessability and specificity) and incremental approach (flexibility). In common with the majority of the other studies examined in this section, performance is measured through manager perceptions. These cover the extent to which the strategy was completed, the degree to which it achieved what was intended and also the level of acceptability of the method and outcomes. She finds that of the ten factors, there are four which are significant for success. These are described as realizers. She draws the conclusion that planning matters: 'the prominence of assessability and specificity among the "realizers" confirms the role of planning, the mainstay of so much orthodoxy' (596). Interestingly, the findings also suggest that the flexibility associated with a more incremental style is not significant. Although these are clearly not sufficient in number to be representative, the cases suggest that a rational style has more benefit than an incremental approach and that it 'may well imply that what is required for successful outcomes is increasingly rational managers' (1997, 596).

Stewart and Kringas (2004) also use a case study methodology in their examination of six Australian public agencies. They do not focus exclusively on implementation style, but elements of this are explored in their study. In particular, they attempt to assess the way in which the strategy is implemented: is it imposed or is there some scope for negotiation? They also examine the ways in which staff were involved through communication. These issues were explored through interviews (72 overall) and documentary sources. Performance was assessed through staff surveys and interviews which explored their 'attitudes towards the change' and also through some performance indicators, although these were not available for three of the case study agencies. The evidence is limited in that performance was not easily measured in each case, but it tentatively suggests that a more incremental or negotiated style may be important for performance: the two agencies in their study that achieved the highest rankings on objective and subjective measures of performance had more scope for negotiation.

Bantel (1997) also finds some evidence in support of an incremental style. She examines one element of the incremental style to implementation: employee empowerment. Her evidence is based on a sample of 166 high technology companies in the US, and may therefore only have limited generalizability. She measures performance through self-reported survey items on research and development performance, profitability, financial stability and growth rate of sales, and finds that employee participation is positively related to performance as measured by growth rate, but not profit or financial stability. Hence, this element of an incremental style to implementation appears to enhance at least one dimension of performance.

As seen above, there is only limited evidence available about the impact of implementation style on performance, and much of this is drawn from studies of private organizations. Both a rational style and an incremental style have some evidence of success. Despite this, the balance of the evidence for an incremental style is less strong than for the rational approach. The range of empirical evidence is limited in places, especially in relation to 'no clear' approach, and here we draw largely on arguments about the importance of established routines (Becker, 2004) and evidence from Hickson et al. (2003) to develop our hypothesis. Given the above evidence, we propose three hypotheses on implementation style and suggest that:

H5.1 A rational approach to implementation is positively related to organizational performance

H5.2 An incremental approach to implementation is positively related to organizational performance, but less so than a rational approach

H5.3 No clear approach to implementation is negatively related to performance.

Strategy implementation, strategy content and performance

One factor that may mediate the impact of implementation style on performance is the strategy of the organization. This reflects the central idea of contingency theory that there is 'no universal best way', but rather that the impact of implementation processes will be contingent on a number of factors. Miles and Snow (1978) make a number of arguments about the link between strategic orientation and the internal characteristics of an organization. These are outlined in Chapter 3 and developed and tested in relation to formulation in Chapter 4. Miles and Snow (1978) focus their arguments largely on formulation processes, but also incorporate elements of implementation. Some predictions on the link between strategy and implementation have also been made by Parsa (1999) and Hart (1992). However, there is virtually no empirical evidence which tests these arguments on the link between strategy content and the performance effects of implementation processes, either for private or public organizations.

As outlined in Chapter 4, Miles and Snow (1978) argue that organizations will perform better if they are able to find an appropriate relationship between their 'entrepreneurial' problem (which strategy to adopt) and the 'administrative' problem (which processes and structures to select). They argue that defenders, prospectors and reactors have very different strategies. Defenders place their emphasis on their core services and efficiency; prospectors seek to innovate; and reactors have no clear strategy but simply respond to the environment. These varied and distinct strategies will therefore require different approaches to strategy processes such as implementation.

Miles and Snow (1978) distinguish between the extent of *planning* associated with different strategies. They argue that defenders plan extensively and that they do this prior to taking any action. Defenders plan carefully so that they can take full advantage of the environmental conditions. This planning activity usually involves the setting of clear objectives and goals for outputs and costs. Hence defenders are rational implementers: they separate the formulation of plans from implementation and focus on control through meeting goals and objectives. Whilst there is little evidence or justification provided, both Parsa (1999) and Hart (1992) also suggest that rational approaches to implementation are likely to be linked to a defender strategy. This is echoed by Veliyath and Shortell (1993, 360–361) who argue that defenders 'will place more emphasis on planning implementation in order to attain maximum efficiency in their key throughput processes'. A rational implementation style is likely to work well for defending strategies as its focus on centralized control through methods such as business plans and targets should enable the efficiency of existing operations to be monitored effectively.

Miles and Snow (1978) indicate that the planning process in a prospector is different. Prospectors do not engage in systematic or detailed planning as their position is more dynamic and fluid as they are ready to expand or contract their activities. Prospectors take a broad and tentative approach to planning, and their planning process is rarely completed before they begin implementation. Prospectors have an incremental approach to implementation with a looser distinction between formulation and implementation. Again, both Parsa (1999) and Hart (1992) predict that more iterative and incremental approaches are associated with prospector organizations. Veliyath and Shortell (1993) suggest that as prospectors emphasize problem finding rather than problem solving, they would have a less formal and rational implementation style. They also argue that prospectors are less likely to have a rational implementation process because there is less of a divide between formulation and implementation and therefore 'procedures for the implementation of strategy are more likely to be ad hoc and experimental' (Veliyath and Shortell, 1993, 363). An incremental style is likely to be helpful for prospecting strategies as there is less centralized control, allowing staff to innovate and experiment as they proceed with implementation. This should therefore enhance the process of 'learning by doing'. An incremental style also allows for more involvement by lower-level staff, and this may enable greater and quicker acceptance of the strategy which may be especially important for prospectors as they implement new strategies.

Finally, reactors will demonstrate a range of approaches to implementation. Miles and Snow argue that reactors do not fully shape the structures and processes of their organization to fit their strategy. It is difficult for reactors to plan as these organizations rely on external pressures to shape their strategy and do not have a clear vision of their own. This, combined with a lack of a clear or consistent approach to implementation is likely to lead to even more confusion and uncertainty and hence worse performance. A lack of a clear approach will lead to worse performance in a reacting strategy as the organization is missing not only a stable strategy but also an established routine for implementation.

There is almost no systematic evidence on the interaction of implementation style, strategic stance and organizational performance in either the private or public sector. Govindarajan (1988) provides some limited evidence that prospecting units operate well with an incremental style: he found that low control over department heads was associated with high performance in units that were differentiating. Bantel (1997) also finds some support for the idea that prospecting and an incremental style of implementation leads to good performance.

Her evidence indicates that a product leadership strategy (similar to a prospector) and employee empowerment together leads to high growth rate, however, this does not affect other elements of performance. She states that 'this implies that managers need to be highly deliberate about developing coordination and congruence between technology based industries product/market strategies and supportive implementation capabilities' (1997, 166). Veliyath and Shortell (1993) examined the implementation style (as well as other factors), stance and performance of for profit and not-for profit hospitals in the US. They found, contrary to their expectations, that prospector hospitals operated a more rational implementation style than defenders. They undertook a profile deviation analysis and found that when prospector hospitals varied from the 'ideal profile' of the top 20 per cent of prospectors in terms of profit, there was a significant negative effect on performance. Interestingly however, the mean score for planning implementation for the study sample were higher than the 20 per cent who were the highest performing prospectors. This leads the authors to suggest that 'increases in these planning system characteristics beyond an optimum point appear to be counterproductive for prospector Hospitals' (1993, 378). Overall, this evidence is limited in a number of ways. There are very few studies in total, and none of them undertakes a systematic study of implementation style, stance and performance. Only one study provides any evidence from the public sector, and in this case the measure of performance used is profitability.

The Miles and Snow theoretical framework, and in some cases evidence, leads us to propose the following hypotheses:

H5.4 A rational approach to implementation is likely to be positively related to performance in an organization with a defender stance

H5.5 An incremental approach to implementation is likely to be positively related to performance in an organization with a prospector stance

H5.6 No clear approach to implementation reinforces the negative effect of a reactor stance on performance.

Measuring strategy implementation

Rational planning and logical incremental factors were constructed for our implementation measures using factor analysis (Table 5.2). Informants were asked four questions on the presence of formal procedures in their approach to implementing strategies in their service. A key element

Table 5.2 Measures of strategy implementation

Variable definition	*X*	SD	F1	F2
We use a project/business plan to implement strategies (R)	5.57	1.04	.77	
When implementing strategies we have clearly defined tasks with targets (R)	5.53	0.93	.91	.85
When implementing strategies we regularly review progress against targets (R)	5.51	1.00	.92	.85
We implement strategies by piloting them initially and then implementing them in full (R)	4.20	1.38	.50	
When implementing strategies we often refine and amend them as we go along (LI)	5.28	0.90		
We improve the implementation of our strategies by getting all of the affected groups involved in their development (LI)	5.12	1.03		
There is no discernible approach to implementing strategies in our service area	2.75	1.09		
N	62			

Note: R = rational, LI = logical incrementalism.c.

of the rational approach is that formulation and implementation are sequential activities (Thompson, 2000). Rational implementers are likely to define tasks clearly, through formal methods such as business or project plans, which identify tasks with targets, and permit reviews of progress (Hart, 1992). As part of the evaluation of appropriate strategies, the organization may also pilot them before full implementation (Bryson, 1995). Each of our measures sought to tap these features of a planned approach to implementation (see Table 5.2). The ICC for the rational implementation approach measures was 0.35 ($p > .001$), and the Cronbach Alpha score was 0.76.

A logical incremental approach to implementation is less rigid. Organization members are active participants in the process of implementation (Rajagopalan and Rasheed, 1995), continually adapting strategies as they are implemented. Our two measures of a logical incremental approach to strategy implementation capture these ideas of adjustment (Hart, 1992) and negotiation (Nutt, 1986). The ICC for the incremental implementation measures was 0.38 ($p > 0.001$), with an acceptable Cronbach Alpha score of 0.60 (Loewenthal, 1996). In addition, we included the statement 'there is no discernible approach to implementing strategies' in order to test directly whether reactors lack consistent processes (Inkpen and Choudhury, 1995).

Statistical results

The results for the statistical tests of the impact of implementation style and strategy are shown in Tables 5.3 and 5.4. The models provide a good statistical explanation of the variations in the performance of local authority services in Wales (the R^2 is satisfactory in both models). This suggests that the models provide a solid foundation for assessing the effects of implementation style, and whether the impact of implementation style is moderated by strategy content.

Strategy implementation and performance

Table 5.3 shows the results for the basic implementation and performance model. None of the implementation approaches has a positive and significant association with performance. Taken at face value, this

Table 5.3 Strategy implementation approach and public service performance

Independent variable	Slope	t-score
Rational implementation	1.5293	.76
Logical incremental implementation	−3.9195	−1.83+
No clear implementation approach	−1.6908	−.96
R^2	.43**	
Adjusted R^2	.34**	
$N = 40$		

Note: Significance levels: $+p \leq 0.10$; $*p \leq 0.05$; $**p \leq 0.01$ (two-tailed tests).

Table 5.4 Implementation approach × strategy content and public service performance

Independent variable	Slope	t-score
RI × defending	5.1663	2.90**
LI × prospecting	4.2130	1.80+
NA × reacting	−1.6271	−.91
R^2	.62**	
Adjusted R^2	.47**	
$N = 40$		

Note: Significance levels: $+p \leq 0.10$; $*p \leq 0.05$; $**p \leq 0.01$ (two-tailed tests).

indicates that style of implementation does not contribute to improvements in performance. Although much of the literature suggests that the style of implementation matters, almost all of the previous studies measured success as the implementation of the strategy, rather than an improvement in performance.

The statistical results do not provide support for Hypothesis 5.1. A rational approach is positively related to performance, however the coefficient is not statistically significant. This contradicts the literature we reviewed which suggests that this approach will enhance performance (e.g. Pinto and Prescott, 1990). It may be that this approach, in which planning and implementation are separate activities, leads to a lack of motivation from staff who are categorized as 'doers' rather than 'thinkers'. Kim (2002), for example finds that a participative management style in the strategic planning process is positively associated with job satisfaction. Another possibility is that the focus on action plans and targets has led to too much rigidity and not allowed enough learning to take place. One of our interviewees from a service under threat of central government intervention stated that the introduction of rational implementation processes in their service had meant that 'the element of creativity has been curtailed at a local level'.

Hypothesis 5.2 is not supported by the findings. A logical incremental implementation approach is certainly less helpful than a rational approach, but is negatively rather than positively related to performance. This is surprising as it contradicts much of the available evidence on the value of staff participation and involvement in strategy implementation. A potential explanation for the negative association between an incremental approach and performance is that it leads to a lack of focus in the implementation process and a tendency to drift (Bourgeois and Brodwin, 1984). For example, a manager in one service with a predominantly incremental approach to implementation noted in interview that 'you feel you're overwhelmed by change, that there's no time to implement all changes properly. Things are happening and they are changing, but we seem to be always behind with what we plan to do'.

Hypothesis 5.3 is not supported by the evidence. There is a negative association between having no discernible approach to implementation and performance, but the coefficient is not statistically significant. There is very little previous evidence on this, but our expectation was that those organizations that had no discernible approach to implementation would have low standards of performance because organizational members would be confused about the approach that they should take and strategies might never be fully implemented. One possibility is that organizations with no discernible style of implementation simply vary their approach, either at random or according to the strategy to be implemented at the time. The randomness of implementation style is evident in a comment from an interviewee who stated that implementation typically depended on 'who decides what the main drivers are and what the priorities are', but that senior officers in the service seemed to be 'pretty unaware of what's happening – we need people who have the authority to commit funding and budgets'.

Taken at face value, these results indicate that no single style of implementation is independently likely to lead to service improvement. This suggestion – that style makes no difference – conflicts with much of the research on strategy processes. It also contradicts most of the available evidence on the impact of implementation style in private organizations. However, many of the previous studies measured success as the implementation of the strategy rather than an improvement in service performance. Another possible interpretation of these results is that they are only true of our public sector sample. It may, for example, be that the nature of performance in the public sector is more complex than for private organizations and that it is therefore less likely that they style of implementation will affect it. The explanation provided by the Miles and Snow model, however, is that it is not implementation style in itself that matters, but the *fit* between implementation style and strategy content. We now proceed to examine this possibility.

Strategy implementation, strategy content and performance

Table 5.4 also shows the results when we introduce the interaction terms for implementation approach and strategic stance into our base model. The results provide support for our fourth hypothesis (Hypothesis 5.4). A rational approach to implementation is positively associated with performance when it is combined with a defender orientation. This suggests that it is important for services to align their strategy with their implementation processes. Indeed, one interviewee in a predominantly defending authority felt that overall the whole organization 'definitely is getting better' as a result of rational planning, stressing that 'if we're going to make progress [in implementing strategy], we've got to pilot it'. Hypothesis 5.5 is also supported. The combination of an incremental approach with prospecting is positively related to performance. A logical incremental style is negatively associated with performance in all of our models, but the effect of this style becomes positive if it is interacted with a prospecting strategy. For this strategic orientation, a logical incremental approach is positively associated with service performance. An interviewee in a prospecting service performing well on the National Assembly for Wales Performance Indicators (NAWPIs) indicated that during strategy implementation there is 'consultation coming out of our ears'. Our final Hypothesis 5.6 is not supported by the statistical results. We expected that a lack of a discernible approach to implementation in conjunction with a reactor strategy would be especially bad for performance. The results show that the lack of a clear style of implementation is no worse (or better) when organizations adopt this strategic orientation.

Overall, these results confirm the suggestions of Miles and Snow (1978) that the link between strategy processes and strategy content has an influence on organizational performance. In particular, we find that strategy content is an important moderator of the relationship between implementation style and performance. A rational style of implementation is positively correlated with performance in organizations that emphasize a strategy of defending. Similarly, a logical incremental style of implementation has a positive impact when it is combined with prospecting. Our findings confirm that a 'fit' between the organization's strategy and its implementation style matters for the performance of public organizations.

Conclusion

Implementation is widely held to be a critical element of strategy, and one which can have a significant impact on performance. However, prior evidence that examines the link between implementation style and performance is largely limited to private sector studies. The findings presented here provide an important step in understanding the effects of implementation style on performance in the public sector. Our results suggest that there is no consistent style of implementation that is likely to lead to improvements in performance. If we ignore the moderating effect of strategy content, a logical incremental style of implementation is negatively associated with performance. In addition, no positive effect was found for rational planning, contradicting much of the literature and government guidance. The idea that strategy and the internal characteristics of an organization should be tightly coupled is one of the classic perspectives in the strategic management literature. We therefore also examined whether the impact of implementation style on performance was influenced by the strategy content of the organization. No known work has systematically examined the links between implementation style, strategy content and performance in either the public or private sectors. Our results show that rational implementation was positively correlated with performance for defending strategies, and that incrementalism was positively correlated with performance for prospecting strategies.

Overall, our findings confirm the importance of implementation style. The approach taken by the organization to put its strategies into practice does matter. However, one of the central messages of this study is that universal recommendations on the appropriate style to adopt are inappropriate. This is because strategic stance is an important mediator of the impact of implementation style on performance. This confirms Miles and Snow's (1978) suggestion that strategic stance and processes should be tightly coupled and that a fit between them is likely to enhance performance. Our evidence shows that the impact of implementation style is clearly contingent on the strategic orientation of the organization.

Our research has a number of practical implications. The most important is that managers should seek to ensure that the implementation style of their organization is matched to its strategic stance. Another significant issue is that universal recommendations on implementation style from governments and regulatory agencies (often in favour of a rational approach) are inappropriate. This style of implementation will not improve performance in all organizations.

These findings are similar to those outlined in Chapter 4 on processes of strategy formulation. In both cases, there was no single style (either rational or incremental) of formulation or implementation that was positive in relation to performance. Similarities between formulation and implementation also emerge when the moderating effect of strategic stance is considered. In relation to both formulation and implementation processes, a logical incremental style is correlated with performance for organizations with a prospecting stance. The importance of fit appears to be more important overall for strategy implementation: a rational style combined with a defending stance was significant for implementation but not for processes of strategy formulation. A number of other factors may also be significant in understanding implementation such as organizational structure (Noble, 1999). We explore this further in Chapter 6. Miles and Snow also argue that it is important to align strategy content and processes to the environment that organizations face and this is examined in Chapter 7.

6
Structure, Strategy and Performance

The allocation and distribution of the authority to make decisions is a critical task of organizational design in the public and private sector. Classical theorists of bureaucracy regarded the relative degree to which decision-making is centralized as integral to understanding how managerial choices are conducive to greater organizational efficiency (Gulick and Urwick, 1937; Weber, 1947). Contingency theory suggests that the extent of centralization within an organization should be dependent upon other key characteristics, especially the strategy content of an organization. In this chapter, we conceptualize centralization in organizations; survey the existing quantitative evidence on the centralization–performance relationship in public organizations; and theorize and empirically assess the separate and combined effects of centralization and strategy on public service performance.

Herbert Simon (1976) stressed that an organization's anatomy was constituted both by the allocation and the distribution of decision-making functions. The extent to which senior or middle managers are responsible for setting strategy and the degree to which other staff are involved in strategic decisions have profound implications for all aspects of organizational behaviour and outcomes. In particular, centralization within organizations may be likely to influence the success with which an organization can pursue its selected strategy. Miles and Snow highlight that organizations will perform better when their structure follows their strategy. If the relative degree of centralization is in close alignment with the content of an organization's strategy, then, in theory, it becomes easier to realize the intended benefits of that strategy. Many recent public service reforms have addressed the allocation and distribution of decision-making in public organizations. Such prescriptions for internal change present an ideal opportunity for public management scholars seeking to understand the relationship between organizational characteristics and performance. What organizational structures are conducive to better performance? How are these related to the strategic management of organizations? Does the interaction of structure and strategy matter? Does performance improve when decision-making within public organizations is tightly aligned with strategy? More precisely, do the effects of organizational structure depend on the content of strategies and how they are formulated and implemented?

In the first part of this chapter, the concept of centralization is outlined, before existing evidence on its relationship with public service performance is reviewed and summarized. We then develop hypotheses on the independent and combined effects of centralization and strategy content and process on performance prior to presenting the results of our statistical analysis of the performance of Welsh local service departments.

What is centralization?

The centralization or decentralization of decision-making within organizations is a key indicator of the pattern of social relationships within any organization. Alternative structures of command and control provide system stability and institutional support for a variety of different organizational values and routines (O'Toole and Meier, 1999). Broadly speaking, such structures reflect two key sets of characteristics. First, the broad 'structural' features that 'define the physical milieu' in which organization members interact, such as the overall size of an organization and the ratio of administrators to production workers. Second, the 'structuring' activities managers undertake in order to deliberately shape the behaviour of organization members (Dalton et al., 1980). Although these two characteristics apply to all organizational structures, in the public sector, managers generally have far less discretion than their private sector counterparts over 'structural' issues. For example, the size of public organizations often reflects statutory duties and responsibilities, and is typically only altered at the behest of overhead political authorities (see Rainey, 1989). By contrast, public managers are likely to have a similar degree of control over 'structuring activities', such as the relative levels of decision participation, as managers in private firms – if not always over where responsibility for the content of decisions ultimately lies.

All organizations are 'a collection of social positions not an aggregate of individuals' (Hage and Aiken, 1967, 77). Organizational structuring is thus primarily concerned with the construction of an idealized 'socially created pattern of rules, roles and relationships' (Dawson, 1996, 111). Hence, 'structuring' activities invariably indicate 'how positions are arranged in the social structure' (Hage and Aiken, 1967, 77). One key 'structuring' activity that is susceptible to managerial control, and which, in turn, may influence organizational performance, is the relative degree to which decision-making is centralized (see especially Hage and Aiken, 1967).

The centralization or decentralization of decision-making is a key indicator of the manner in which an organization allocates resources and determines policies and objectives. It is, moreover, an issue that has long been recognized as a critical area of research on organizational behaviour (see Pugh et al., 1968). For organizational theorists, the relative degree of centralization within an organization is signified by the 'hierarchy of authority' and the 'degree of participation in decision-making', aspects of structure that reflect the exercise and distribution of power across the entire organization (Carter and Cullen, 1984; Glisson and Martin, 1980; Hage and Aiken, 1967, 1969). Indeed, a large number of studies of organizational structure in the public, private and nonprofit sectors measure the extent of centralization by assessing both of these dimensions (Allen and LaFollette, 1977; Carter and Cullen, 1984; Dewar et al., 1980; Glisson and Martin, 1980; Hage and Aiken, 1967, 1969; Jarley et al., 1997; Negandhi and Reimann, 1973). Hierarchy of authority refers to the extent to which the power to make decisions is exercised at the upper levels of the organizational hierarchy, while participation in decision-making pertains to the degree of staff involvement in the determination of organizational policy.

A centralized organization will typically have a high degree of hierarchical authority and low levels of participation in decisions about policies and resources; while a decentralized organization will be characterized by low hierarchical authority and highly participative decision-making. Thus, where only one or a few individuals make decisions, an organizational structure may be described as highly centralized. By contrast, the least centralized organizational structure possible is one in which all organization members are responsible for and involved in decision-making. Organizations can be designed in such a way as to increase or decrease the relative degree of centralization. Evaluation of the costs and benefits of hierarchical control and decision participation for organizational performance is therefore a critical task for managers and researchers alike.

Evidence on centralization and public service performance

There is a growing literature on structures of decision-making in the public sector, especially as it pertains to the street-level bureaucrats responsible for directly providing public services, such as teachers, police officers and social workers (e.g. Lipsky, 1980; Maynard-Moody and Musheno, 2003; Riccucci, 2005). However, there is still comparatively little research systematically investigating the effects of centralization within public organizations on performance. A wide array of studies assess the effects of the structure of the organizational population: (de)centralization on local (e.g. Boyne, 1992) and regional governments (e.g. Andrews and Martin, 2010), but rather less is known about the impact of central control of decisions or staff participation in decision-making on public service performance. Moreover, few studies utilize a theoretical model of centralization within organizations. Rather than examine the dimensions of centralization proposed by Hage and Aiken (1967), they tend to focus on either hierarchy of authority (e.g. Schmid, 2002) or the degree of decision participation (e.g. Ashmos et al., 1998).

A thorough review of the available empirical evidence on centralization and performance requires the adaptation of additional search terms for relative levels of hierarchy of authority and decision participation (e.g. control, involvement), in conjunction with those for performance (e.g. achievement, effectiveness). Our extensive search revealed only 11 studies that sought to quantitatively analyse the relationship between centralization and organizational performance in the public sector. These studies were mostly undertaken in the US (9), with one each being carried out in Israel and Sweden. The content of the studies is summarized in Table 6.1.

The reviewed studies offer an initial basis upon which to form judgements about the relationship between centralization and performance. The evidence covers a wide range of public services ranging from hospitals to US federal agencies, but is exclusively focused on single-purpose organizations. At the same time, most of the studies typically draw on only a small sample of organizations, though some utilize multiple dependent variables, including measures of efficiency and effectiveness. Formal tests of statistical significance are used in each study, and most implement multivariate techniques to control for the potential effects of other relevant contextual variables. As in our study, many researchers (Glisson and Martin, 1980; Martin and Segal, 1977; Moynihan and Pandey, 2005; Richardson et al., 2002; Schmid, 2002; Whetten, 1978) draw directly on or adapt one or more of the survey indices utilized in

Table 6.1 Studies of centralization and public service performance

Study	**Organizations and sample size**	**Dimension of centralization**	**Measure of performance**	**Net effect on performance**
Anderson (1995)	National Corporation of Swedish Pharmacies, 1971–90	Hierarchy of authority	Productivity	
Ashmos et al. (1998)	52 Texan hospitals	Participation in decision-making	Staff perceptions of output and efficiency	– –
Fiedler and Gillo (1974)	55 community college faculties in Washington state	Participation in decision-making	Perceptions of teaching performance	NS
Glisson and Martin (1980)	30 organizations in one US city	Hierarchy of authority Participation in decision-making	Productivity Efficiency	+ +
Holland (1974)	1 Massachusetts mental health institution	Hierarchy of authority Participation in decision-making	Outcomes	–
Martin and Segal (1977)	23 halfway houses for alcoholics in Florida	Hierarchy of authority	Outcomes	–
Maynard-Moody et al. (1990)	2 community correctional facilities in Oregon and Colorado	Participation in decision-making	Perceptions of implementation success	–
Moynihan and Pandey (2005)	83 US state-level health and human service agencies	Hierarchy of authority	Staff perceptions of effectiveness	–
Schmid (2002)	41 Israeli boarding schools	Hierarchy of authority	Staff perceptions of effectiveness	
Whetten (1978)	67 New York manpower agencies	Participation in decision-making	Output Staff perceptions of effectiveness	+ –
Wolf (1993)	44 US cabinet agencies	Hierarchy of authority	Bureaucratic effectiveness	NS

Hage and Aiken's (1967) study of the structural properties of 16 social welfare and health agencies. In that study, Hage and Aiken developed an index of hierarchy of authority based on five items gauging the extent to which organization members required the approval of superiors in order to make decisions. An index of participation in decision-making was also constructed from four questionnaire items asking how frequently organization members participated in hiring and promotion decisions, and policy and program adoption decisions.

Overall, the studies of centralization and performance in the public sector uncover contrasting effects associated with centralized decision-making. Schmid's (2002) study of therapeutic boarding schools in Israel failed to uncover statistically significant relationships between hierarchy of authority and performance. Nevertheless, other researchers do find such relationships. Glisson and Martin's (1980) study of human service organizations in the US reveals that Hage and Aiken's index of centralization measuring hierarchy of authority and participation in decision-making has a large statistically significant positive effect on productivity, even when controlling for other aspects of organizational 'structuring' such as formalization. Glisson and Martin (1980) also find a small positive effect on efficiency. However, although this study implies that centralization may play an important role in determining the quantity of organizational output, its effects may be related in a different manner to alternative measures of service performance. For instance, Whetten (1978) finds that participation in decision-making has a negative effect on the output of US manpower agencies, but a positive one on staff perceptions of effectiveness. This study suggests that centralization facilitates production-orientated goals because it reduces environmental uncertainty and provides a clear indication of the service mission to middle managers and front-line staff. Nevertheless, increased levels of decision participation can maximize the points of contact between service managers and users, potentially leading to more responsive service development.

Anderson (1995) indicates that decentralization of authority (measured using semi-structured interviews) was associated with high performance in the National Corporation of Swedish Pharmacies between 1971 and 1990. Evidence from the mental health-care sector also suggests decentralizing decision-making (measured using a single-survey item) enables managers to provide clients with more individual attention leading to better clinical outcomes (Holland, 1973). Maynard-Moody et al.'s (1990) analysis of street-level bureaucracy highlights that program implementation in two contrasting US community correctional organizations was best where there was 'greater street-level influence in policy processes' (845). They ascertain this by deriving a measure of decision participation based on several questions assessing the extent of influence different occupation groupings have in making policy in community correction facilities. Other researchers too have furnished evidence suggesting that excluding professional staff from decision-making is likely to result in poor quality public services (e.g. Ashmos et al., 1998; Martin and Segal, 1977).

Research which has drawn exclusively on subjective ratings of organizational effectiveness has found little or no relationship between centralization and performance. Moynihan and Pandey (2005) uncover a negative connection between centralization (measured using an adapted version of the Hage and Aiken scale) and perceptions of effectiveness in 83 US human and health services. However, Wolf's exhaustive (1993) case survey of bureaucratic effectiveness, which coded the extent of hierarchy of authority observed in each study on a five-point scale, found no relationship between centralization and performance in a range of US federal agencies. Similarly, in an earlier investigation, Fiedler and Gillo (1974) show that decentralizing decision-making, gauged using a single questionnaire item asking respondents about their influence over policy decisions, had little effect on the perceived achievements of different faculties within community colleges.

Limitations of the existing evidence on centralization and public service performance

Despite the many merits of the studies reviewed above, their content is nevertheless limited in a number of ways. Many of the quantitative empirical studies utilize subjective survey-based measures of effectiveness that may not be as robust and reliable as administrative indicators of performance. Indeed, Dalton et al. (1980) identify this as a weakness of research on structure and performance more generally. To build confidence in the evidence on centralization and public service performance, it is essential to draw on administrative measures that reduce the prospect for common source bias to contaminate the findings.

At the same time, the impact of centralization on public service outcomes rarely occurs in isolation from other relevant internal organizational characteristics. In particular, configurational and contingency theorists highlight that strategy content and process is likely to constitute an important boundary condition of the structure–performance relationship (Miles and Snow, 1978; Mintzberg, 1979). Richardson et al. (2002), for example, show that organizational growth strengthens the relationship between participation in decision-making and profitability in health-care treatment centres in the US. Thus, it is conceivable that the effects of centralization may be more likely to be felt in combination with other theoretically relevant organizational attributes. Indeed, it is a core argument of contingency theorists that the benefits of any given organizational characteristic will occur only in combination with other complementary characteristics. According to Miles and Snow, this means that the relative degree of centralization within an organization must be in alignment with the content of the strategy selected by top management. To understand the potential benefits of centralization for performance, it is therefore necessary to consider how and in what ways it might interact with organizational strategy.

Hypotheses on centralization and performance

The level of centralization within an organization is a key indicator of the strategic approach adopted to achieving effective coordination and control. The allocation of roles and responsibilities in this way simultaneously constrains and prescribes the behaviour of organization members (Hall, 1982). It also performs a symbolic function indicating that someone is 'in charge' (Pfeffer and Salancik, 1978). As a result, it may reasonably be expected that the degree of centralization will have a significant effect on the resolution of principal–agent dilemmas that may be a key determinant of organizational outcomes. Indeed, some researchers contend that even modest improvements in organizational structuring can generate large gains for customers, employees and managers (see Starbuck and Nystrom, 1981). However, despite its pervasiveness, the impact of centralization is contingent on many other organizational characteristics, such as strategy content and processes (Pettigrew, 1973; Pfeffer, 1981). It is therefore likely that the degree of hierarchy of authority and participation in decision-making may have mixed effects on performance.

On the one hand, it has been suggested that centralized decision-making is necessary to make big bureaucracies manageable (e.g. Goodsell, 1985; Ouchi, 1980). For example, Frederick Taylor (1911) argued that the 'scientific' management of organizations was only possible where decision-making was restricted to a small cadre of planners. On the other hand, centralization is associated with many of the dysfunctions of bureaucracy identified by public choice theorists, especially abuses of monopoly power, rigidity and red tape (e.g. Downs, 1967; Niskanen, 1971; Tullock, 1965). For instance, Lipsky (1980) highlights that bureaucratic controls may lead front-line staff to devote disproportionate time to finding ways to by-pass established decision-making procedures, thereby damaging internal and external accountability.

Broadly speaking, then, the potential effects of centralization on performance can be summarized in two rival positions. Proponents of centralized decision-making suggest that it leads to better performance by facilitating greater decision speed, providing firm direction and goals and establishing clear lines of hierarchical authority. All of which may render principal–agent dilemmas redundant. By contrast, supporters of more participative decision-making suggest that centralization harms performance by preventing middle managers and street-level bureaucrats from making independent professional decisions, enshrining inflexible rules and procedures and undermining responsiveness to changing environmental circumstances. The plausibility of both views thus implies that centralization may have inconsistent, contradictory or even no meaningful effects on performance. The costs and benefits of any given structural arrangement might therefore simply cancel each other out. This leads to the following null hypothesis:

H6.0 Centralization is unrelated to organizational performance.

Centralization and public service performance: the moderating effects of strategy content and process

Contingency theorists argue that the best way to maximize organizational effectiveness is by developing appropriate linkages between different internal management characteristics (Doty et al., 1993). Strategic choices must therefore be made about how to achieve the optimum fit between the articulation and achievement of an organization's goals (Chandler, 1962). The content of those strategic choices and how they are formulated and subsequently implemented are all likely to have an important influence on the relationship between centralization and performance. According to Miles and Snow (1978), appropriate structures and processes hold the key to the successful pursuit of any given strategy. Thus, it is necessary to ensure that a *fit* is established between the internal characteristics of an organization and the strategy that is pursued. A misalignment between structure and strategy will hinder performance. As a result, organizations face not only an 'entrepreneurial' problem (which strategy to adopt), but also an 'administrative' problem (the selection of structures that are consistent with the strategy).

Miles and Snow (1978) argue that, for defenders, 'the solution to the administrative problem must provide management with the ability to control all organizational operations centrally' (41). This is because a defender is attempting to maximize the efficiency of internal procedures. A defender resembles a classic bureaucracy in which 'only top-level executives have the necessary information and the proper vantage point to control operations that span several organizational subunits' (Miles and Snow 1978, 44). By contrast, the prospector's administrative system 'must be able to deploy and coordinate resources among many decentralized units and projects rather than to plan and control the operations of the entire organization centrally' (Miles and Snow 1978, 59). Decisions are therefore devolved to middle managers and front-line staff so that they can apply their 'expertise in many areas without being unduly constrained by management control' (Miles and Snow, 1978, 62). Finally, reactors, unlike defenders or prospectors, have no predictable organizational structure: some may be centralized while others are decentralized. Therefore, they 'do not possess a set of mechanisms which allows them to respond consistently to their environments' (Miles and Snow 1978, 93).

This set of arguments led Miles and Snow to suppose that prospectors would be decentralized, while defenders would be centralized, and that where these relationships between strategy and structure obtain a good fit, organizations would perform well. Chandler's (1962) analysis of industrial enterprises, too, suggests that organizations that adapt their structure to meet new strategic goals operate more efficiently and are more likely to achieve their goals. Nonetheless, Miles and Snow posit that this relationship will not hold for organizations adopting a reacting strategy, as reactors are unable to develop structures consistent with their changeable strategic choices. The application of this model to the public sector therefore leads to the following hypotheses:

H6.1 Centralization is likely to be positively related to performance in an organization with a defender stance
H6.2 Decentralization is likely to be positively related to performance in an organization with a prospector stance
H6.3 Neither centralization nor decentralization is related to performance in an organization with a reactor stance.

According to contingency theories, internal characteristics, such as structure and process, should also be in alignment to create the complementary effects required to drive an organization forward. Hence, for Miles and Snow (1978), certain contingent relationships between an organization's internal characteristics will prove more successful than others to realization of an organization's goals, and the design task for top management is therefore to determine the most effective *fit* between them. In terms of the combined effects of structure and strategy process on performance, the contingent relationships likely to result in better organizational functioning will reflect the kind of goals associated with more or less centralized organizations.

Organizational theory has long emphasized that centralized organizations tend to pursue the goal of processing tasks efficiently (Weber, 1947). To do this effectively, they tend to adopt a mechanistic-type of structure characterized by strong planning systems (Burns and Stalker, 1963). Miles and Snow (1978) highlight formal planning procedures, systematic market analysis and target-setting are all likely to enhance the positive effects of central control over decision-making. By contrast, decentralized organizations tend to pursue more diffuse and broad goals rather than focusing narrowly on efficiency or core business development. As a result, the goals of a decentralized organization are more likely to be realized where the processes by which decisions are made and implemented are in a state of some flux – albeit one that is framed by some kind of overarching strategic goal (Miles and Snow, 1978). Decentralized organizations require 'looser' more organic processes to cope better with the accumulation of diverse and potentially conflicting views on how best to deliver services as well as on how best to accommodate a wider range of demands from a wider client base. This, in turn, implies that senior and middle managers must negotiate operational and strategic decisions on a comparatively ad hoc and informal basis in a decentralized organization, whereas analytical exercises to determine how to execute centrally set decisions are required to maintain the chain of command in a centralized organization. Inevitably, set against the strategic decisions linking centralization and decentralization to specific types of strategy process, misalignment or the absence of structure or process would be likely to result in worse organizational performance. Thus, we anticipate that:

H6.4 Centralization is likely to be positively related to performance in an organization with a planned strategy process

H6.5 Decentralization is likely to be positively related to performance in an organization with an incremental strategy process

H6.6 Neither centralization nor decentralization is related to performance in an organization with an absent strategy process.

Measuring centralization

Our measures of organizational centralization are based on variables which evaluate both the power to make decisions and the degree of involvement in decision-making at different levels within the sample organizations (Hage and Aiken, 1967). Four items from the survey of Welsh local authorities were used to measure hierarchy of authority and participation in decision-making. Hierarchy of authority was gauged by combining two items focusing on whether strategy making was carried out by the Chief Executive Officer alone or collectively within the senior management team. Participation in decision-making was assessed by combining two items gauging the degree of staff involvement in decision-making. The resulting measures of *hierarchy of authority* and *participation in decision-making* exhibit strong Cronbach's Alpha internal reliability scores of 0.74 and 0.89, respectively (Nunnally, 1978). The descriptive statistics for each survey item are shown in Table 6.2.

Statistical results

Our statistical models are presented in the following sequence: the separate effects of our *hierarchy of authority* and *participation in decision-making* measures are exhibited in Table 6.3. The centralization × strategy content interaction terms are shown in Table 6.4 to illustrate when controlling for other strategy–structure configurations whether strategic stances moderate the effects of *hierarchy of authority* and *participation in decision-making*. Following that, centralization × strategy formulation interactions are exhibited in Table 6.5. This highlights the extent to which the effects of centralization may be contingent upon the approach to strategic decision-making that is generally adopted within the sample organizations. Finally, the centralization × strategy implementation interaction terms are shown in Table 6.6. These interactions indicate the extent to which the approach to implementing strategies may enhance or weaken the effects of centralization.

Table 6.2 Measures of centralization

	Mean	**Min**	**Max**	**s.d.**
Strategy for our service is usually made by the Chief Executive	2.23	1.00	6.00	1.19
Strategy for our service is usually made by the Corporate Management Team	3.30	1.00	7.00	1.65
Participation in decision-making				
All staff are involved in the strategy process to some degree	4.70	1.00	7.00	1.53
Most staff have input into decisions that directly affect them	4.79	1.67	7.00	1.34

Table 6.3 Centralization and performance

Independent variable	Slope	t-score	Slope	t-score
Hierarchy of authority (HA)	−.020	1.00		
Participation in decision-making (PD)			−.019	1.12
R^2	.63**		.68**	
Adjusted R^2	.59**		.65**	
$N = 53$				

Note: Significance levels: **$p \leq 0.01$ (two-tailed tests).
All equations include control variables entered in the models shown in Table 2.7.

Table 6.4 Centralization × strategy content and performance

Independent variable	Slope	t-score	Slope	t-score
HA × defending	.044	2.93**		
HA (reversed) × prospecting	.421	.97		
HA × reacting	.862	1.15		
PD (reversed) × defending			1.721	2.15*
PD × prospecting			1.020	2.24*
PD × reacting			.603	1.52
R^2	.73**		.78**	
Adjusted R^2	.68**		.74**	
$N = 53$				

Note: Significance levels: *$p \leq 0.05$; **$p \leq 0.01$ (two-tailed tests).
All equations include control variables entered in the models shown in Table 2.7.

Table 6.5 Centralization × strategy formulation and performance

Independent variable	Slope	t-score	Slope	t-score
HA × rational approach	.020	1.70+		
HA (reversed) × incremental approach	−.016	−1.25		
HA × no approach	.027	2.79**		
PD (reversed) × rational approach			.004	.57
PD × incremental approach			−.013	−1.79+
PD × no approach			−.004	−.54
R^2	.79**		.74**	
Adjusted R^2	.75**		.69**	
N = 53				

Note: Significance levels: +$p \leq 0.10$; **$p \leq 0.01$ (two-tailed tests).
All equations include control variables entered in the models shown in Table 2.7.

Table 6.6 Centralization × strategy implementation and performance

Independent variable	Slope	t-score	Slope	t-score
HA × rational approach	1.177	3.02**		
HA (reversed) × incremental approach	.555	1.16		
HA × no approach	.345	.85		
PD (reversed) × rational approach			.060	.13
PD × incremental approach			−.248	−.80
PD × no approach			.183	.50
R^2	.92**		.90**	
Adjusted R^2	.89**		.88**	
$N = 40$				

Note: Significance levels: $^{**}p \leq 0.01$ (two-tailed tests).
All equations include control variables entered in the models shown in Table 2.7.

The models generally provide a very good level of statistical explanation of variations in the performance of local authority services in Wales. The average R^2 is above 70 per cent and is significant at 0.01 or better. This suggests that the models provide a sound foundation for assessing the separate and combined effects of centralization and strategy content and process.

Centralization and performance

The results shown in Table 6.3 support our null hypothesis for centralization and performance. The coefficients for *hierarchy of authority* and *participation in decision-making* are statistically insignificant, and make no difference to the explanatory power of the models.

The statistical results suggest that neither centralized nor decentralized decision-making has an independent effect on public service performance. As speculated earlier, it is conceivable that the supposed costs and benefits of centralization for service performance cancel each other out: fast decision-making may be counterbalanced by a need for building support for decisions. The latter requirement may be especially acute in public organizations which are held accountable by many different stakeholders, including politicians, service users, the media and employees. Alternatively, it may simply be the case that the degree of both hierarchy of authority and participation in decision-making are unrelated to how well services perform. The actual process of service delivery and its outcomes are not affected if an organization concentrates the opportunity and power to make decisions in only a few hands or if decision-making is distributed more evenly throughout an organization. A further possibility is that the effects of centralization are moderated by other critical determinants of performance, especially organizational strategy. The introduction of centralization–strategy content interactions within the model provides strong support for this explanation.

Centralization, strategy content and performance

The statistical results presented in Table 6.4 are consistent with Hypothesis 6.1: the coefficients for '*hierarchy of authority* times defending' and '*participation in decision-making* (inverted) times defending' are positive and statistically significant. However, the evidence is only partially consistent with Hypothesis 6.2: the coefficient for '*participation in decision-making* times prospecting' is statistically significant with a positive sign, while the coefficient for '*hierarchy of authority* (inverted) times prospecting' is not statistically significant. The results furnish support for Hypothesis 6.3: the coefficients for the structure-reacting interactions are all statistically insignificant. The findings thus provide a clear indication that centralized defenders are likely to have high performance: the coefficients for both '*hierarchy of authority* times defending' and '*participation in decision-making* (inverted) times defending' are positive and statistically significant, even when controlling for alternative strategy–structure configurations. The models also suggest that prospecting will improve performance if carried out in combination with a high level of decision participation, but that it makes no difference to service achievements when combined with a low degree of hierarchical authority. F-tests revealed that the R^2 change when interaction terms are introduced was statistically significant at the 0.01 per cent level. This highlights that the degree of 'fit' between structure and strategy content is an important determinant of public service performance.

Organizations that adopt a defending strategy enhance their performance if they centralize authority and reduce decision participation. Centralized decision-making can sometimes increase goal ambiguity by enabling the enactment of frequent changes in overall strategic direction (Pandey and Wright, 2006). However, centralization may be conducive to maintaining stable service priorities where top management teams adopt a defending strategy of making operations more efficient. Whetten's (1978) study of manpower agencies suggests that centralization facilitates such production-orientated goals because it reduces environmental uncertainty and furnishes a clear indication of the service mission to middle managers and front-line staff. Indeed, one of our interviewees in a defending service suggested that management and decision-making in the service had become more centralized as the Corporate Management Board sought to respond to an increasingly hostile operating environment. This had increased efficiency by reducing the 'inconsistencies' sometimes associated with decentralized decision-making, especially intra-organizational communication and office administration costs. Centralization may also have had a positive influence on the recent introduction of performance management and planning in Welsh local government (Boyne et al., 2002). Miles and Snow (1978) argue that such organizational processes are key characteristics of successful defenders. In another defending service, an interviewee highlighted that the implementation of a new performance management framework had hinged on 'a lot of pulling together with the director and the [authority's] Chief Executive Officer'.

Organizations which encourage staff involvement in decision-making provide better services if they are prospectors, but are unlikely to reap improvements by delegating the authority to make decisions. Involving staff in decision-making may enable senior managers to more effectively identify opportunities for improving service delivery. Decision participation can maximize the points of contact between service managers and users, leading to more responsive service development. Evidence from the mental health-care sector suggests decentralizing decision-making enables managers to provide clients with more individual attention (Holland 1973). Similarly, Maynard-Moody et al. (1990) stress that street-level bureaucrats 'savvy about what works as a result of daily interactions with clients, should have a stake in the decision-making process' (845). Decision participation can permit greater leeway for independent thinking to influence strategic management. An interviewee from a successful prospecting education service indicated that their high performance had been partly due to increased involvement of school head-teachers in strategic decision-making.

By contrast, the statistical results suggest that prospecting organizations are unlikely to achieve gains in performance by devolving control over strategic decisions. It seems to make no difference (for our sample) whether prospecting organizations have a low or high degree of hierarchical authority. Our findings therefore suggest that participation in decision-making may be the most influential aspect of centralization in determining organizational outcomes. This buttresses Hage and Aiken's (1967) conclusion that 'participation in decision-making seems to be the more important dimension of the distribution of power than hierarchy of authority' (p. 88).

Evidence corroborating our results for prospecting and decision participation is provided by a number of researchers. McMahon (1976), Richter and Tjosvold (1980) and Tannenbaum (1962) all find that extending participation in decision-making increases organizational effectiveness by enhancing mutual influence, motivation and satisfaction. Indeed, in one prospecting service, an interviewee stated that more decentralization meant that 'staff morale has improved, because there is more feedback on how they are performing'. Such affective consequences may be less evident in organizations with a low degree of hierarchy, because middle managers and front-line staff may simply be held individually rather than collectively responsible for decisions. In other words, the potentially positive influence of professionalization on organizational performance is likely to be contingent on decision participation rather than the design of the chain of command (see Hage and Aiken, 1967). The combined effect of different aspects of decentralization and employee norms and motivation within public organizations is an issue which merits extended empirical investigation.

The degree of hierarchy of authority and participation in decision-making made no difference to the performance of reacting organizations. For reactors, strategy is typically set by external circumstances. It is therefore conceivable that the relative degree of centralization does not influence service outcomes in reacting organizations because it has no substantive impact on the content of their decisions. For example, a manager in one reacting service indicated in an interview that their decisions were essentially determined by a national strategic framework and local political issues. In such circumstances, both senior and middle managers have far less scope to positively influence service delivery decisions. An alternative explanation is that reacting organizations simply do not have the capacity to make authoritative decisions or encourage meaningful participation in decision-making even if they are presented with an opportunity to do so. In another reacting service, a manager noted in interview that their department benefited from strong regulatory direction because there was 'limited ability to recognize issues and deal with them'. This is consistent with evidence that the development of structures for coping with uncertainty is critical for managers seeking to increase their ability to make and implement decisions (Hinings et al., 1974).

Overall, Miles and Snow's (1978) hypotheses on structure and strategy content are given broad confirmation: high performance appears to be more likely for public organizations that match their decision-making structure with their strategic stance. Defending organizations with a high degree of hierarchical authority and low staff involvement in decision-making, in particular, perform better, but prospecting organizations with high decision participation are also likely to do well. By contrast, hierarchy of authority and participation in decision-making make no difference to the performance of reacting organizations. We turn now to the interactive effects of centralization and strategy process.

Centralization, strategy processes and performance

F-tests revealed that improvement in the R^2 when the structure × strategy process interaction terms are introduced in the formulation and implementation models is statistically significant at the 0.01 per cent level. This indicates that the degree of 'fit' between centralization and strategy formulation and implementation adds further explanatory power to the statistical model. However, the results presented in Tables 6.5 and 6.6 provide mixed support for each of the hypotheses. Hypothesis 6.4 receives partial confirmation: the coefficients for HA × rational approach to strategy formulation and for HA × rational approach to strategy implementation are both positive and statistically significant. However, the coefficients for HA (reversed) × incremental strategy processes are not statistically significant – though the signs for the coefficients are in the expected direction. Hypothesis 6.5 receives no support, and is directly contradicted by the result for the coefficient for PD × incremental implementation approach, which is statistically significant but with a negative rather than the anticipated positive sign. Hypothesis 6.6 is also contradicted in one instance: the coefficient for HA × no formulation approach is positive and statistically significant. However, each of the other three relevant coefficients is not statistically significant, thereby corroborating the expectation that an absence of strategy process is unlikely to influence the relationship between centralization and performance.

The findings provide some indication that centralization and strategic planning may be likely to result in better performance, but that this appears to be the case only when the power to make decisions is exercised at the top of the organization rather than when staff are restricted from participating in decision-making. In one service department controlled largely by the Corporate Management Team, a manager indicated that their success in delivering high-quality services was attributable to 'a rolling programme of options appraisals' that guided the formulation of strategies. In another, a service manager indicated that a formal business planning guide which 'assists people at the lower level to match their business' to service and corporate priorities had enabled resources to be allocated more fairly to the front-line to implement new strategies.

By contrast, decentralization and incremental processes do not seem to complement one another in a way that results in better performance, at least for this sample and time period. In fact, decentralization combined with incremental formulation of strategies appears to result in worse performance. One of our interviewees in a community safety department suggested that the service had struggled to cope with a loose organizational structure, wherein the CEO 'tried to make managers manage'. In a manner redolent of Lipsky's (1980) arguments about street-level bureaucracy this manager claimed that a 'focus on people-management, rather than case-management', was to the detriment of service delivery.

On balance, it seemed to be the case that the influence of relative levels of centralization on performance was unlikely to be affected by an absence of strategy process. Nevertheless, one of the benefits associated with the exercise of authority at the top of the organizations appears to be a greater prospect of better performance in the absence of an established approach to the formulation of strategies. This is suggestive of benefits associated with fast decision-making at the top of an organization that are untrammelled by the need to provide any systematic or negotiated account of the origins of the content of decisions. In one service in which performance was improving, the Head of Department was no longer involved in strategy formulation and implementation, which had been taken over by the Corporate Management Board. This points towards the need to examine the context behind the structure–process relationship before drawing firm conclusions about effects on outcomes.

Our findings on centralization, strategy and performance can be summarized as follows. The first hypothesis we advance in this chapter receives strong support: centralization has neither a positive nor a negative independent effect on performance. Our hypotheses on the combined effects of centralization and strategy content on performance are also confirmed: centralization benefits defending organizations, decentralization prospecting ones and makes no difference to those that are reactive. However, our hypotheses on the combined effects of centralization and strategy process and performance receive more mixed support: in combination, centralization and rational planning are, as anticipated, associated with higher performance, but decentralization does not elicit any benefits for organizations with a more incremental type of strategy process. For the most part, though, centralization is, as expected, unrelated to performance when combined with an absent strategy process.

Conclusions

This chapter has explored the separate and joint effects of centralization and strategy content and process on public service performance. The statistical results show that variations in public service performance are unrelated to hierarchy of authority and the degree of participation in decision-making when these variables are examined in isolation; but that the effect of structure on performance is mediated by strategy content and (to a lesser degree) strategy formulation, even when controlling for past performance, service expenditure and external constraints. However, strategy implementation appears to make little difference to the relationship between centralization and performance. As a result, we conclude that Miles and Snow (and other contingency theorists) offer some hope for public management scholars seeking to explain the impact of organizational structure on service performance. However, their arguments appear to hold only for certain combinations of internal organizational characteristics. Our findings provided strong support for the idea that appropriate connections between structure and strategy content make a difference to organizational success, but that this is less likely to be so for the joint effects of structure and strategy process.

The contingent relationships between internal organizational characteristics that we identify in Chapters 3–6 confirm many of the hypotheses we develop based on the Miles and Snow model of organizational strategy. In Chapter 3, we found that strategy content matters in the ways predicted. Prospecting and defending lead to better performance than does reacting. The findings presented in Chapters 4 5 illustrate that strategy process rarely makes a difference to performance on its own. Although incremental strategy implementation seems to lead to poorer performance, it is, on the whole, only when in alignment with appropriate strategy content that alternative types of strategy formulation and implementation matter to the achievements of our sample of organizations. In particular, incremental strategy processes are likely to result in better performance for prospecting service departments. In this chapter, we find that strategy content is again a key moderator of the impact of another internal organizational characteristic – the relative degree of centralization within an organization. However, only some of the expected combined effects of structure and process on performance are present for our sample of organizations. This leaves open the question of how best to align organizational structures with strategy processes, or, even, if it is possible or desirable to seek such alignment. At the same time, the findings we present in Chapters 3–6 raise important questions about the relationship between the organization and its environment that were touched upon in Chapter 2, where we identified the important impact that the organizational environment has on performance.

To fully explore how public organizations can benefit from the pursuit of strategic fit, it is essential to trace the combined effects of the environment and strategy content on performance, as well as the combined effects of the environment and strategy process. Miles and Snow (1978) suggest that organizations need to adapt their strategy content and process to the environmental circumstances that they face. Investigation of the relationship between environmental 'fit' and performance will therefore provide important information on the strategic choices that senior managers should make to enhance the effectiveness of public service provision. Thus, in Chapter 7, we turn to the interactive effects of the organizational environment and strategic management on performance.

7
Strategy, Environment and Performance

The central theoretical perspective of this book has been provided by the contingency theory developed by Miles and Snow. According to Miles and Snow, not only is it important to achieve alignment between the internal characteristics of organizations, but a fit between those characteristics and the environment is also critical to organizational success. Miles and Snow (1978, 3) note the demands that this places on organizations at the outset of the book: 'For most organizations, the dynamic process of adjusting to environmental change and uncertainty – of maintaining an effective alignment with the environment while efficiently managing internal interdependencies – is enormously complex.' In the introduction to the Classic Edition (as published in the 2003 reprint, xviii) they argue that they were 'less certain about how consistency across strategy, structure and process contributed to firm success. Eventually, we decided that the concept of *fit* could be used to explain the dynamics of organizational adaptation and effectiveness.' In view of the need for fit, in Chapters 4–6, we examined how strategy interacts with key internal characteristics to influence performance. In this chapter, we explore how strategy content, formulation and implementation interact with the technical and institutional environment confronted by public organizations to affect organizational outcomes. More precisely we examine how the independent effects of strategy are moderated by environmental forces, by strengthening or weakening them.

The technical environment faced by public organizations is widely recognized to be a major influence on their subsequent performance. Indeed, in Chapter 2 we uncovered strong statistical relationships between the relative munificence and dynamism faced by our sample organizations and their service achievements. The allocation of financial resources to public service providers in developed countries by political principals often compensates them for the difficulty of their operating circumstances. For example, in the UK, local governments receive large block grants from central government that reflect judgements about the level of need amongst the population that they serve. However, despite an acknowledgement of variations in the challenges posed by the technical environment, political principals still tend to expect that public organizations can adapt to their environment in ways that are more or less conducive to better social outcomes. In this respect, contingency theory may hold the key to understanding successful strategic adaptation in the public sector.

In addition to adapting to the demands of the technical environment, public organizations arguably face greater pressure to address external institutional forces than their private sector counterparts (Rainey, 2010). The institutional environment confronted by public service providers has seen major change over recent years. From large-scale restructuring inspired by New Public Management thinking in the 1990s through to an emphasis on network forms of organization and public governance in more recent times, public agencies have been subject to an array of reforms promoting new models of service delivery. One of the more important developments, and the topic examined in this chapter, has been changes in the style and content of the regulation faced by public service providers. Regulation was initially used as a tool to monitor marketized services. However, the policy premise at the time of our empirical work, in the early 2000s, was that regulation in general, and inspection in particular, can place pressures on organizations to deliver services more efficiently and effectively. Critically, it is widely acknowledged that the service improvement approach to regulation will only work where the relationship between regulator and regulatee is a productive and cooperative one and where there is genuine commitment to managing services better (see Martin, 2010). As a result, great pressure has been placed upon public organizations to adopt strategies and processes that can enable them to effectively adapt to the environment in which they operate.

In this chapter, we explore empirically the links between the technical and institutional environment, strategic management and performance. To what extent is performance affected positively by the combination of particular internal and external variables? Do certain strategies and environments reinforce or counteract each other? We seek to answer these questions in a number of stages. In the first part of this chapter, we present theoretical arguments from the field of contingency theory on why the joint effects of organizational strategy and environment might be expected to influence organizational performance. We then go on to develop hypotheses specifically addressing the joint impact of strategy content and process and technical and institutional environments on public service performance. In the third part, we present and interpret the results of a series of statistical tests examining the relationships between strategy, environment and performance. Finally, we draw conclusions on the implications of our findings for strategic management in the public sector.

Strategy, technical environment and performance

The strategy–environment fit is an important element in the Miles and Snow model. However, it receives comparatively less attention in their work than the alignment of internal structures and processes with strategic choices. Nevertheless, it is clear that Miles and Snow believe that organizations have the discretion to adopt the strategy that is best suited to the technical circumstances that they face. Whilst in principle any given organizational strategy may be more likely to succeed where there are fewer environmental challenges to be overcome, Miles and Snow provide a firm indication of the circumstances in which one might expect prospecting and defending to flourish best. In this they follow Burns and Stalker's (1961) classic arguments about the contingent nature of the relationship between the organization and its environment.

Burns and Stalker suggest organic organizational structures are required in a complex, uncertain and changing environment, whereas mechanistic structures perform better in a simple, predictable and stable environment. Thus, in Miles and Snow's view, prospecting should work best in a challenging environment, while defending should be especially effective in one that is beset with fewer difficulties. At the same time, Miles and Snow's arguments suggest that reacting will not be consistently linked to any set of external circumstances, since reactors 'do not possess a set of mechanisms which allows them to respond consistently to their environments over time' (Miles and Snow, 1978, 93). The theoretical rationale for these arguments enables us to develop a set of testable hypotheses regarding the moderating effects of each of the three dimensions of the technical environment that we identified earlier on the relationship between strategy and performance. We now outline these hypotheses, beginning with the likely moderating effects of munificence on strategic management.

Chapter 2 sets out how a munificent environment is one that is characterized by the relative abundance of critical resources needed for an organization to perform its core tasks at an optimum level of effectiveness. It is, thus, generally regarded by management researchers to be a critical aspect of the technical environment in which organizations and managers operate (see, for instance, Castrogiovanni, 1991). An organization that is able to appropriate more slack resources from its external environment in order to achieve its goals operates in a context that offers fewer problems for effective strategic management. We expect, therefore, that, at a minimum, in munificent resource-rich settings the time and money required to guarantee the success of any given organizational strategy or approach to formulating and implementing strategy will be less than in more straitened circumstances. That is, that greater slack within the technical environment permits organizations to allocate a higher level of resource to the pursuit of whatever strategy content or process is selected by managers. This expectation leads to our first hypothesis:

H7.1 Munificence strengthens positive relationships between strategy content and process and performance.

Turning to Dess and Beard's (1984) second dimension of the environment, complexity, we can begin to sketch out more fully the likely shape of the contingent environment-strategy effects on performance. Adapting to environmental complexity requires that organizations seek to meet the diverse range of service needs and demands that are placed on them by their clientele. Public organizations are typically expected to accomplish this in an effective, efficient and equitable manner. Although public bureaucracies once sought to provide one-size-fits-all solutions to the diverse client groups whom they served, it is increasingly recognized that organizations should now seek to explore a multitude of alternative service delivery approaches in order to meet the very specific requirements of different groups. This is especially so, for example, in providing services to groups which are hard-to-reach, economically disadvantaged or socially excluded. This implies that organizations that continually strive to find new and better ways of providing services rather than stick to an established 'tried and tested' approach may be better able to adapt to myriad client needs or to the challenges posed by client dispersion. By contrast, those that persist with a narrow focus on what worked in the past may fall victim to the perils of threat-rigidity and become increasingly unable to cope with the demands of a heterogeneous or dispersed client population. Organizations with a reactive strategy are likely to fare no worse or better under conditions of complexity because any potential benefits of waiting for signals from the environment rather than persisting with a bad strategy may be outweighed by the continued absence of a clear strategic approach to managing the environment. Therefore, our second hypothesis is that:

H7.2 Complexity strengthens the relationship between prospecting and performance and weakens the relationship between defending and performance, but does not alter the relationship between reacting and performance.

In addition to representing an important influence on the likely effects of strategy content on performance, the relative degree of environmental complexity may also have a distinctive impact on the relationship between strategy process and performance. As noted above, contingency theory suggests that the adoption of more 'organic' organizational characteristics is likely to enhance responsiveness to environmental complexity and change. Thus, for example, Mintzberg (1979) suggests that complex environmental pressures tend to give rise to 'adhocracies' – organizations that adopt fluid or informal planning processes which permit more nuanced context-sensitive and adaptive decision-making rather than the tightly defined and prescribed approaches to making strategic decisions characteristic of large 'machine bureaucracies'. Within the context of the Miles and Snow model this indicates that incremental processes of strategy formulation and implementation may prove to be particularly successful for organizations confronting a high degree of environmental complexity. By contrast, the adoption of rational planning may constrain the options available to organizations for responding to the need to understand and accommodate myriad client needs and demands within strategic decision-making. An absence of a distinctive approach to strategy processes may again be expected to make little positive or negative contribution to the ability of an organization to manage a complex environment. Hence, we anticipate that:

H7.3 Complexity strengthens the relationship between incremental processes and performance and weakens the relationship between rational planning and performance, but does not alter the relationship between process absence and performance.

The relative instability and unpredictability of the technical environment is likely to have a similar interactive impact on the performance effects of strategy content as environmental complexity. The more flexible the strategic orientation of an organization, the more likely that it will be able to respond effectively to any sudden changes in the circumstances that it faces. By contrast, if the technical environment is predictable, then there is no need to expend resources of time and money in seeking to adapt to new or complicated challenges as the needs and demands of clients are stable and well-known. Organizations with a reactive strategic orientation will be blown this way and that by environmental change in ways that may unwittingly enhance or harm performance but rarely in a manner from which useful practical lessons can be drawn. Thus, we expect that:

H7.4 Dynamism strengthens the relationship between prospecting and performance and disrupts the relationship between defending and performance, but does not alter the relationship between reacting and performance.

In a similar vein, the combined effect of environmental dynamism and ad hoc processes of strategy formulation and implementation on performance is likely to be positive. Fluid processes permit organizations to alter, amend and adjust the way strategic decisions are made and implemented as new information about the changing needs and demands of clients emerges. In contradistinction, the combined effect of dynamism and rigid planning processes is likely a negative one because the existence of highly formal processes of strategy formulation and implementation inevitably constrain the ability of organizations to change track in the face of large or unexpected environmental shifts. An absence of a consistent approach to strategy process may again have both costs and benefits in such circumstances, but will likely offer little prospect of being susceptible to the evaluation that might guide subsequent managerial interventions. As a result, we hypothesize that:

H7.5 Dynamism strengthens the relationship between incremental processes and performance and weakens the relationship between rational planning and performance, but does not alter the relationship between process absence and performance.

Strategy, institutional environment and performance

In Chapter 3, we found no evidence for the impact of the institutional environment on organizational performance. Neither the extent of inspection nor whether regulation was perceived as supportive was statistically associated with the effectiveness of local services. It is conceivable though that inspection and regulation have no separate effects on service standards but have joint effects with strategy. In particular, external intervention in service provision may interact with organizational strategy, and weaken or reinforce its impact on performance. Although a few studies have examined the impact of regulation on performance in the private sector, none has considered the combined effect of regulation and strategy on performance. Some studies consider the impact of the regulatory environment on performance but omit the impact of organizational strategy (Gruca and Nath, 1994; Wade et al., 1998), and others examine the impact of strategy in a regulated environment, but treat regulatory pressures as constant across all the organizations in their sample (Fox-Wolfgram et al., 1998; Ramaswamy et al., 1994). Thus, new hypotheses on the moderating effect of regulation on the relationship between strategy and performance must be developed.

We draw upon the literature that applies cybernetic theory to processes of organizational control in the public sector to illustrate the likely impact of regulation on strategy and performance (Boyne et al., 2002; Dunsire, 1978; Hood et al., 1999). Cybernetic theory posits that regulation (or in this case the subsection of regulation that is inspection) is a tripartite process that involves setting standards, gathering information on attainment against these standards in organizations in the target population and effecting change and modifying behaviour if standards are not met. An organization that is subject to inspection has to understand the standards that it is going to be required to attain, have systematic information on these standards and comply with the recommendations that emerge from the inspection visit.

Inspection regimes are focused on achieving organizational improvements. However, there are a number of factors that may influence the inspection outcome and the impact on the inspectees. Boyne et al. (2002) summarize these to include aspect of the inspection regime (the technical and managerial skills of the inspectors, the clarity of the standards, the quality of the data supporting the inspection event and relationship between the inspectors and inspectees) and potential problems of the inspection process (e.g. resistance, ritualistic compliance, capture and performance ambiguity). The complexities of an inspection visit, together with the range of potential problems that can arise from the process suggest that an inspection event is inevitably disruptive for an organization. Effort is displaced from implementing the existing strategy to preparing for the inspection visit (e.g., writing documents and collating data, and managing impressions rather than managing services). Moreover, in the aftermath of the inspection, resources must be devoted to responding to inspectors' recommendations to effect change, and to altering service delivery in a way that at least appears to comply with their requests.

In short, we argue that inspection is likely to destabilize the link between all aspects of organizational strategy and performance. Where a particular strategy is a force for good (see Chapter 4 e.g.), then inspection events will have a detrimental impact on performance because they add to the costs associated with realizing the content of that strategy. At the same time, where a particular strategy is already harmful to performance, inspection will only serve to compound this performance trajectory – inspection alone cannot suffice to mitigate the negative effects of a bad strategy, because it is only when that strategy is abandoned that a change in performance can be anticipated.

Given the evidence we have presented thus far, we anticipated the following relationships. For strategy content the positive effects of prospecting and defending will be (at least partly) reversed by inspection, whereas organizations displaying high levels of reacting will continue to be poor performers. We argue this because the standards associated with an inspection may not relate to the goals of a prospector or defender – they may not be in keeping with the innovative strategies of a prospector or could be at odds with the core business of a defender – thereby requiring them to divert their attention away from activities which are, in theory, most conducive to higher organizational performance.

In relation to the strategy processes of formulation and implementation the relationship might be expected to be more complex. Where there is an absence of strategy formulation processes, inspection will compound poor performance. Similarly, for organizations with incremental processes the disruption arising from an inspection will likely add to the costs of strategy making because the process of negotiation with stakeholders will have to incorporate the interests of a new and extremely powerful set of actors. By contrast, it is possible that rational processes will work well with inspection.

As noted above (and in Chapter 3), inspection events prompt a review of progress to date and turn an organization's attention to new horizons.

In drawing upon a formal assessment of existing performance and future needs, inspection events can be synchronized with other tools of rational planning already being used within organizations, such as cost–benefit analysis, action plans and targets. It is therefore possible that in this case inspection may strengthen the relationship between process and performance. It is, however, important to note that in Chapter 4 we did not uncover any support for our hypothesis that rational planning increases performance. We, therefore, suggest that the relationship between rational planning and performance is moderated by inspection, because inspection works as a mechanism to formally identify key deficiencies and propel an organization towards higher levels of performance. These arguments apply in the case of both strategy formulation and implementation. Thus we hypothesize that:

H7.6 Inspection weakens the relationship between strategy (content, process and implementation) and performance, except in the case of rational planning where the relationship will be strengthened.

We have mounted a case that the institutional environment, as experienced through the process of inspection is more likely than not to have a detrimental effect on performance. However, given that regulatory regimes typically require blanket coverage of all relevant organizations, there are likely to be substantial variations in the way an inspection is conducted and perceived by those being inspected. In Chapter 3, we rehearsed some arguments on why this was so, notably that any potential inspection problems are reduced by stronger co-production of inspection outcomes. In this chapter, we move on to suggest that the extent to which regulation is perceived to be supportive is also likely to affect the relationship between strategy and organizational success. More specifically, supportive regulation may help public managers to pursue their preferred strategy more effectively.

To illustrate this proposition, we take the example of organizations characterized by reacting and strategy absence. A reactor takes its cues from the external organizational environment. Since processes of inspection and oversight are now a key feature of the environment faced by public organizations, those with a reactor strategy are likely to be especially responsive to the recommendations of regulators. Added to that, the experience of a supportive inspection event is likely to make it even easier for reacting organizations to move forward in ways that are conducive to better performance. Further, within the context of an improvement-focused regulatory regime, reactors may continue to receive additional signals which enable them to be steered towards enhanced outcomes.

By contrast, regulation that is viewed as unsupportive by service managers is likely to undermine their attempts to make organizational strategies work. The level of support in the institutional environment is likely to be important for the group of public organizations that are examined in this book because of the extent of inspection in the early twenty-first century in Wales. All public services, therefore including those in this study, were subject to inspection. For example, schools were regulated by Estyn, social service departments by the Social Services Inspectorate for Wales, benefits and revenues by Benefits and Revenues Inspection Service, and all services not included by a dedicated regulatory came under the auspices of the Audit Commission in Wales. Thus, if a service displaying a defender or prospector strategy feels that the institutional environment is not supporting their particular approach, it is likely to be harmful to organizational performance. Our seventh hypothesis is, therefore:

H7.7 Supportive regulation shifts the relationship between strategy (content, process and implementation) and performance in a positive direction.

Statistical results

The results for the statistical tests of the impact of strategy and the technical and institutional environment on public service performance are now described. The measures of strategy content and processes were discussed in Chapters 3 and 4 and those of the technical and institutional environment in Chapter 2. We commence our discussion with the technical environment.

Strategy, technical environment and performance

The results of the statistical data testing the relationship between the organizational strategy, the technical environment and performance are presented in Tables 7.1–7.3. Table 7.1 presents evidence on the moderating effects of the technical environment on the relationship between strategy content and performance. Table 7.2 illustrates the moderating effects of the environment on the strategy formulation–performance relationship, and Table 7.3 shows those for the strategy implementation–performance relationship. The statistical results

Table 7.1 Strategy content (SC) × technical environment and performance

Independent variable	Prospecting		Defending		Reacting	
	Slope	t-score	Slope	t-score	Slope	t-score
SC × munificence	.0116	1.39	.0124	1.50	−.0363	−3.31**
SC × complexity	−.0223	−2.17*	−.01900	−1.96+	.0038	.30
SC × dynamism	0.0004	.14	−.0003	−.13	−.0043	−1.85+
R^2	0.70**		.77**		.70**	
Adjusted R^2	.61**		.71**		.62**	
N = 51						

Note: Significance levels: $+p \leq 0.10$; $*p \leq 0.05$; $**p \leq 0.01$.
All equations include control variables entered in the models shown in Table 2.7.

Table 7.2 Strategy formulation (SF) × technical environment and performance

Independent variable	Planning		Incrementalism		Absence	
	Slope	t-score	Slope	t-score	Slope	t-score
SF × munificence	−.0095	−.91	.0055	.57	−.0062	−.70
SF × complexity	.0050	.38	−.0119	−1.17	.0032	.24
SF × dynamism	.0059	1.85+	.0026	1.24	−.0035	−1.22
R^2	.67**		.67**		.67**	
Adjusted R^2	.57**		.58**		.58**	
N = 50						

Note: Significance levels: $+p \leq 0.10$; $*p \leq 0.05$; $**p \leq 0.01$.
All equations include control variables entered in the models shown in Table 2.7.

Table 7.3 Strategy implementation (SI) × technical environment and performance

Independent variable	Planned		Incremental		Absence	
	Slope	t-score	Slope	t-score	Slope	t-score
SI × munificence	−4.4325	−2.09*	−8.3049	−3.45**	9.1813	4.05**
SI × complexity	3.9209	1.17	8.1959	2.20*	−9.6960	−2.91**
SI × dynamism	.3086	.34	1.1164	2.09*	−1.0149	−1.85+
R^2	.54**		.63**		.62**	
Adjusted R^2	.35**		.49**		.47**	
N = 40						

Note: Significance levels: $+p \leq 0.10$; $*p \leq 0.05$; $**p \leq 0.01$.
All equations include control variables entered in the models shown in Table 2.7.

presented in these three tables offer very limited support for Hypotheses 7.1–7.5; indeed the balance of evidence leads us to reject these hypotheses.

Hypothesis 7.1 suggested that there would be a positive relationship between munificence and any strategy approach. Of the nine coefficients presented in Tables 7.1–7.3 that test this hypothesis, only one is positive and statistically significant: this is for strategy implementation absence × munificence. The coefficients do not attain significance in the strategy formulation model (Table 7.2), nor for the strategy content characteristics of prospecting or defending. However, the coefficients are negative and significant on three occasions: in relation to reacting and planned and incremental approaches to implementation.

Hypotheses 7.2 and 7.3 examined the relationships between complexity and organizational strategy. Hypothesis 7.2 dealt with strategy content, and the data offer mixed support (Table 7.1). The proposition that complexity weakens the relationship between defending and performance was supported by the results (though at the lower 10 per cent level of significance). The coefficient for reacting × complexity did not achieve statistical significance, thereby supporting the hypothesis that complexity does not alter the relationship. The coefficient for prospecting × complexity did achieve statistical significance. However the direction of the coefficient was not as predicated, it was negative and thereby contradicts Hypothesis 7.2.

Hypothesis 7.3 focused on the interaction between complexity and strategy processes of formulation and implementation. Table 7.2 presents the results for strategy formulation. None of the coefficients in this table attained statistical significance. The hypothesis is rejected for planning and incremental formulation, however non-significance was predicted for complexity × formulation process of absence so this aspect of the hypothesis is upheld. Table 7.3 offers mixed, and somewhat complex, results again. One part of the hypothesis is supported, that pertaining to incremental formulation processes – here the coefficient was positive and significant. While no support was offered for planned implementation, as the coefficient was not significant, the hypothesis is rejected for complexity × strategy formulation absence because the coefficient is statistically significant and negative.

Hypothesis 7.4, on the interaction between dynamism and strategy context, is rejected outright (Table 7.1). None of the results are as anticipated. The coefficient for prospecting is not significant yet was predicted to be positive, while the coefficient for defending which was anticipated to be positive does not attain statistical significance. A non-significant result was argued for in relation to reacting, whereas the coefficient in Table 7.1 is negative and significant. Two of the six coefficients provide support for Hypothesis 7.5, two are contrary to the hypothesis and two are not significant (Tables 7.2 and 7.3). The coefficient for dynamism × strategy formulation absence is not significant and does not alter the relationship between absence and performance as predicted in Hypothesis 7.5. Incremental implementation processes are shown to have a positive impact on performance when interacted with dynamism, and thereby also support Hypothesis 7.5 (Table 7.3). A negative and statistically significant result is found for an implementation absence (where a non-significant result was expected), and the coefficient for planning formulation was positive and significant (rather than negative). While both these results were recorded at the lower 10-per cent level of statistical significance, they reject the hypothesis. Finally, the coefficients for incremental formulation and planned implementation were not significant. Overall, these are, again, weak results suggesting that the predicted environmental contingencies do not hold up in this data set.

The strongest finding to emerge from this analysis is that reacting is not a good strategy in munificent or dynamic environments, but is unaffected by the challenges posed by a complex environment. By contrast, environmental complexity appears to pose problems for prospecting and defending organizations. Whereas both types of strategy exhibit a positive relationship with performance (see Chapter 3), they appear to result in worse performance when pursued in a complex environment.

In general, the various strategy formulation–technical environment combinations make no difference to performance. The same cannot be said of strategy implementation approaches. While the relationships here are complicated, they do suggest that in a munificent environment having no clear approach may be an advantage, however no clear implementation approach is not an advantage when the environment is complex and dynamic. For example, organizations that display incremental strategy implementation approaches appear to struggle in munificent environments, perhaps because there is no need to expend time and resources in building stakeholder support for strategic and operational responses within such a favourable context, but, as contingency theory suggests, such processes thrive in those that are complex and dynamic. By contrast, a planned approach to strategy implementation appears likely to result in worse performance in a munificence environment – though the same finding is not observed for planned strategy formulation, and makes no difference in complex or dynamic environments. It is possible that in a munificent environment it simply matters less how middle managers and front-line staff choose to implement strategic choices. The benefits of adopting a rational approach to implementation are, in effect, not great enough to strengthen the already great advantages of operating in a munificent environment. At the same time, the costs associated with a rational implementation approach, such as the increased resources required to run pilot schemes, draft and update suitable action plans, and carry out continual performance management and monitoring, may be so great as to overturn any possible performance gains.

Institutional environment, strategy and performance

The results for the regressions of the institutional environment on strategy and performance are presented in Tables 7.4–7.6. Table 7.4 tests for interactions between regulation and strategy content, Table 7.5 for strategy formulation and Table 7.6 for strategy implementation. Hypothesis 7.6 is tested by the inspection × strategy interaction and Hypothesis 7.7 by the regulatory support × strategy interaction in each of the three tables. On balance, the evidence presented in Tables 7.4 through 7.6 provides lacklustre support for Hypotheses 7.6 and 7.7, respectively.

Hypothesis 7.6 predicted that inspection would weaken the relationship between strategy content and strategy implementation and performance and strengthen it in the case of rational planning. The coefficients in Table 7.4 offer support for this moderated relationship in relation to prospecting and reacting. The coefficient for prospecting × extent of inspection has a statistically significant negative sign, and the coefficient for reacting × extent of inspection also has a negative sign (at the lower significance level of 10 per cent). Thus both prospectors and reactors that are inspected perform worse

Table 7.4 Strategy content (SC) × institutional environment and performance

Independent variable	Prospecting		Defending		Reacting	
	Slope	t-score	Slope	t-score	Slope	t-score
SC × inspection	−.0344	−3.13**	.0035	.27	−.0294+	−1.78+
SC × regulatory support	.0110	2.29*	.0046	1.12	.0156	2.60*
R^2	.79**		.72**		.68**	
Adjusted R^2	.74**		.66**		.61**	
N = 51						

Note: Significance levels: $+p \leq 0.10$; $^*p \leq 0.05$; $^{**}p \leq 0.01$.
All equations include control variables entered in the models shown in Table 2.7.

Table 7.5 Strategy formulation × institutional environment and performance

Independent variable	Planning		Incrementalism		Absence	
	Slope	t-score	Slope	t-score	Slope	t-score
Inspection × formulation approach	.0353	1.91+	.0184	1.34	.0084	.62
Regulatory support × formulation approach	−.0164	−2.12*	−.0101	−1.85+	.0058	.87
R^2	.73**		.76**		.69**	
Adjusted R^2	.67**		70**		.62**	
N = 50						

Note: Significance levels: $+p \leq 0.10$; $^*p \leq 0.05$; $^{**}p \leq 0.01$.
All equations include control variables entered in the models shown in Table 2.7.

Table 7.6 Strategy implementation × institutional environment and performance

Independent variable	Planned		Incremental		Absence	
	Slope	t-score	Slope	t-score	Slope	t-score
Inspection × implementation approach	2.1963	.66	−3.1491	−.79	−.0726	−.02
Regulatory support × implementation approach	−1.7552	−1.13	1.4250	1.08	−.2106	−.13
R^2	.54**		.53**		.52**	
Adjusted R^2	.40**		.39**		.37**	
N = 40						

Note: Significance levels: $+p \leq 0.10$; $^*p \leq 0.05$; $^{**}p \leq 0.01$.
All equations include control variables entered in the models shown in Table 2.7.

than their counterparts who are not inspected. However, full support for Hypothesis 7.6 is not found because the coefficient for defending × inspection does not have the expected negative sign and is not statistically significant.

Inspection of the interactions in Tables 7.5 and 7.6 indicates no further overall support for Hypothesis 7.6 – five of the six coefficients do not reach statistical significance. The only coefficient to achieve significance (at the lower level of $p < 0.1$) is for inspection × planning formulation. In this case, the sign is positive indicating that inspection assists with performance as was anticipated. Thus, the derivation of benefits from rational processes involving the systematic examination of goals, collection of performance data and the availability of alternative strategic choices is assisted by inspection.

A similar pattern is of results is uncovered in relation to the findings for Hypothesis 7.7 as was for Hypothesis 7.6. The results for regulatory support × strategy content offer some support for the hypothesis, whereas those for strategy formulation and strategy implementation do not. The coefficients in Table 7.4 confirm that supportive regulation has a positive effect on the relationship between strategy and performance: there are statistically significant positive signs for prospecting × supportive regulation and reacting × supportive regulation. As expected, supportive regulation adds a positive twist to these strategies, and produces stronger effects than prospecting and reacting alone would otherwise achieve. By contrast, the results for defending × supportive regulation offer no support for Hypothesis 7.7: the coefficient while positive does not attain statistical significance. The evidence presented in Table 7.5 on the relationship between regulatory support × strategy formulation does not confirm or disconfirm Hypothesis 7.7 in the case of strategy absence, while the coefficient is positive, it does not reach levels of statistical significance. However, the findings for regulatory support × planning formulation and regulatory support × incrementalism formulation are statistically significant and negative. These findings reject the case made for the positive impact of regulatory support on performance. Statistical significance is not recorded for any of the coefficients in Table 7.6 that examines strategy implementation.

We now turn to a discussion of these results by strategy approach. The evidence on strategy content suggests that prospecting organizations which are subject to inspection are likely to perform worse than they would in the absence of inspection, but that those experiencing supportive regulation are likely to perform better. Formal inspection may hamper innovative organizations as they are required to focus on preparing for and responding to the rigours of the regulatory process, thereby diverting attention from service development. To achieve high performance, it is likely to be necessary for prospectors to explore less well-travelled 'improvement journeys'. A manager in one prospecting service indicated in interview that: 'I'm clear what's expected of me and I'm left to manage. Authority is delegated to me to achieve what we set out to achieve.' Regulators may need to adopt a more laissez-faire approach to ensure such prospecting behaviour can be carried out with conviction; indeed, most UK regulatory regimes during the early 2000s acknowledge that 'freedoms and flexibilities' should be accorded to the best performing public organizations. Our evidence suggests that those with a strong prospecting orientation are likely to fall into this category, and that inspection events may be counterproductive for them. However, we also argued that improvement-orientated regulation that is perceived to be supportive could contribute towards better outcomes, potentially reinforcing the positive effect of prospecting on performance. For prospectors, improvement-orientated regulation is likely to consist of general advice about how to innovate successfully, rather than the intense scrutiny of a potentially hostile and disruptive site visit.

The relationship between regulation, strategy and performance for reacting organizations mirrors that of prospecting organizations. This suggests that reactors perform better when they are subject to regulation that complements their existing strategic orientation, but that formal inspection is likely to harm their performance. Detailed inspectors' recommendations may excessively constrain the ability of reactors to respond effectively to pressures from other external agencies. By contrast, if they receive less direct and forceful instructions from a single regulatory body, reactors can continue to change services in accordance with each new challenge to their existing provision. For example, a manager in one reactive service highlighted in interview that it was necessary: '... to plan for political issues as and when they arise ...', and as a result, decisions were often '... made at the last minute ...'. This strategic style is unlikely to be acceptable to inspectors who are looking for evidence of formal planning and corporate control (Andrews et al., 2003), but may be seen as a positive action by an organization to requests made by regulators that are more distant than inspectors.

Defending organizations perform no better or worse as a result of inspection; nor does the perceived supportiveness of regulators influence the impact of a defending stance on performance. The relationship between defending and performance may be impervious to the effects of regulation because this strategic stance is characterized by a commitment to the status quo. One manager of a defending service indicated in interview that their organization no longer required dedicated strategy staff, as their strategy had been set by the Corporate Management Board. It is possible that neither formal inspection nor informal regulatory pressure affect the strategic choices of defending services, which appear to be insulated from these external pressures. Defenders may also be particularly adept at efficiently processing and accommodating the burden of compliance with regulation.

The main effect of regulation, from these results, would appear to be on strategy content and not strategy processes. In particular, there appears to be no statistical relationship between inspection and regulatory support and strategy implementation. This may be because the implementation style of the organization is a feature of its relatively enduring administrative culture. If implementation style is 'the way we do things round here', then it may be fairly difficult for inspection or supportive regulation to influence it.

For strategy formulation a weak relationship, as anticipated, is found for the positive impact of inspection on rational planning, but no such results emerge for the interactions with regulatory support. This may be a function of where inspection and regulation are targeted. The growth of regulation in UK public services during the period under discussion was, as we noted earlier in this chapter, focused on service improvement – regulation prior to this was often aimed at controlling quasi-markets. If the focus is upon delivering better outcomes, it is perhaps feasible to see the main effects in strategy content, that is organizational action to achieve desired goals, rather than the processes through which strategic decisions are made (Hart, 1992).

Conclusion

In this chapter, we have explored the joint effects of the external environment and organizational strategy on public service performance. This is, as far as we are aware, the first analysis of these important issues that has been undertaken. Our main findings are as follows. First, the technical environment made some difference to the strategy–performance relationships that we uncover. Statistically significant interaction effects were observed for the majority of the environment–implementation relationships, but fewer were detected for either strategy content or formulation. Second, the institutional environment also has some effects on the relationship between strategy and performance. In particular, inspection events weaken the positive effect of prospecting. Indeed, our evidence suggests that both prospectors and reactors perform better in the absence of inspection, and that the impact of defending is neither helped nor hindered by an inspection visit. By contrast, regulation that is viewed as supportive by service managers is likely to reinforce the effectiveness of a successful strategy, and to shift a neutral strategy in a positive direction. In other words, if the regulatory regime is seen as helpful, then the impact of local strategies for service improvement is enhanced. The results of the tests we carried out

Table 7.7 Moderating effects of the environment on the strategy–performance relationship

	Technical environment			Institutional environment	
	Munificence	**Complexity**	**Dynamism**	**Inspection event**	**Regulatory support**
Content					
Prospecting		–		–	+
Defending		–			
Reacting	–		–	–	+
Formulation					
Planned			+	+	–
Incremental					–
Absence					
Implementation					
Planned	–				
Incremental	–	+	+		
Absence	+	–	–		

Note: + = positive and statistically significant; – = negative and statistically significant; empty space = not statistically significant.

examining the moderating effects of the environment on the strategy–performance relationship are summarized below in Table 7.7. The table highlights that for the most part we did not identify the anticipated moderating effects.

The empirical results presented in this chapter indicate that achieving a hypothetical fit between an organization's strategy and the munificence, complexity and dynamism in the operating circumstances that it faces appears to make a difference to performance in only very specific circumstances. Indeed, on those occasions that a moderating effect is observed, it often runs counter to that hypothesized. Unexpectedly, then, this implies that the insights of Miles and Snow (and contingency theory more widely) may not be entirely relevant to public organizations seeking to adapt to their technical environment. It is also suggestive of the need for alternative propositions to be developed regarding effective strategic responses to environmental munificence, complexity and dynamism in the public sector. At the same time, our statistical results suggest that, on the whole, the institutional environment (that aspect of the external context which is especially distinctive to the public sector) makes little impression on the strategy–performance relationship. Thus, our evidence highlights that much more work in other organizational settings and countries is required to establish whether all of the elements of the Miles and Snow model are truly applicable to public organizations. In providing a thoroughgoing application of this comprehensive theory of organizational strategy, we have though furnished a strong template for future studies that seek to understand strategic management and public service performance.

8
Conclusions

The idea that public organizations perform better if they adopt the 'right' strategy is prevalent in generic management theory, public management literature, policy debates, governmental reforms and popular culture. Various stakeholders and pressure groups, depending on their ideological position and policy priorities, exhort public organizations to follow different strategies: to be more innovative, 'stick to the knitting' and focus on efficiency, or react more directly to the external demands placed upon them by government agencies. Similarly, public managers are sometimes pressed to develop and implement strategies in a rational manner and follow processes that rely on planning and data, whereas at other times they are asked to be more flexible and intuitive, and pay less attention to technical procedures and more attention to organizational politics.

Are any of these strategic stances and strategy processes better than the others? Is there 'one best way' to organizational success, which comprises a particular route for strategy development, the adoption of a specific strategy and a superior approach to strategy implementation? Indeed, is it desirable to have identifiable and clear strategic stances and processes at all, or is it more productive to 'let chaos rule' and have strategic ambiguity and unpredictable processes of formulation and implementation?

In this book, we have sought to provide the first comprehensive answers to these questions in the public sector by exploring the underlying theories about strategic management that were developed in research on private organizations, and developing and applying these to a set of public organizations. In addition, we have gone beyond the simple notion of 'one best strategy' by examining whether the concept of 'strategic fit' is relevant to the public sector. This concept implies that high performance does not follow universally from the adoption of specific strategies or processes, but that instead the link between strategic management and organizational achievements depends on the internal and external circumstances faced by an organization. In other words, public managers should not seek 'the one strategy' but instead attempt to identify and accommodate the many contingencies that shape the success of different strategies.

Our analysis has taken a number of these contingencies into account, and tested whether strategy content and process *interact* with them to produce organizational success or failure. In particular, we have examined whether the impact of strategic management is influenced by the internal structure of public organizations, and by the conditions in their external environment. Whereas most previous research on strategic fit and performance has considered only the technical environment, we have also examined fit with the institutional environment. This is especially important in the public sector because organizations are subject to strong institutional pressures, as a result of laws and regulations imposed by higher levels of government and policed by bodies such as auditors and inspectors. In addition to such external contingencies, we have looked at contingencies *within* strategic management itself, by exploring whether particular combinations of strategy content and process are more likely to be associated with better performance.

In taking all of these contingencies into account, we have sought to capture the full Miles and Snow model of strategic management, which in turn has influenced and been influenced by other models which suggest that what counts is the *combination* of strategy with other influences on organizational outcomes. Such models suggest that performance is influenced by the fit between strategic stance, processes of formulation and implementation, organizational structure and the external environment. In this final chapter, we summarize whether our results are consistent with 'universal' or contingency views of organizational strategy, and outline the theoretical and practical implications of our findings.

First we summarize our findings on the separate effects of strategy content and strategy processes. What are the consequences for performance of different strategic stances and alternative approaches to formulation and implementation? Second, we review our evidence on whether the coupling of specific types of content and process leads to better or worse performance. For example, does prospecting work best when combined with incremental processes? The third stage is to bring organizational structure into the picture, and to examine whether the impact of strategic management is contingent on this internal characteristic of public organizations. For example, is prospecting the optimal strategy in a decentralized organization? In the next section of this conclusion, we consider the final set of moderating variables, which relate to the external environment. Here we examine whether strategy effects are contingent on technical and institutional constraints. For example, how do resource munificence and regulatory intervention alter the effectiveness of different strategies? Finally, we draw the main strands of our arguments and evidence together, and summarize whether and under what circumstances strategic management makes a difference to public service performance.

The initial models: the separate effects of strategy content and strategy processes

In Chapters 3–5, we developed and tested propositions on the impact of three aspects of strategic management on performance: (1) strategy content, (2) strategy formulation and (3) strategy implementation. These propositions were largely derived from the Miles and Snow model, but with some significant modifications. First, we argued that strategies are continuous not categorical, so rather than being exclusively a prospector, defender or reactor, an organization is likely to be pursuing a mix of all three strategic archetypes simultaneously. Second, we extended the Miles and Snow focus on strategy processes to include not only formulation but also implementation, and examined whether each stage of the strategy process is characterized by rationalism, incrementalism or no discernable pattern ('strategy process absence').

The evidence in Chapter 3 showed that strategies that are consistent and identifiable are more likely to lead to better performance. Both prospecting and defending turned out to have positive links with organizational achievements. Moreover, these two strategies, of exploring new markets and services, and sticking with the existing pattern of services while trying to enhance their efficiency, had roughly equal positive effects on service effectiveness. It is important to note here that all three strategies were included together in our statistical models, so our results show the impact of prospecting, defending or reacting when the extent of the other two strategies is held constant. Therefore, the similarity of the coefficients for prospecting and defending suggests that adding some innovation to a focus on core services is as valuable as adding extra weight to efficiency in a search for new markets and products. In line with our argument that organizational strategies are continuous not categorical, the statistical evidence confirms that it is the presence of a mix of strategies that makes a difference to performance, not the singular pursuit of only one strategic orientation.

Both prospecting and defending were found to be better than a stance of reacting to external constraints and instructions. In other words, strategies that are internally selected seem to work better than those that are imposed by external events and stakeholders. We had expected that a reacting strategy might be beneficial in the public sector, because of the responsibility of organizations to respond to the demands of citizens and higher levels of government. Yet, it seems that responsiveness and effectiveness may be more easily achieved if an organization pursues strategies of prospecting and defending. This finding has direct policy implications, because many government reform programmes seek to *impose* a specific strategic orientation on public organizations. This is a strategy of reacting taken to extremes, and seems likely to be counterproductive for at least two reasons. First, different strategies (prospecting and defending) can be equally effective so it is inappropriate to emphasize one to the exclusion of the other; and second, reacting appears to be the worst strategic option, not only on the basis of the evidence in this book but also according to the results of prior studies conducted in the UK and USA (see Chapter 3). Rather, our evidence suggests that organizations should be left to pursue prospecting and defending, and to choose the combination of these that fits their requirements and is most likely to improve their performance. This is not to argue that organizations should be unresponsive to the demands of stakeholders because, as we discuss below, the external circumstances that influence the impact of prospecting and defending include the complexity of service needs. Yet the very expression 'strategy' implies a measure of choice by public managers, so it seems important to allow an organizational strategy to be selected and followed through, rather than requiring frequent reactions to the shifting and perhaps inconsistent agendas of other levels of government.

In Chapter 4, we explored the effects of different approaches to strategy formulation. Does it matter if an organization's strategy content is developed through a process of rational planning, an incremental process of 'muddling through' and political bargaining or a melange of processes that have no stable characteristics? Our evidence shows that the last of these approaches to formulating strategy, 'strategy process absence', is a liability for public organizations. This type of process is likely to appear unpredictable or even random to those involved in it, and may seem chaotic and unreliable to external stakeholders such as partners in service provision. The statistical results show that the absence of a clearly discernable and consistent method of developing strategies is associated with lower performance than either rational planning or incrementalism. These two styles of strategy formulation are largely neutral in their consequences for organizational achievements: more emphasis on one or the other neither helps nor hinders public service improvement. Thus, as with strategy content, our main finding is that it is better to have a clear approach in place that communicates purpose and process to organizational members, rather than leaving them to guess what is desired or how to contribute effectively to higher performance. Just as prospecting and defending are better options than reacting, so these strategies are more likely to lead to success alongside planning or incrementalism than the absence of a clear approach to strategy formulation.

The main policy implication is again that it appears inappropriate for governments to push all public organizations towards a particular approach to strategy formulation. At different times the political pendulum has swung strongly towards rational planning (with an emphasis on the use of data, techniques such as cost–benefit analysis, performance indicators and targets), and strongly in the other direction (fluid rather than formal processes, broad directions rather than specific measurable objectives). During the era of new public management, the emphasis has shifted sharply in the direction of planning and performance measurement and monitoring. However, our results suggest that this method of strategy formulation is no better (or worse) than logical incrementalism. Perhaps the costs associated with incrementalism, such as insufficient evaluation of policy options and political drift, are roughly the same as those involved in rational planning, such as the managerial time and effort that must be devoted to establishing and running a data-hungry method of strategy formulation. The net result appears to be that rationalism and incrementalism have much the same performance consequences, but that each is better than the absence of a strategy process that is recognizable by the members of an organization.

We turned our attention to the implementation phase of the strategy process in Chapter 5. Once a strategic orientation has been selected (in practice, as our data show, a particular blend of prospecting, defending and reacting), how should this be put into effect? To answer this question, we used process models that have traditionally been applied to strategy formulation, and adapted and extended these to strategy implementation. Thus our analysis of formulation and implementation ran in parallel, and we examined whether the latter stage of the strategy process was also characterized by planning, incrementalism or an absence of a discernable approach to turning a broad stance into specific operations. Planning in the implementation phase is distinguished by clearly defined tasks and targets, the evaluation of pilots and formal progress reviews; and incrementalism comprises frequent amendments of strategy and political bargaining between the affected groups as implementation proceeds.

Our evidence suggests that, after an organization has adopted a strategy, the worst of the three processes that we investigated for putting it into practice is incrementalism. This may be a product of the strategic dilution and political conflict associated with this type of strategy process. However, it is important not to attach great weight to this evidence because it is preliminary in two senses. First, no other direct tests of the impact of strategy implementation on the performance of public organizations have been conducted, so we have no information on whether this effect of incrementalism holds elsewhere. It is possible that it is specific to this empirical context or time period. Second, as we discuss below, an incremental approach to implementation has beneficial effects when combined with a prospecting strategy. Another main conclusion from our evidence on strategy implementation is that neither rational approaches, nor the absence of a discernable process, make much difference to organizational performance. At face value, this suggests that the content of the strategy matters more than precisely how it is implemented. However, as we discuss below, this interpretation is altered when the effects of different combinations of strategy content and implementation style are taken into account.

Internal contingencies: content, processes and structure

So far in this chapter, we have summarized our evidence on strategy content and processes when each of these aspects of strategic management is examined separately from the other. We now take our analysis a stage further by considering whether different *combinations* of strategy content and processes make a difference to public service performance. Is the impact of particular strategies strengthened or weakened when they are pursued jointly with specific processes of formulation or implementation? We also reflect on the implications of our evidence on a further internal contingency: does it matter whether strategic management is combined with a centralized or decentralized organizational structure?

In Chapters 4 and 5, we tested a variety of propositions, derived from the Miles and Snow model, concerning the interactive effects of strategy content and processes. Does the 'alignment' of these aspects of strategic management lead to better performance? First, in Chapter 5, we examined whether prospecting works better when it is combined with an incremental formulation process, defending has stronger positive effects in conjunction with a rational process of strategy development and whether the worst strategic stance, reacting, is even more likely to lead to failure when no clear process is followed. We found support for only one of these three propositions on strategic alignment: prospecting and incrementalism interact to produce a stronger effect than when they operate separately. In other words, organizations that emphazise a strategy of innovation get an even higher payoff when they fit this strategy to a process that is characterized by flexibility and negotiation with powerful stakeholders. By contrast, neither the supposed strategic fit of defending and planning, nor the strategic misfit of reacting and the absence of a clear formulation process, seems to make any difference to organizational results. These combinations of content and process lead to no better or worse performance than when their two elements are pursued separately. This suggests that the applicability of the concept of strategic fit is itself contingent on which combinations of content and process are examined.

The joint effects of strategy content and implementation processes were considered in Chapter 5. As we noted above, prospecting and defending have positive effects on performance, but the only implementation effect is that, on average and across all strategies, an incremental style of implementation is associated with poorer performance. Does this mean that all organizations, regardless of their strategy should avoid incrementalism, and that a rational style of implementation is irrelevant to performance? To explore this issue we examined the combinations of strategy content and strategy implementation that are assumed to constitute organizational alignment. Building on the Miles and Snow model of strategic fit, we examined whether the alignment of prospecting and an incremental implementation style, and defending and a rational implementation style, led to better performance than each element of strategy content and strategy process in isolation.

Our results support both of these forms of fit: the positive impact of prospecting on performance is enhanced when it is combined with an implementation process that emphasizes adaptation to new circumstances, and defending works better in conjunction with planned implementation that involves clear tasks, targets and progress reviews.

Thus, the two strategic stances that have positive effects on performance, prospecting and defending, have even stronger effects when they are complemented by the specific styles of implementation that are assumed to match them in the Miles and Snow model. By contrast, as with the results for strategy formulation, the absence of a clear implementation process makes the effects of the lemon of strategic stances, reacting, no more or less bitter.

A comparison of the evidence on strategic fit for formulation and implementation suggests that the latter matters more than the former: strategy content interacts with only one type of formulation process (incrementalism), but with both rational and incremental styles of implementation. This implies that as long as an effective strategy is adopted, how it is formulated is a relatively minor issue. By contrast, even a good strategy needs to be accompanied by an appropriate implementation style in order to maximize its impact on organizational achievements. This reinforces the validity of our argument in Chapter 5 that greater attention should be paid in strategy research to implementation style, and that more theory and evidence on this topic would be beneficial. A practical implication of our findings is that public organizations, and especially those that emphasize a defending stance, should devote their attention to tailoring their implementation rather than their formulation process to fit their strategy. This is less likely to be true, however, for organizations that prioritize prospecting. Our evidence suggests that this strategy works best when aligned with a consistently incremental approach to both formulation and implementation. Moreover, when all of the evidence on these aspects of strategic management is taken together, innovation in strategy content and flexibility and adaptation throughout the strategy process appear to offer the best route to organizational success.

In Chapter 6, we turned our attention to another important internal contingency: organizational structure. Our focus here, following the Miles and Snow model, was on the extent of centralization within organizations, and the interactive effects of strategy and structure on performance. We examined aspects of structure that are especially relevant to strategic management: the extent to which strategic decisions are made by the chief executive and the senior management team (as an indicator of a hierarchical, and thereby centralized, form of authority over strategy content), and the degree of involvement of all or most staff in the strategy process (as a measure of participation in decision-making). When we tested the separate effects of these aspects of structure, neither centralized strategic decisions nor widespread participation in the strategy process made a difference to organizational performance. However, this pattern of evidence changed when we considered the interactive effects of centralization with strategy content and, to a lesser extent, strategy formulation and implementation.

According to the Miles and Snow model, centralization is a good fit with a defending strategy and a poor fit with a prospecting strategy. The former requires tight control over internal operations and a strong focus on efficiency, whereas the latter requires flexibility and autonomy for organizational sub-units so that they can respond in innovative ways to new circumstances and opportunities. We found evidence to support both of these propositions: strategic decision-making by top managers, and limited participation in the strategy process by other groups, reinforce the positive effect of defending on performance. Similarly, the benefits of prospecting are reinforced when it is combined with widespread participation in decision-making. Thus, both of these strategies work better if alignment with organizational structure is achieved. By contrast, and in accordance with our other findings, a reacting strategy remains worse than prospecting and defending, regardless of whether it is combined with centralization or decentralization.

The final stage of our analysis of organizational structure was to examine whether strategy processes and centralization had joint effects on performance. Our major finding here was that rational processes, both at the formulation and implementation stage, are more likely to be successful in a hierarchical organization where senior managers have control over strategy. Correspondingly, rational processes may enhance the impact of centralization by providing the top management team with a planned and coordinated approach to developing and implementing strategy. As noted above, centralization and a defending strategy also have mutually reinforcing effects. All of this is consistent with an image of a 'mechanistic' organization in which power and processes are tightly controlled in pursuit of a fixed strategy of stability and efficiency. Furthermore, our evidence suggests that 'triple alignment' of strategy content, rational processes and a centralized structure is required for public organizations to make the most of a defending strategy.

In sum, our research in this book shows that strategies of prospecting and defending not only have significant effects by themselves but also have important joint effects with organizational processes and structures. This evidence provides substantial support for the assumption in the Miles and Snow model that that the extent of 'internal fit' is a significant moderator of the impact of strategy on organizational results.

We turn next to consider whether the same conclusion holds for the alignment of strategic management with the external circumstances faced by public organizations.

External contingencies: the technical and institutional environment

We began our empirical analysis of service performance by examining the separate effects of the external environment on public organizations in Chapter 2. At the time of the development of the Miles and Snow model in the mid-1970s, and for some years afterwards, academic work on strategic management largely focused on the technical environment (such as the social and economic conditions faced by organizations). For private organizations in particular, this environment was conceptualized as being mostly fixed, and beyond their immediate control. Subsequently, definitions of the environment widened to include institutional forces that constrain and direct organizational decisions, most importantly the coercive pressures that are applied by governmental and regulatory agencies. In contrast to the technical environment, the institutional environment is less fixed and more open to interpretation by managers; put another way, whereas technical constraints may be viewed as 'hard and factual', institutional constraints are more 'soft and malleable'. Nevertheless, both sets of constraints are expected to make a difference to organizational performance.

In Chapter 2, we tested the impact of these environmental conditions on public service effectiveness. We examined three aspects of the technical environment: (1) resource munificence, (2) the complexity of service needs and (3) the rate of change or 'dynamism' of these needs. Our evidence showed that all three of these external constraints make a difference to performance. Public organizations are more likely to succeed if resources are abundant, and needs are simple and changing in slow and predictable ways. Similarly, they are more likely to fail if resources are scarce, and the needs of clients are complex and shifting quickly and unexpectedly. Thus our results confirm that socio-economic circumstances are important influences on public service standards, and set limits on the capacity of organizations to achieve high performance. Our evidence also suggests that the technical environment may constrain the effectiveness of different approaches to strategic management.

We also examined two aspects of the institutional environment that were especially important to our sample of public organizations in the UK during the study period: the incidence of external visits by government inspectors, and local perceptions of the supportiveness of the inspection process. How often were organizations subjected to direct institutional pressures to manage their services in specific ways that were viewed as legitimate by central government, and did they find the inspection process to be constructive or disruptive? These variables turned out to have no separate impact on performance, thereby, at face value, contradicting the recent emphasis in the academic literature on the strong role of institutional pressures. Indeed, our results in Chapter 2 imply that technical rather than institutional constraints make a difference to organizational achievements. It is possible that responsiveness to institutional pressures makes a difference to organizational legitimacy, but that technical conditions make a more direct and forceful contribution to organizational effectiveness. Yet, it is also important to consider interactive effects with strategic management before drawing conclusions on the relative effects of the technical and institutional environment.

We addressed this issue in Chapter 7 where we explored the joint effects of external constraints with strategy content, strategy formulation and strategy implementation. Our evidence shows that the positive effects of prospecting and defending are weaker when service needs are complex. In other words, both strategies work better if the technical environment is simple, and even these successful strategies are blunted when the characteristics of clients are heterogeneous. Thus, as predicted by the Miles and Snow model, defending works better in a straightforward environment; however, we found no evidence for their proposition that prospecting comes into its own in a challenging environment. The worst generic strategy, reacting, becomes even more of a liability when service needs are changing substantially and rapidly, perhaps because environmental turbulence defeats the ability of managers to keep shifting to new strategic positions. Thus difficult technical conditions provide significant obstacles to the success of all three strategic orientations, and reduce the effectiveness of prospecting, defending and reacting. Our evidence suggests that the prospects for the positive impact of strategy content are best when the external environment is simple and stable.

We also found that the effects of strategy processes were moderated by the technical environment, but mostly for implementation rather than formulation, which again confirms the significance of this stage of the strategy process for public service performance. As we noted above, an incremental approach to implementation is generally associated with lower performance. However, incrementalism works better in complex and dynamic external circumstances, because adaptive and flexible processes are required to deal with these challenges. By contrast, although the absence of a settled approach to strategy implementation has neutral effects on average (see above), these effects become negative in the face of resource scarcity and complex and dynamic service needs. Perhaps unsurprisingly, 'strategy process absence' is an ineffective implementation style when the going gets tough.

Finally, our evidence shows that the institutional environment has some interactive effects with strategic management, but mostly with strategy content rather than strategy processes. Direct regulatory interventions by government inspectors are disruptive for strategic management in public organizations. Inspection visits are associated with weaker positive effects for prospecting strategies, and turn the effects of reacting strategies from neutral to negative. However, the negative effects of the inspection visits are partly offset when the regulatory process is viewed by public managers as supportive. Thus, although institutional pressures have little effect on performance by themselves, they moderate the impact of strategic management on public service effectiveness. Nevertheless, institutional effects are still less prevalent than technical effects, both separately and in combination with strategy content and processes. Therefore our conclusion is that the relationship between strategic management and organizational performance is shaped more strongly by the socio-economic environment than the regulatory environment.

Putting the pieces together: does strategic management matter?

In this book, we have shown that strategic management makes a difference to the performance of public organizations. Furthermore, all three of the major elements of strategic management matter for the effectiveness of public services: (1) strategy content, (2) formulation and (3) implementation. Often, however, it is impossible to provide a straightforward answer to the question 'does strategic management matter?' Rather, as our evidence demonstrates, the most appropriate response to this question is 'it all depends'. In particular, it depends on which aspects of strategy content and processes are pursued together, and how these in turn are combined with organizational structure and the technical and institutional environment. Our findings suggest that managers need to pay attention to the connections between these contingencies in order to get the best out of whatever strategy their organization has adopted. The links between strategy and performance are complex and varied, not simple and uniform, and it is conceivable that different strategies will be equally effective, depending on the internal and external circumstances of public organizations.

We have used the Miles and Snow framework to structure our analysis of strategy and performance, and examined the major contingencies of process, structure and environment that are identified in this conceptual model. Future work could usefully examine whether the contingencies that we have identified hold in other national, institutional and organizational contexts. In addition, it will be important to move beyond the Miles and Snow model to explore a wider set of contingencies. Prominent among these should be organizational performance itself. First, we have examined only service effectiveness, but the impact of strategy may well differ across dimensions of performance. For example, defending seems likely to work best if organizations prioritize efficiency, prospecting may be the optimal strategy if the major goal is to respond to new service needs, and reacting may be the safest strategy in political systems where public organizations are accountable to a single dominant political principal. Second, the performance baseline may affect the relevance of different approaches to strategic management. If an organization is already performing poorly, a defending strategy by itself is unlikely to produce the improvements that are required; by contrast, if it is already performing well, a more balanced mix of defending and prospecting may help it to maintain its success.

Other contingencies also merit close attention in future research. Prominent amongst these should be organizational size. Public management reforms often focus on the size of organizations, but little is known about how this alters strategic management and its link with performance. This could include an examination of how size moderates the relationship between processes and performance: it is possible that incrementalism works better in small organizations (which may in any case lack the capacity for rational planning) and very large organizations (which are too big for a rationalist process that requires tight control of many sub-units). In this book, we have examined only one aspect of the institutional environment – the extent of public service regulation. Other potentially relevant institutional pressures include the policy environment in which organizations deliver services (e.g. rationalist processes of formulation and implementation may lead to better results in a technocratic regime that is sympathetic to this style of management), and the extent of fiscal austerity (defending is likely to be regarded as superior to prospecting if cost reductions are viewed as an end in themselves).

These examples are simply illustrative of the contingencies that could be included in further work on strategic management and performance. Indeed, a wider implication of our findings is that *all* models that seek to explain variations in public service performance, regardless of their theoretical emphasis and the explanatory variables that they prioritize, should be recast as contingency models. This is likely to require extensive theoretical refinement as well as methodological progression beyond simple additive models where all variables have separate effects. Whatever direction the broader research programme on the performance of public organizations takes, the evidence presented in this book strongly suggests that a focus on strategy content and processes will be essential. Thus for both academic researchers and public organizations, strategic management is likely to be an important part of the difference between success and failure.

Appendix 1: Welsh Local Government

This study is located in Wales which is one of the four countries that constitutes the United Kingdom of Great Britain and Northern Ireland. The 2001 Census put its population at 2,903,085 and its area measures 8018 square miles. The principality is predominately rural in its character, and its most densely populated areas are in the industrialized South East.

The organizational context of our analysis is local authorities in Wales. These organizations were first established in 1888, when 13 county councils responsible for administering a range of public functions were created across Wales. Further reforms sub-divided these areas into lower-tier district councils during the 1890s. Following a period of comparative stability, in 1974, almost 184 local government units in Wales were consolidated into 45 units. The county boroughs were abolished and absorbed into a two-tier structure of 8 counties and 37 districts. Then, in the 1990s, this two-tier system was replaced by the 22 unitary authorities that make up the local government system in Wales today.

Welsh local authorities are democratically accountable through elections held every 4 years. They are governed by a Westminster-style cabinet system of political management. In a Westminster political system such as the UK, the cabinet represents the *de facto* executive branch of government, and is usually made up of senior members of the ruling political party, all of whom collectively decide public policy and government strategy. Welsh local authorities are multipurpose organizations providing education, social care, regulatory services (such as land use planning and waste management), housing, welfare benefits, leisure and cultural services. Around £4 billion a year is spent on these services, though expenditure levels vary considerably between larger urban authorities such as Cardiff and smaller rural ones like Anglesey. The bulk of this expenditure is funded by central government (80 per cent), with the remaining 20 per cent raised through local taxation.

Central funding for Welsh local authorities is distributed by the Welsh Assembly Government, an elected regional body which also sets the broad policy agenda for local government in Wales. The Assembly Government is the executive arm of the National Assembly for Wales, which was established in 1999 following a referendum on the devolution of powers held by the then Labour Party-led UK national government. Unlike the Scottish Parliament that was set up at the same time, the National Assembly for Wales was not granted primary law-making or tax-raising powers, and has no control over several other 'reserved matters', such as defence; employment and economic affairs; energy policy; foreign affairs; and policing which remain under the control of the UK national government. Nevertheless, the Assembly is responsible for overseeing the implementation of legislation in many areas of the public sector, including education, health, housing, sport and leisure and other local government services. As a result, it has some scope to develop different policy initiatives from those adopted in England. The tiers of government are represented in Figure A1.1.

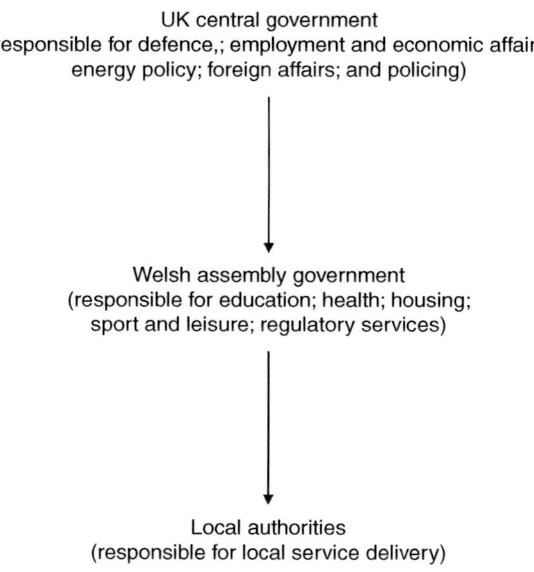

Figure A1.1 Governance in Wales

As is the case in many countries, local authorities in England and Wales are subject to pressure from central government to improve their services and in 1999 a policy of Best Value was introduced to achieve this. The policy required local authorities in England and Wales to undertake detailed and comprehensive reviews of their services, set targets outlined in formal plans and produce action plans to monitor and report against targets. In addition, all services that were not covered by existing dedicated inspectorates were to be inspected by the new Best Value Inspectorate. In Wales, dedicated inspectorates in relation to local authority services include Estyn (education and youth services), Social Services Inspectorate Wales (social care of adults and children) and Benefits and Revenues Inspectorate (welfare benefits). Best Value was extremely unpopular in Wales, and the regime was abandoned in 2002 and replaced by the Wales Programme for Improvement. This policy continued the focus on improving services, but placed less emphasis on the formal processes that local authorities had to go through.

The units of analysis that are used for our study are the service departments within the local authorities. We study the strategy–performance hypothesis in different departments in order to identify whether the relationship between the variables is consistent with the Miles and Snow model. Although local authorities themselves may have varying managerial and political priorities, individual departments can participate in their determination and often have distinctive approaches to strategic issues (see Dibben, 2006). Thus, by analysing service departments in a single local government system, other potentially salient influences on strategy, structure and process, such as the policies of higher tiers of government or legal and regulatory constraints, are held constant.

Appendix 2: Survey Methodology and Questionnaires

Section A: Survey methodology

Data sources

Data for our study of strategy and performance in Welsh local government are drawn from a number of primary and secondary data sources. Data for the dependent measure of performance were drawn from the National Assembly for Wales Performance Indicators (NAWPIs). Multiple informant surveys of managers in Welsh local governments were undertaken in 2002 and 2003. These surveys recorded the majority of our independent variables (the survey instruments are found in Section B). Measures of the environment were typically recorded in the 2001 Census; we use these sources and versions of the data published by government departments.

Survey

Our statistical analysis was conducted on 90 cases in 2002 and 62 of those cases in 2003.[1] This represented a 46-per cent response rate in 2002 and 31 per cent in 2003. In each year, we surveyed senior and middle managers. The 2002 survey examined strategy content and strategy formulation, and the 2003 survey explored strategy implementation processes. The distribution of the service departments in our sample is shown in Table A2.1. The departments are representative of the diverse operating environments faced by Welsh local authorities, including urban, rural, socio-economically deprived and predominantly Welsh- or English-speaking areas.

Survey data were derived from an electronic questionnaire of managers in Welsh local authorities. Electronic surveys offer a number of advantages over postal surveys, such as cost-effectiveness and user responsiveness (see Enticott, 2003). The survey explored informants' perceptions of organization, management and performance (for a copy of the surveys, see Section B of this appendix). For each question, informants placed their service on a seven-point Likert scale ranging from 1 (disagree with the proposed statement) to 7 (agree with the proposed statement).

Data were collected from different tiers of management to ensure that our analysis took account of different stakeholder perceptions within the service departments. This surmounts sample bias and measurement error problems associated with surveying informants from only one organizational level. Much of the public management literature that draws on surveys adopts an elite survey approach; that is, surveying single organizational leaders. This approach often taps the aspirations of organizational leaders, overlooks the range of different perceptions within an organization, provides inaccurate accounts of front-line staff and can result in an overly positive portrayal of the organization (Bowman

Table A2.1 Units of analysis by service departments

	2002	2003
Benefits and revenues	12	5
Education	10	8
Highways	9	6
Housing	8	7
Leisure and culture	11	5
Planning	8	4
Public protection	10	7
Social services	13	12
Waste management	9	8

and Ambrosini, 1997; Phillips, 1981; Podsakoff and Organ, 1986; Purcell, 1999). The reliance when drawing on a sample on one senior manager in an elite survey can also obfuscate tensions and disagreement in the top management team, and between the higher echelons of an organization and lower levels of management (Hambrick and Mason, 1984; Phillips, 1981). Research evidence drawn from public agencies points towards varying priorities between layers of managers in the hierarchy (Lipsky, 1980; Purcell, 1999; Walker and Brewer, 2008; Walker and Enticott, 2004). Such evidence has led some of the authors of this book to express concern about the reliability of evidence drawn from elite surveys (Enticott et al., 2009; Walker and Enticott, 2004).

The multiple informant survey approach adopted in this study seeks a more accurate account by surveying a number of actors located in different parts of the organization. It adopted a number of decision rules codified by Enticott et al. (2009). Survey respondents could be differentiated by managerial level, department or any other method which reflects a variety of views within the organization. Given that Welsh local government has distinctive groups of managers with common interests and job functions, we surveyed heads of service and middle managers. These organizational groups have been called social positions (Aiken and Hage, 1968), hierarchical positions (Payne and Mansfield, 1973), tiers of bureaucracy (Brewer, 2005, 2006) and echelons (Aiken and Hage, 1968). An echelon is defined as 'the level of stratum in the organization and the department or type of professional activity' (Aiken and Hage, 1968, 918).

Research – some of which has been conducted on Welsh local governments near neighbour English local government – has shown that attitudes differ between hierarchical levels within organizations (Enticott et al., 2009; Payne and Mansfield, 1973; Walker and Brewer, 2009; Walker and Enticott, 2004). Validity for our approach is provided by way of t-tests that revealed statistically significant differences between the mean scores of each echelon for the majority of our survey items, whereas the spread of responses across the items for each echelon was broadly similar. Table A2.2 shows that senior managers tended to hold stronger views about strategy content and formulation than middle managers, who tend to hold stronger views about the relative degree of centralization in their organizations. Far fewer statistical differences were observed for the strategy

Table A2.2 T-test results for differences between mean scores (on 1–7 scale) in each echelon

Measures	**Senior managers**	**Middle managers**
Strategy content		
We continually redefine our service priorities	**3.7**	**3.0**
We seek to be first to identify new modes of delivery	**4.0**	**3.4**
Searching for new opportunities is a major part of our overall strategy	**3.5**	**2.9**
We often change our focus to new areas of service provision	3.9	3.7
We seek to maintain stable service priorities	**3.4**	**2.8**
The service emphasizes efficiency of provision	**3.1**	**2.7**
We focus on our core activities	**5.0**	**5.8**
We have no definite service priorities	**3.5**	**2.7**
We change provision only when under pressure from external agencies	**5.5**	**6.1**
We give little attention to new opportunities for service delivery	**5.4**	**5.9**
The service explores new opportunities only when under pressure from external agencies	**5.6**	**6.0**
We have no consistent response to external pressure	**4.4**	**4.9**
Strategy formulation		
Strategy making is a formal procedure in our service	3.2	2.7
Strategy is based on formal analysis of the service's needs	**3.7**	**2.9**
We assess alternative strategies	**4.5**	**3.0**
We follow precise procedures to achieve targets	**4.3**	**3.4**
Targets in the service are matched to specifically identified citizen needs	**4.3**	**3.3**
Strategy is made on an on-going basis	**3.0**	**2.6**
Strategy develops through negotiation with external stakeholders (e.g. voluntary/private sector groups)	3.3	3.1
There is no discernable strategy process	**5.1**	**5.8**
Strategy implementation		
We use a project/business plan to implement strategies	2.8	2.5
When implementing strategies we have clearly defined tasks with targets	**2.9**	**2.5**
When implementing strategies we regularly review progress against targets	2.6	2.6
We implement strategies by piloting them initially and then implementing them in full	3.0	2.7
When implementing strategies we often refine and amend them as we go along	4.1	3.8

Table A2.2 (Continued)

Measures	**Senior managers**	**Middle managers**
We improve the implementation of our strategies by getting all of the affected groups involved in their development	3.2	3.0
There is no discernible approach to implementing strategies in our service area	5.1	5.2
Centralization		
Strategy for our service is usually made by the Chief Executive	**3.4**	**2.9**
Strategy for our service is usually made by the Corporate Management Team	3.9	3.9
All staff are involved in the strategy process to some degree	**3.2**	**3.8**
Most staff have input into decisions that directly affect them	**3.4**	**4.1**

Bold = statistically significant differences at $p > 10$.

implementation measures. Furthermore, resources were sufficiently plentiful to allow us to target more than one informant in each service department in our population.

Survey data were collected in the autumn of 2002 and the autumn of 2003. Information (including email addresses) for up to ten key senior and middle managers in every service department were provided by the corporate policy unit in 17 of the 22 Welsh authorities agreeing to participate in the study. The sampling frame consisted of 198 services and 830 informants in 2002, and 198 services and 860 informants in 2003. Responses were received from 46 per cent of services (90) and 29 per cent of individual informants (237) in 2002, and 31 per cent of services (62) and 25 per cent of informants (216) in 2003. The 2002 survey explored strategy content and strategy formulation processes, and the 2003 survey examined strategy implementation processes. Time-trend tests for nonrespondent bias (Armstrong and Overton, 1977) revealed no significant differences in the views of early and late respondents in either year.

The survey was sent to informants as an Excel file attached to an email. Informants were assured of the confidentiality of their responses. Informants' responses within each service were aggregated to generate organizational-level data suitable for our analysis. The average score of respondents within a service was taken as representative of that service. So, for instance, if in one authority there were two informants from the social services department, one from services for elderly people and another from children's services, then the mean of their responses was used.

Following piloting in 2002 and 2003, we improved the survey instrument by adding a glossary of terms, and further questions about the nature of services, and stressed the need for respondents to provide an 'honest appraisal' (see Section B of this appendix for copies of the full survey instruments). We also clarified the split between service-level and authority-wide questions and made the technical terms used in the instrument more accessible.

We used two techniques to control for the potential influence of common method bias on survey respondents. First, psychological and temporal remedies were used in the design of our questionnaire (Podsakoff and Organ, 1986). The items measuring strategy in the 2002 survey were placed in a different section of the questionnaire than those measuring structure and process. The order of individual items measuring specific concepts such as rational planning and logical incrementalism was also partially merged to control for priming effects. In addition, items drawn from our 2003 survey generated on average a 72-per cent difference from the 2002 survey in the composition of the respondents for each service. Second, our piloting process improved many survey questions and increased the emphasis on respondent anonymity, reducing the likelihood of item ambiguity and evaluation apprehension (Tourangeau et al., 2000).

Finally, we tested for the presence of common method biases on the survey data using two partial correlation procedures. Partialling out respondents' perceptions of staff satisfaction as a proxy for the potential influence of 'general affectivity' (Brief et al., 1988) and the average correlation between population density, as an independent 'marker variable' (Lindell and Whitney, 2001), and the other variables used in our analysis revealed broadly similar results. These tests indicated that common methods bias is not a serious problem.

In all the statistical models run the average Variance Inflation Factor (VIF) score is less than 2 for all the independent variables. The results are therefore not distorted by multicollinearity (Bowerman and O'Connell, 1990). To correct for nonconstant error variance, the models were estimated with robust regression: a technique that relies on an iterative process of downweighting extreme cases until they meet the assumptions of OLS regression (Western, 1995).

Interviews

In addition to carrying out the survey, we undertook interviews with 32 managers in a sample of local authority services in Wales during the period April to July 2003, and a further set of interviews with 32 managers in a sample of local authority services in Wales during the period August to November 2004. The interviewees were selected respondents from our survey who were willing to discuss the strategic management in their service in more depth. Semi-structured interview schedules were used, subject to strict principles of confidentiality. The interviews explored issues arising from the survey return for each respondent's service. These interviews provided further information on the links between implementation, strategy and performance across a range of service areas and authorities. We use the information obtained from these interviews to help us to interpret the results of our statistical models.

Section B: Questionnaires

Strategy and service improvement in local government

Strategy formulation survey 2002

The Local and Regional Government Research Unit at Cardiff University is conducting a large research project examining the impact of strategic management on service improvement in Welsh local government. This is a major piece of independent research, funded by the Economic and Social Research Council, that runs until 2004. The questionnaire is the main method we will be using to survey local authorities in Wales. We will also undertake short follow-up interviews with members and officers. The research findings will be fed back to local authorities on an on-going basis to help you to continue to improve. They will also be presented to the Wales Improvement Network and at other improvement forums in Wales.

How to complete the survey

We are interested in finding out which strategies work best in which circumstances. There are, therefore, no right or wrong answers to each of the questions. We are interested in your perceptions and impressions. We would like you to answer as frankly as possible. Answers will not be treated as a reflection on either your reputation or that of your service or authority. All questionnaires will be received in complete confidence. It will not be possible to identify respondents from the results. A glossary of terms is included at the end of the questionnaire to help you understand the terminology used in the questionnaire. Please respond to the survey independently.

The questionnaire is in 4 parts:

PART A asks you about strategy making in your specific service area;
PART B asks you about the content of strategies in your specific service area;
PART C asks you about the performance of your specific service area;
PART D asks you about factors affecting your specific service area.

The pilot project carried out in May 2002 indicated that the questionnaire will take on average about 15 minutes to complete. To answer the questions either: Highlight the appropriate circle by clicking it with your mouse button:

Or type the answer in the space provided.

Please give your views freely. If you do not know an answer, please leave blank.

Once you have finished, please save the file and email it to: serviceimprovement@cardiff.ac.uk Please return the file by no later than 31st January 2003. Please note, all responses will be treated in COMPLETE CONFIDENCE. For more information and assistance contact: Rhys Andrews, Tel: 029 2087 6014, email: AndrewsR@cardiff.ac.uk

Introduction

Your role

Your Job Title
Responsibilities of your role
Your Service
Description of your service's functions
Your Department
Your Authority
Your Improvement Review if you are being reviewed (and the date)
Length of service in the Authority

When did you join this Authority (in any capacity)
Please indicate if you were involved in completed Best Value Reviews during:
2000/2001
2001/2002
2002/2003

Part A: Strategy-making

The following set of questions asks you to think about strategy making in your service (By strategy making we mean the way the authority decides how to deliver services or the ways you go about selecting new approaches to service delivery.)

Section 1: The way we make our strategies

The questions in this section explore how strategies are made in your service. Please indicate the extent to which you agree with the following statements about strategy making in your service. (Please click the circle closest to your own view.)

1. We are regularly challenged with new goals and aspirations for the service:
2. Strategy in our service reflects broad goals:
3. Strategy making is a formal procedure in our service:
4. Strategy is based on formal analysis of the service's needs:
5. We assess alternative strategies:
6. We follow precise procedures to achieve targets:
7. Targets in the service are matched to specifically identified citizen needs:
8. Strategy is made on an on-going basis:
9. Strategy develops through negotiation with external stakeholders (e.g. voluntary/private sector groups):
10. Strategy develops through consultation with local citizens:
11. People in the service are willing to take risks:
12. Strategy in the service develops through experimentation:
13. Strategy is based on little analysis of the service's needs:
14. Strategy in the service evolves slowly:
15. Strategy is usually based on existing practices:
16. There is no discernible strategy-making process:
17. Strategy making is deliberately avoided:

Section 2: The role of people in strategy making

The questions in this section explore the influence of different people on strategy making in your service. Please indicate the extent to which you agree with the following statements about strategy making in your service. (Please click the circle closest to yourown view.)

18. Strategy for our service is usually made by the Chief Executive:
19. Strategy for our service is usually made by the Corporate Management Team:
20. Strategy for our service is usually made by the Head of Service:
21. Strategy for our service is usually made by elected members:
22. Strategy for our service is usually made by external agencies:
23. The service's mission is determined by the Chief Executive:

24. The service's mission is determined by the Corporate Management Team:
25. The service's mission is determined by the Head of Service:
26. The service's mission is determined by elected members:
27. The service's mission is determined by external agencies:
28. Managers in the service serve as personal examples of how our people should behave:
29. The strategy we follow is dictated by our way of doing things:
30. Our targets are strictly defined by external agencies:
31. All staff are involved in the strategy-making process to some degree:
32. Most staff have input into decisions that directly affect them:
33. Strategy reflects the interaction of different interests in the service:
34. Staff throughout the service understand what needs to be accomplished to deliver continuous improvement:
35. There is strong resistance to rapid change within the service:
36. Strategy develops through negotiation between higher-level management and officers:
37. Strategy develops through negotiation between higher-level management and external agencies:
38. There is no internal pressure to create or develop strategy:
39. There is no discernible pattern of responses to pressure from external agencies:

Part B: Strategy of the service

The following set of questions asks about the strategy of your service. (By strategy we mean the overall outlook and direction of the service, rather than the strategic plan or other documents for the service.) The questions examine how your service seeks to position itself and the typical content of its strategic decisions.

Section 1: The content of strategies in the service

The questions in this section explore the content of the strategic choices taken by your service. Please indicate the extent to which you agree with the following statements about your service. (Please click the circle closest to your own view.)

1. We continually redefine our service priorities:
2. We seek to be first to identify new modes of delivery:
3. Searching for new opportunities for service delivery is a major part of our overall strategy:
4. We often change our focus to new areas of service provision:
5. We seek to maintain stable service priorities:
6. The service emphasizes efficiency of provision (e.g. high quality and low cost):
7. We give little attention to new opportunities for service delivery:
8. We focus on our core activities:
9. We have no definite service priorities:
10. We change provision only when under pressure from external agencies:
11. The service explores new opportunities only when under pressure from external agencies:
12. We have no consistent response to external pressures:
13. The service invests heavily in marketing and/or PR:

14. We provide existing services to new users:
15. The service invests heavily in research and development:
16. We provide new services to new users:
17. We expand the range of services we provide:
18. We provide new services to existing users:
19. We have discontinued some services altogether:
20. The service is adopting new approaches to budgeting (e.g. to assess the outcomes achieved in major policy areas):
21. The service frequently obtains additional internal funding:
22. The service frequently obtains additional external funding (e.g. from the Welsh Assembly Government (WAG)):
23. We obtain additional resources by increasing charges to users:
24. We pursue a policy of contracting/outsourcing (e.g. the same/similar service delivered by another agency under contract):
25. We pursue a policy of externalization (e.g. passing/selling a service to another agency):
26. The service works in partnership with users:
27. The service works in partnership with the voluntary sector:
28. The service works in partnership with the private sector:
29. The service works in partnership with other local or public authorities:
30. The service works in partnership with other departments within the authority:
31. The service is creating new internal structures (e.g. new business/service units):
32. Services are moving between departments:
33. Our service is merging with other services:
34. We pursue a policy of decentralizing services (e.g. organizing services on a neighbourhood basis):
35. We pursue a policy of centralizing services:
36. The service has a policy of delayering its management (e.g. reduces the tiers of staff):
37. The service has a policy of relayering its management (e.g. adding new tiers of staff):
38. The service has introduced new managerial roles and teams:

Section 2: Autonomy of the service

Please indicate the extent to which you agree with the following statements about the autonomy of your service. (Please click the circle closest to your own view.)

39. Our service has a great deal of autonomy:
40. Our service has more autonomy than other services in the authority:
41. Our service has more autonomy than similar services in similar authorities do:

Part C: Performance of the service

We would like to know how you assess the performance of the service. We would like you to think about the performance of the service relative to similar services in similar authorities and to estimate its current performance. To what extent do you agree that your service performs well in comparison with others in relation to: (please click the circle closest to your own view).

1. Quality of outputs (e.g. how reliably your services are delivered):
2. Quantity of Outputs (e.g. the volume of service delivered):
3. Efficiency (e.g. cost per unit of service delivery):
4. Effectiveness (e.g. whether your objectives were achieved):
5. Value for Money (cost-effectiveness):
6. Consumer satisfaction:
7. Equity (e.g. how fairly your services are distributed amongst citizens):
8. Staff satisfaction
9. Promoting the social, economic and environmental well-being of local people:
10. Overall, to what extent would you agree that your service is performing well:

Part D: Factors affecting the service

The following set of questions explores how a range of issues inside and outside your service are affecting it

Section 1: The socio-economic context

Please indicate the extent to which you agree with the following statements about the socio-economic context of your service. By socio-economic context we mean levels of deprivation, social change, population change and so on. (Please click the circle closest to your own view.) The socio-economic context in which the service operates

1. is unpredictable (i.e. changes in unexpected ways):
2. is changing rapidly:
3. is very complex:
4. is favourable:
5. Please indicate the extent to which you agree that the service is able to influence the socio-economic context:

Section 2: The financial context

Please indicate the extent to which you agree with the following statements about the financial context of your service. By financial context we mean levels of funding made available and so on. (Please click the circle closest to your own view.) The financial context the service operates in

6. is unpredictable (i.e. changes in unexpected ways):
7. is changing rapidly:
8. is very complex:
9. is favourable:

10. Please indicate the extent to which you agree that the service is able to influence the financial context:

Section 3: The external political context

Please indicate the extent to which you agree with the following statements about the external political context of your service. By external political context we mean relationships with central government and its departments, relationships with other agencies and so on. (Please click the circle closest to your own view.)
The external political context the service operates in

11. is unpredictable (i.e. changes in unexpected ways):
12. is changing rapidly:
13. is very complex:
14. is favourable:
15. Please indicate the extent to which you agree that the service is able to influence the external political context:

Section 4: The internal political context

Please indicate the extent to which you agree with the following statements about the internal political context of your authority. By internal political context we mean relationships between departments, members and officers, relationships between senior management and front-line staff and so on. (Please click the circle closest to your own view.) The internal political context the service operates in

16. is unpredictable (i.e. changes in unexpected ways):
17. is changing rapidly:
18. is very complex:
19. is favourable:
20. Please indicate the extent to which you agree that the service is able to influence the internal political context:

Section 5: The level of support

Please indicate the extent to which you agree with the following statements about the level of support your service receives from other agencies. (Please click the circle closest to your own view.)

21. Central government agencies (e.g. Wales Assembly Government, Welsh Development Agency and so on) are supportive of the service:
22. Regulatory agencies (e.g. External inspectorates such as the Audit Commission, Estyn, Social Services Inspectorate for Wales and so on) are supportive of the service:
23. Advisory agencies and professional bodies (e.g. WLGA, IDeA and so on) are supportive of the service:

24. Finally, could you please indicate below how long it took you to complete the questionnaire and add any other comments you wish to make about the questionnaire and strategy and service improvement.

Glossary of terms used in the questionnaire

Advisory agencies Non-governmental bodies whose function is to advise local authorities (e.g. Syniad).
Audit Commission The organization established by the government to ensure that public money is being used economically, efficiently and effectively.
Central government agencies Centrally established Government bodies such as the National Assembly for Wales or the Welsh Development Agency.
Continuous improvement The statutory requirement placed on local authorities by the Local Government Act 1999 to deliver continuous improvement in the economy, efficiency and effectiveness of their functions.
Contracting out/Outsourcing A function of a local authority service being delivered by another agency under contract.
Core activities Those functions which are the primary service areas of a department.
Economic and Social Research Council (ESRC) The UK's leading research funding agency providing research to business, the public sector and government on economic and social concerns.
Estyn The inspectorate responsible for inspecting education in Wales.
External stakeholders External statutory, voluntary or private sector organizations involved in the delivery of public services.
Externalization A function of a local authority service being sold or passed to another agency.
Improvement and Development Agency (IDeA) The organization established by and for local government to help councils deliver leadership, cultural change and performance improvement.
Professional bodies Agencies representing the interests of particular professions or sectors.
Regulatory agencies Inspectorates with responsibility for inspecting the delivery of public services in the UK.
Research and Development Policy and delivery-orientated research (i.e. not market research).
Service Improvement The general activity of improving service delivery.
Social Services Inspectorate for Wales (SSIW) The inspectorate responsible for inspecting social services in Wales.
Strategic management The set of decisions and actions within an organization resulting in the formulation and implementation of a strategy.
Strategy The overall direction and outlook of an organization.
Strategy making The way an organization decides how to deliver its service and products.
Strategy content The typical content of an organization's strategy.
Targets Measurable aims for service delivery.
Wales Improvement Network The all-Wales Improvement forum for local authorities coordinated by Syniad.

Welsh Development Agency (WDA) The organization established to coordinate economic development projects in Wales.
Welsh Local Government Association (WLGA) The professional body representing the interests of local authorities in Wales.

Strategy and service improvement in local government

Strategy implementation survey 2003

The Centre for Local and Regional Government Research at Cardiff University is conducting a large-scale research project examining the impact of strategic management on service improvement in Welsh local government. This is a major piece of independent research funded by the Economic and Social Research Council, running until 2004. Questionnaires are being used to survey Welsh local authorities. Short follow-up interviews will also be undertaken with selected respondents. Findings will be fed back to councils on an on-going basis. The questionnaire will take approximately 15–20 minutes to complete.

How to complete the survey

We want to find out which ways of implementing strategies work best in which circumstances. Please give your perceptions and impressions about the service area your work mostly involves. Answers will not be treated as a reflection on either your reputation or that of your service or authority. All responses will be treated in complete confidence. It will not be possible to identify respondents from the results.

The questionnaire is in 3 parts:

PART A asks you about how strategies are implemented in your service area;
PART B asks you about the performance of your specific service area;
PART C asks you about factors affecting your service areas;

To answer the questions either: Highlight the appropriate circle by clicking it with your mouse button. Or type in the spaces provided. If you do not know an answer, please leave blank. Your help with this research is greatly appreciated.

A glossary of terms explaining the terminology used is included at the end of the questionnaire. We would be very grateful if you could complete and return the questionnaire by 19th December 2003. Once you have finished, please save the file and email it to: serviceimprovement @cardiff.ac.uk. Please return the file by 19th December 2003. For more information on the project and assistance contact: Rhys Andrews, tel: 029 2087 6014, email: serviceimprovement@cardiff.ac.uk Centre for Local and Regional Government Research, www.clrgr.cf.ac.uk

Introduction

Your role

Your job title:
Your Service Area:
Your Department:
Your Authority:
Length of service in the Authority

Part A: Implementing strategies

The following set of questions asks you to think about how strategies are implemented in your service area.

Section 1: Approaches to strategy implementation

The questions in this section explore how strategies are implemented in your service area. Please indicate the extent to which you agree with the following statements about strategy implementation in your service.

1. Strategies are implemented in ways directed by senior officers:
2. Strategies are implemented in ways directed by cabinet members:
3. We use a project/business plan to implement strategies:
4. When implementing strategies we have clearly defined tasks with targets:
5. When implementing strategies we regularly review progress against targets:
6. When implementing strategies a new vision of where this service will be is communicated to all staff:
7. When implementing strategies a number of significant changes are made to illustrate the new vision:
8. Implementation is usually straightforward because we have already created common values amongst staff (e.g. a customer focus):
9. When implementing strategies we often refine and amend them as we go along:
10. We implement strategies by piloting them initially and then implementing them in full:
11. We improve the implementation of our strategies by getting all of the affected groups involved in their development:
12. Our managers encourage staff to develop and implement strategies:
13. Our front-line staff are willing to implement innovation and change:
14. Our middle managers are willing to implement innovation and change:
15. Our front-line staff and middle managers take the initiative in developing and implementing strategies:
16. We implement our strategies gradually:
17. There is no discernible approach to implementing strategies in our service area:
18. When implementing strategies we frequently communicate with affected groups within the organization (e.g. giving talks, opportunities to discuss change):
19. When implementing strategies we frequently communicate with affected groups outside the organization:
20. We use rewards and sanctions to ensure that staff implement new strategies (e.g. performance-related pay):

Section 2: Enablers and Barriers to Implementation

The questions in this section explore barriers to the implementation of strategies in your service area. Please indicate the extent to which you agree with the following statements about strategy implementation in your service.

21. The organization generally assigns appropriate levels of funding to the implementation of strategies:
22. The organization generally assigns appropriate levels of staff resources to the implementation of strategies:
23. It often takes longer to implement strategies than originally anticipated:
24. The established culture has made it difficult to implement new strategies:
25. Established ways of working have made it difficult to implement new strategies:
26. Staff generally understand the objectives of new strategies:
27. We usually have adequate technical/professional knowledge to enable us to implement new strategies:
28. If we do not have adequate technical/professional knowledge, we are sent on courses/conferences to enable us to implement new strategies:
29. Affected groups usually support the implementation of new strategies:
30. Front-line staff usually support the implementation of new strategies:
31. Middle managers usually support the implementation of new strategies:
32. Senior managers usually support the implementation of new strategies:
33. Elected members usually support the implementation of new strategies:
34. The implementation of our strategies often relies on other departments in the authority:
35. The implementation of our strategies often involves other organizations outside the authority:
36. Uncontrollable factors in the external environment often have an adverse impact on the implementation of our strategies:
37. Competing internal activities often distract attention from implementing strategies:

Section 3: Extent of Implementation

The questions in this section explore the extent to which strategies are implemented in your service area. Please indicate the extent to which you agree with the following statements about strategy implementation in your service.

38. Our strategies are implemented in full:
39. Our strategies usually achieve their intentions:
40. The actual implementation of our strategies does not deviate significantly from the planned implementation:
41. We generally implement all of our strategies in the same way:

Section 4: The Content of Implemented Strategies

The questions in this section explore the content of the strategies which are implemented in your service area. Please indicate the extent to which you agree with the following statements about your service.

42. Searching for new opportunities for service delivery is a major part of our strategies:
43. We emphasize stability and efficiency of provision (e.g. high quality and low cost):

44. Our strategies are strongly shaped by external pressures:
45. We provide existing services to new users:
46. We provide new services to existing users:
47. We provide new services to new users:
48. The service seeks additional funding (e.g. from the Welsh Assembly Government):
49. The service works in partnership:
50. The management structure of the service has changed:

Part B: Performance of the service

We would like to know how you assess the performance of your service. Please think about the performance of the service relative to similar services in similar authorities to estimate its current performance. To what extent do you agree that your service performs well in comparison with others in relation to

1. Quality of outputs (e.g. how reliably your services are delivered):
2. Quantity of outputs (e.g. the volume of service delivery):
3. Efficiency (e.g. cost per unit of service delivery):
4. Effectiveness (e.g. whether your objectives were achieved):
5. Value for Money (cost-effectiveness):
6. Consumer satisfaction:
7. Equity (e.g. how fairly your services are distributed amongst local citizens):
8. Staff satisfaction:
9. Promoting the social, economic and environmental well-being of local people:
10. Overall, to what extent would you agree that your service is performing well:

Part C: Factors affecting the service

The following set of questions explores how a range of internal and external issues affect your service.

Section 1: The Socio-economic context

Please indicate the extent to which you agree with the following statements about the socio-economic context of your service. By socio-economic context we mean levels of deprivation, social change, population change and so on. (Please click the circle closest to your own view.) The socio-economic context in which the service operates

1. is unpredictable (i.e. changes in unexpected ways):
2. is changing rapidly:
3. is very complex:
4. is favourable:
5. The service is able to influence the socio-economic context:

Section 2: The financial context

Please indicate the extent to which you agree with the following statements about the financial context of your service. By financial context we mean levels of funding made available and so on. (Please click the circle closest to your own view.) The financial context in which the service operates

6. is unpredictable (i.e. changes in unexpected ways):
7. is changing rapidly:
8. is very complex:
9. is favourable:
10. the service is able to influence the financial context:

Section 3: The external political context

Please indicate the extent to which you agree with the following statements about the external political context of your service. By external political context we mean relationships with the Welsh Assembly Government and its departments, relationships with other agencies and so on. (Please click the circle closest to your own view.) The external political context in which the service operates

11. is unpredictable (i.e. changes in unexpected ways):
12. is changing rapidly:
13. is very complex:
14. is favourable:
15. The service is able to influence the external political context:

Section 4: The internal political context

Please indicate the extent to which you agree with the following statements about the internal political context of your service. By internal political context we mean relationships between departments, members and officers, relationships between senior management and front-line staff and so on. (Please click the circle closest to your own view.) The internal political context in which the service operates

16. is unpredictable (i.e. changes in unexpected ways):
17. is changing rapidly:
18. is very complex:
19. is favourable:
20. The service is able to influence the internal political context:

Section 5: The level of support

Please indicate the extent to which you agree with the following statements about the level of support your service receives from other agencies. (Please click the circle closest to your own view.)

21. Central government agencies (e.g. Wales Assembly Government, Wales Development Agency and so on) are supportive of the service:
22. Regulatory agencies (e.g. external inspectorates such as the Audit Commission, Estyn, Social Services Inspectorate for Wales and so on) are supportive of the service:

23. Advisory agencies and professional bodies (e.g. WLGA, IDeA and so on) are supportive of the service:

Further comments

Finally, could you please add any further comments you wish to make about the questionnaire and strategy and service improvement.

Glossary of terms used in the questionnaire

Advisory agencies Non-governmental bodies whose function is to advise local authorities (e.g. Syniad).
Audit Commission The organization established by the government to ensure that public money is being used economically, efficiently and effectively.
Central government agencies Centrally established Government bodies such as the National Assembly for Wales or the Welsh Development Agency.
Economic and Social Research Council (ESRC) The UK's leading research funding agency providing research to business, the public sector and government on economic and social concerns.
Estyn The inspectorate responsible for inspecting education in Wales.
External stakeholders External statutory, voluntary or private sector organizations involved in the delivery of public services.
Improvement and Development Agency (IDeA) The organization established by and for local government to help councils deliver leadership, cultural change and performance improvement.
Professional bodies Agencies representing the interests of particular professions or sectors (e.g. the WLGA).
Regulatory agencies Inspectorates with responsibility for inspecting the delivery of public services in the UK.
Service Improvement The general activity of improving service delivery.
Social Services Inspectorate for Wales (SSIW) The inspectorate responsible for inspecting social services in Wales.
Strategic management The set of decisions and actions within an organization resulting in the formulation and implementation of a strategy.
Strategy The overall direction and outlook of an organization.
Strategy implementation The way an organization implements its strategies.
Targets Measurable aims for service delivery.
Wales Improvement Network The all-Wales Improvement forum for local authorities coordinated by Syniad
Welsh Development Agency (WDA) The organization established to coordinate economic development projects in Wales.
Welsh Local Government Association (WLGA) The professional body representing the interests of local authorities in Wales.

Notes

Appendix 2: Survey Methodology and Questionnaires

1. Similar results to those presented in this book were obtained for the 2002 data when the cases were restricted to the sub-set for 2003 (available on request).

References

Aiken, M. and J. Hage. 1968. 'Organizational interdependence and intra-organizational structure', *American Sociological Review,* 33, 5, 912–30.

Allen, B. H. and W. R. LaFollette. 1977. 'Perceived organizational structure and alienation among management trainees', *Academy of Management Journal,* 20, 2, 334–41.

Anderson, S. 1995. 'Organizational status and performance: The case of the Swedish pharmacies', *Public Administration,* 73, 2, 287–301.

Andrews, R. 2004. 'Analysing deprivation and local authority performance: The implications for CPA', *Public Money & Management,* 24, 1, 19–26.

Andrews, R. and G. A. Boyne 2008. 'Organizational environments and public service failure: An empirical analysis', *Environment and Planning C – Government and Policy,* 26, 4, 788–807.

Andrews, R., G. A. Boyne, K. J. Meier, L. J. O'Toole Jr. and R. M. Walker. 2008. 'Strategic fit and performance: Testing Miles & Snow', *Organizational strategy, structure, and process: A reflection on the research perspective of Miles and Snow conference.* Cardiff, UK, December. Available from http://www.cf.ac.uk/carbs/research/groups/clrgr/research/public/how_public.html, accessed 7th September 2010.

Andrews, R., G. A. Boyne and R. M. Walker. 2006a. 'Strategy content and organizational performance: An empirical analysis', *Public Administration Review,* 66, 1, 52–63.

Andrews, R., G. A. Boyne and R. M. Walker. 2006b. 'Subjective and objective measures of organizational performance: An empirical exploration'. In G. A. Boyne, K. J. Meier, L. J. O'Toole and R. M. Walker (eds), *Public service performance: Perspectives on measurement and management.* pp. 14–34. Cambridge: Cambridge University Press.

Andrews, R., G. A. Boyne and G. Enticott. 2006c. 'Performance failure in the public sector: Misfortune or mismanagement?', *Public Management Review,* 8, 2, 273–2969.

Andrews, R., G. A. Boyne, J. Law and R. M. Walker. 2003. 'Myths, measures and modernisation: A comparative analysis of local authority performance in England and Wales', *Local Government Studies,* 29, 4, 54–78.

Andrews, R., G. A. Boyne, J. Law and R. M. Walker. 2005a. 'External constraints and public sector performance: The case of comprehensive performance assessment in English local government', *Public Administration,* 83, 4, 639–56.

Andrews, R., G. A. Boyne, K. J. Meier, L. J. O'Toole Jr. and R. M. Walker. 2005b. 'Representative bureaucracy, organizational strategy, and public service performance: An empirical analysis of English local government', *Journal of Public Administration Research and Theory,* 15, 3, 489–504.

Andrews, R. and S. Martin. 2007. 'Has devolution improved public services? An analysis of the comparative performance of local public services in England and Wales', *Public Money & Management,* 27, 2,149–156.

Andrews, R. and S. Martin. 2010. 'Regional variations in public service outcomes: The impact of policy divergence in England, Scotland and Wales', *Regional Studies*, 44, 8, 919–34.

Ansoff, H. I. 1991. 'Critique of Henry Mintzberg's the "design school": Reconsidering the basic premises of strategic management', *Strategic Management Journal*, 12, 6, 449–61.

Aragon-Sanchez, A. and G. Sanchez-Marin. 2005. 'Strategic orientation, management characteristics and performance: A study of Spanish SMEs', *Journal of Small Business Management*, 43, 3, 287–308.

Armstrong, J. S. and T. S. Overton. 1977. 'Estimating non-response bias in mail surveys', *Journal of Marketing Research*, 14, 3, 396–402.

Ashmos, D. P., D. Duchon and R. R. McDaniel, Jr. 1998. 'Participation in strategic decision-making: The role of organizational predisposition and issue interpretation', *Decision Sciences*, 29, 1, 25–51.

Ashworth, R., G. A. Boyne and R. Delbridge. 2009. 'Escape from the Iron Cage? Organizational change and isomorphic pressures in the public sector', *Journal of Public Administration Research and Theory*, 19, 1, 165–87.

Ashworth, R., G. A. Boyne and R. M. Walker. 2002. 'Regulatory problems in the public sector: Theories and cases', *Policy & Politics*, 30, 2, 195–211.

Audit Commission. 2002. *Comprehensive performance assessment*. London: Audit Commission.

Bailey, A., Johnson, G. and Daniels, K. 2000. 'Validation of a multi-dimensional measure of strategy development processes', *British Journal of Management*, 11, 1, 151–62.

Bantel. K. A. 1997. 'Performance in adolescent, technology-based firms: Product strategy, implementation and synergy', *Journal of High Technology Management Research*, 8, 2, 243–62.

Barney, J. B. 1991. 'Firm resources and sustained competitive advantage', *Journal of Management*, 17, 1, 99–120.

Becker, M. C. 2004. 'Organizational routines: A review of the literature', *Industrial and Corporate Change*, 13, 4, 643–677.

Bennett, R. 1982. *Central grants to local governments*. Cambridge: Cambridge University Press.

Birch, S. and Maynard, A. 1986. 'Performance indicators and performance assessment in the UK National Health Service: Implications for management and planning', *International Journal of Health Planning and Management*, 1, 3, 287–306.

Blair, T. 2002. *The courage of our convictions: Why reform of the public services is the route to social justice*. Fabian Ideas 603. London: Fabian Society.

Boaden, N. T. and Alford, R. R. 1969. 'Sources of diversity in English local government decisions', *Public Administration*, 47, 3, 203–23.

Bohte, J. and K. J. Meier. 2000. 'Goal displacement: Assessing the motivation for organizational cheating', *Public Administration Review*, 60, 2, 173–82.

Boschken, H. L. 1988. *Strategic design and organizational change*. Tuscaloosa: University of Alabama Press.

Boulding, K. E. 1978. *Ecodynamics*. Beverly Hills, CA: Sage.

Bourgeois, L. J. 1981. 'On the Measurement of Organizational Slack', *Academy of Management Review*, 6, 1, 29–39.

Bourgeois, L. J. 1984. 'Strategic management and determinism', *Academy of Management Review,* 9, 4, 586–96.

Bourgeois, L. J. and D. R. Brodwin. 1984. 'Strategic implementation: Five approaches to an elusive phenomenon', *Strategic Management Journal,* 5, 3, 241–64.

Bowerman, B. L. and R. T. O'Connell. 1990. *Linear statistical models: An applied approach,* 2nd ed. Belmont, CA: Duxbury.

Bowman, C. and V. Ambrosini. 1997. 'Using single respondents in strategy research', *British Journal of Management,* 8, 1, 119–31.

Bowman, E. and C. Helfat. 2001. 'Does corporate strategy matter?', *Strategic Management Journal,* 2, 1, 1–23.

Boyd, B. K. and S. Gove. 2006. 'Managerial Constraint: The Intersection between Organizational Task Environment and Discretion'. In D. Ketchen and D. Bergh (eds), *Research Methodology in Strategy and Management, Volume 3.* pp. 57–96. Oxford: JAI Press.

Boyne, G. A. 1992. 'Local government structure and performance: Lessons from America?', *Public Administration,* 70, 3, 333–57.

Boyne, G. A. 2001. 'Planning, performance and public services', *Public Administration,* 79, 1, 73–88.

Boyne, G. A. 2002. 'Public and private management: What's the difference?', *Journal of Management Studies,* 39, 1, 97–122.

Boyne, G. A. 2003a. 'Sources of public service improvement: A critical review and research agenda', *Journal of Public Administration Research and Theory,* 13, 2, 367–94.

Boyne, G. A. 2003b. 'What is public service improvement?', *Public Administration,* 81, 2, 211–28.

Boyne, G. A. 2004. 'Explaining public service performance: Does management matter?', *Public Policy and Administration,* 19, 4, 100–17.

Boyne, 2006. 'Add to References: Strategies for Organizational Turnaround: Lessons from the Private Sector?', *Administration and Society,* 38, 365–388.

Boyne, G. A. and A. Chen. 2007. 'Performance targets and public service improvement', *Journal of Public Administration Research and Theory,* 17, 3, 455–77.

Boyne, G. A., P. Day and R. M. Walker. 2002. 'Towards a theory of public service inspection', *Urban Studies,* 39, 7, 1197–212.

Boyne G. A. and J. S. Gould-Williams 2003. 'Strategic planning and the performance of public organizations: An empirical analysis', *Public Management Review,* 5, 2, 115–32.

Boyne, G. A., J. S. Gould-Williams, J. Law and Richard M. Walker. 2002. 'Plans, performance information and accountability: The case of Best Value', *Public Administration,* 80, 4, 691–710.

Boyne, G. A., J. S. Gould-Williams, J. Law and R. M. Walker. 2004. 'Problems of rational planning in public organizations: An Empirical assessment of the conventional wisdom', *Administration & Society,* 36, 3, 328–50.

Boyne, G. A., S. Martin and R. M. Walker. 2004. 'Explicit reforms, implicit theories and public service improvement: An evaluation of management reform', *Public Management Review,* 6, 2, 189–210.

Boyne, G. A. and K. J. Meier. 2009. 'Environmental change, human resources and organizational turnaround', *Journal of Management Studies,* 46, 5, 835–63.

Boyne, G. A. and R. M. Walker. 2004. 'Strategy content and public service organizations', *Journal of Public Administration Research and Theory,* 14, 2, 231–52.

Bozeman, B. 1987. *All organizations are public.* San Francisco: Jossey-Bass.

Bozeman, B. and J. Straussman (eds). 1990. *Public management strategies.* San Francisco: Jossey-Bass.

Brewer, G. A. 2005. 'In the eye of the storm: Frontline supervisors and federal agency performance', *Journal of Public Administration Research and Theory,* 15, 4, 505–27.

Brewer, G. A. 2006. 'All measures of performance are subjective: More evidence on U.S. federal agencies'. In G. A. Boyne, K. J. Meier, L. J. O'Toole, Jr. and R. M. Walker (eds), *Public service performance: Perspectives on management and measurement.* Cambridge: Cambridge University Press.

Brewer, G. A. and Selden, S. C. 2000. 'Why elephants gallop: Assessing and predicting organizational performance in Federal agencies', *Journal of Public Administration Research and Theory,* 10, 4, 685–711.

Brief, A. P., M. J. Burke, J. M. George, B. S. Robinson and J. Webster. 1988. 'Should negative affectivity remain an unmeasured variable in the study of job stress?', *Journal of Applied Psychology,* 73, 2, 191–98.

Bryson, J. M. 1995. *Strategic planning for public and non-profit organizations.* San Francisco: Jossey-Bass.

Bryson, J. M. 2010. 'The future of public and nonprofit strategic planning in the United States', *Public Administration Review,* S1, S255–67.

Bryson, J. M., F. S. Berry and K. Yang. 2010. 'The state of public strategic management research: A selective literature review and set of directions', *American Review of Public Administration,* 40, 5, 495–521.

Burns, T. and Stalker, G. M. 1961. *The management of innovation.* London: Tavistock.

Capon, N., J. Farley and J. Hulbert. 1987. *Corporate strategic planning.* New York: Columbia University Press.

Carter, N. M. and J. B. Cullen. 1984. 'A comparison of centralization/decentralization of decision making concepts and measures', *Journal of Management,* 10, 2, 259–68.

Case, P., S. Case and S. Catling. 2000. 'Please show you're working: a critical assessment of the impact of OFSTED inspections', *British Journal of Sociology of Education,* 21, 4, 605–21.

Castrogiovanni, G. J. 1991. 'Environmental munificence: A theoretical assessment', *Academy of Management Review,* 16, 4, 542–65.

Cespedes, F. V. and N. F. Piercy. 1996. 'Implementing marketing strategy', *Journal of Marketing Management,* 12, 2, 135–60.

Chandler, A. D. 1962. *Strategy and structure: Chapters in the history of the industrial enterprise.* Cambridge, MA: MIT Press.

Chapman, C. 2001. 'Changing classrooms through inspection', *School Leadership and Management,* 21, 1, 59–73.

Chun, Y-H. and H. Rainey, 2005. 'Goal ambiguity and organizational performance in U.S. federal agencies', *Journal of Public Administration Research and Theory,* 15, 3, 529–57.

Chustz, M. H. and J. S. Larson. 2006. 'Implementing change on the front lines: A management case study of West Feliciana Parish Hospital', *Public Administration Review,* 60, 5, 725–9.

Clapham, D. 1984. 'Rational planning and politics: The example of local authority corporate plannning', *Policy & Politics,* 12, 1, 31–52.

Conant, J. S., M. P. Mokwa and P. R. Varadarajan. 1990. 'Strategic types, distinctive marketing competencies and organizational performance: A multiple measures-based study', *Strategic Management Journal,* 11, 5, 365–83.

Crittenden, W., V. Crittenden and T. Hunt. 1988. 'Planning and Stakeholder satisfaction in religious organization', *Journal of Voluntary Action Research,* 17, 1, 60–73.

Croll, P. 2002. 'Social deprivation, school-level achievement and special educational needs', *Educational Research,* 44, 1, 43–53.

Cullingford, C. and S. Daniels. 1999. 'Effects of Ofsted inspections on school performance'. In C. Cullingford (ed.), *An Inspector Calls – OFSTED and Its Effect on School Standards*. pp. 59–96. London: Kogan Page.

Cyert, R. M. and J. G. March. 1963. *A behavioral theory of the firm.* Englewood Cliffs, NJ: Prentice-Hall.

Dalton, D. R., W. D. Todor, M. J. Spendolini, G. J. Fielding and L. W. Porter. 1980. 'Organizational structure and performance: A critical review', *Academy of Management Review,* 5, 1, 49–64.

Danziger, J. 1978. *Making budgets.* London: Sage.

Darnell, N. and S. Sides. 2008. 'Assessing the performance of voluntary environmental programs: Does certification matters?', *Policy Studies Journal,* 36, 1, 95–117.

Dawson, S. 1996. *Analysing organizations.* Basingstoke: Macmillan.

Day, P. and R. Klein. 1987. *Accountabilities.* London: Tavistock.

Dean J. W. and M. P. Sharfman. 1996. 'Does decision process matter? A study of strategic decision making effectiveness', *Academy of Management Journal,* 39, 4, 368–96.

Department of Environment, Transport and Regions. 2000. *Indices of multiple deprivation.* London: Department of Environment, Transport and Regions.

Desarbo, W. S., A. C. Di Benedetto, M. Song and I. Sinha. 2005. 'Revisiting the Miles and Snow strategic framework: Uncovering interrelationships between strategic types, capabilities, environmental uncertainty, and firm performance', *Strategic Management Journal,* 26, 1, 47–74.

Dess, G. G. and D. W. Beard 1984. 'Dimensions of organizational task environments', *Administrative Science Quarterly,* 29, 1, 52–73.

Dewar, R. D., D. A. Whetten and D. Boje. 1980. 'An examination of the reliability and validity of the Aiken and Hage scales of centralization, formalization, and task routineness', *Administrative Science Quarterly,* 25, 1, 120–128.

Dibben, P. 2006. 'The "socially excluded" and local transport decision making: Voice and responsiveness in a marketized environment', *Public Administration,* 84, 3, 655–72.

DiMaggio, P. and W. Powell 1983. 'The iron cage revisited: Institutional isomorphism and collective rationality in organizational fields', *American Sociological Review,* 48, 4, 497–518.

Donaldson, L. 1996. *For positivist organizational theory: Proving the hard core*. London: Sage.

Donaldson, L. 2001. *The contingency theory of organizations*. Thousand Oaks, CA: Sage.

Doty, D. H., W. H. Glick and G. P. Huber. 1993. 'Fit, equifinality, and organizational effectiveness: A test of two configurational theories', *Academy of Management Journal*, 36, 6, 1198–250.

Downs, A. 1967. *Inside bureaucracy*. Boston: Little, Brown and Company.

Dror, Y. 1973. *Public policy making re-examined*. Bedfordshire: Leonard Hill.

Dunsire, A. 1978. *Control in a bureaucracy*. Oxford: Martin Robertson.

Dutton, J. M., L. Fahey and V. K. Narayanan. 1983. 'Toward understanding strategic issue diagnosis', *Strategic Management Journal*, 4, 3, 307–23.

Easton, D. 1953. *The Political System*. Alfred Knopf: New York.

Eisenhardt, K. M. and L. J. I Bourgeois. 1988. 'Politics of strategy decision making in high-velocity environments: Towards a midrange theory', *Academy of Management Journal*, 31, 4, 737–70.

Elbanna, S. 2006. 'Strategic decision-making: Process perspectives', *International Journal of Management Reviews*, 8, 1, 1–20.

Emery, F. E. and E. L. Trist. 1965. 'The causal texture of organizational environments', *Human Relations*, 18, 1, 21–32.

Enander, R. T., R. N. Gagnon, R. C. Hanumara, E. Park, T. Armstrong and M. Gute. 2007. 'Environmental health practice: Statistically based performance measurement', *American Journal of Public Health*, 97, 5, 819–24.

Enticott, G. 2003. 'Researching local government using electronic surveys', *Local Government Studies*, 29, 2, 52–67.

Enticott, G. and R. M. Walker. 2008. 'Sustainability, performance and organizational strategy: an empirical analysis of public organizations', *Business Strategy and the Environment*, 17, 1, 79–92.

Enticott, G., G. A. Boyne and R. M. Walker. 2009. 'The use of multiple informants in public administration research: Data aggregation using organizational echelons', *Journal of Public Administration Research and Theory*, 19, 2, 229–53.

Evans, J. D. and C. L. Green 2000. 'Marketing strategy, constituent influence, and resource allocation: An application of the Miles and Snow typology to closely held firms in Chapter 11 Bankruptcy', *Journal of Business Research*, 50, 2, 225–31.

Ferlie, E. 2002. 'Quasi-strategy: strategic management in the contemporary public sector'. In A. Pettigrew, R. Whittington and H. Thomas (eds), *Handbook of Strategy and Management*. pp. 279–98. London: Sage.

Fernandez, S. and H. G. Rainey. 2006. 'Managing successful organizational change in the public sector: An agenda for research and practice', *Public Administration Review*, 66, 2, 1–25.

Fiedler, F. E. and M. W. Gillo. 1974. 'Correlates of performance in community colleges', *Journal of Higher Education*, 45, 9, 672–81.

Fox-Wolfgramm, S., K. Boal and J. Hunt. 1998. 'Organizational adaptation to institutional change: A Comparative study of first-order change in prospector and defender banks', *Administrative Science Quarterly*, 43, 1, 87–126.

Frederickson, J. 1984. 'The comprehensiveness of strategic decision processes', *Academy of Management Journal*, 27, 3, 445–66.

Frumkin, P. and J. Galskiewicz. 2004. 'Institutional isomorphism and public sector organizations', *Journal of Public Administration Research and Theory,* 14, 3, 283–307.

Ginter, P. M., L. E. Swayne and W. J. Duncan. 2002. *Strategic management of health care organizations,* 4th ed. Oxford: Blackwell.

Glisson, C. A. and P. Yancey Martin. 1980. 'Productivity and efficiency in human service organizations as related to structure, size and age', *Academy of Management Journal,* 23, 1, 21–37.

Golden, B. R. 1992. 'Is the past the past – or is it? The use of retrospective accounts as indicators of past strategies', *Academy of Management Journal,* 35, 4, 848–60.

Goodsell, C. T. 1985. *The case for bureaucracy: A public administration polemic,* 2nd ed. Chatham, NJ: Chatham House Publishers.

Gordon, I. and Monastiriotis, V. 2006. 'Urban size, spatial segregation and inequality in education outcomes', *Urban Studies,* 43, 1, 213–36.

Govindarajan, V. 1988. 'A contingency approach to strategy implementation at the business-unit level: Integrating administrative mechanisms with strategy', *Academy of Management Journal,* 31, 4, 828–53.

Grace, C. 2005. 'Change and improvement in audit and inspection: A strategic approach for the twenty-first century', *Local Government Studies,* 31, 5, 575–96.

Greenwood, R. 1987. 'Managerial strategies in local government', *Public Administration,* 65, 4, 295–312.

Greenwood, R., C. R. Hinnings and S. Ranson. 1975a. 'Contingency theory and the organization of local authorities. Part I: Differentiation and integration', *Public Administration,* 53, 1, 1–23.

Greenwood, R., C. R. Hinnings and S. Ranson. 1975b. 'Contingency theory and the organization of local authorities. Part II: Contingencies and structure', *Public Administration,* 53, 2, 169–90.

Grosskopf, S. and Yaisawamg, S. 1990. 'Economies of scope in the provision of local public services', *National Tax Journal,* 43, 1, 61–74.

Gruca, T. and D. Nath. 1994. 'Regulatory change, constraints on adaptation and organizational failure: An empirical analysis of acute care hospitals', *Strategic Management Journal,* 15, 5, 345–63.

Gutiérrez-Romero, R. Haubrich, D. and McLean, I. 2008. 'The limits of performance assessments of public bodies: External constraints in English local government', *Environment and Planning C: Government and Policy,* 26, 4, 767–87.

Gulick, L. and L. Urwick (eds). 1937. *Papers on the science of administration.* New York: Columbia University.

Hage, J. and M. Aiken. 1967. 'Relationship of centralization to other structural properties', *Administrative Science Quarterly,* 12, 1, 72–93.

Hage, J. and M. Aiken. 1969. 'Routine technology, social structure, and organizational goals', *Administrative Science Quarterly,* 14, 3, 366–76.

Hair, J. K. F. Jr., Rolph, E. Anderson, Ronald, L. Tatham and William C. Black. 1998. *Multivariate data analysis,* 5th ed. Upper Saddle River, NJ: Prentice Hall.

Hall, J. C. and Leeson, P. T. 2010. 'Racial fractionalization and school performance', *American Journal of Economics and Sociology,* 69, 2, 736–58.

Hall, R. H. 1982. *Organizations: Structure and process,* 3rd ed. Englewood Cliffs: Prentice-Hall.

Hambrick, D. C. 1983. 'Some tests of the effectiveness and functional attributes of Miles and Snow's strategic types', *Academy of Management Journal*, 26, 1, 5–26.

Hambrick, D. C. 2003. 'On the staying power of defenders, analyzers, and prospectors', *Academy of Management Executive*, 17, 4, 115–18.

Hambrick, D. C. and Cannella, A. A. 1989. 'Strategy implementation as substance and selling', *Academy of Management Executive*, 3, 4, 278–85.

Hambrick, D. C. and P. Mason. 1984. 'Upper echelons: The organization as a reflection of top managers', *Academy of Management Review*, 9, 1, 193–206.

Hargreaves, D. H. 1995. 'Inspection and school improvement', *Cambridge Journal of Education*, 25, 1, 53–61.

Harrington. R. J. 2004. 'The environment, involvement and performance; implications for the strategic process of food service firms', *International Journal of Hospitality Management*, 23, 3, 317–41.

Hart, S. 1992. 'An integrated framework for strategy-making processes', *Academy of Management Review*, 17, 2, 327–51.

Hart, S. and C. Banbury. 1994. 'How strategy-making processes can make a difference', *Strategic Management Journal*, 15, 3, 251–69.

Hawes, J. M. and W. F. Crittenden. 1984. 'A taxonomy of competitive retailing strategies', *Strategic Management Journal*, 5, 3, 275–87.

Hawkins, K. 1984. *Environment and enforcement: Regulation and the social definition of inspection*. Oxford: Oxford University Press.

Hendrick, R. 2003. 'Strategic planning environment, process, and performance in public agencies: A comparative study of departments in Milwaukee', *Journal of Public Administration Research and Theory*, 13, 4, 491–519.

Hirschman, A. O. 1970. *Exit, voice and loyalty: Responses to decline in firms, organizations and states*. Cambridge, MA: Harvard University Press.

Hickson, D. J., S. J. Miller and D. C. Wilson. 2003. 'Planned or prioritized? Two options in managing the implementation of strategic decisions', *Journal of Management Studies*, 40, 7, 1803–36.

Hill, M. and Hupe, P. 2002. *Implementing public policy*. London: Sage.

Hinings, C. R., D. J. Hickson, J. M. Pennings and R. E. Schneck. 1974. 'Structural conditions of intraorganizational power', *Administrative Science Quarterly*, 19, 1, 22–44.

Hodge, G. A. 2000. *Privatization: An international review of performance*. Boulder, CO: Westview Press.

Hoggett, P. 2006, 'Conflict, ambivalence, and the contested purpose of public organizations', *Human Relations*, 59, 2, 175–94.

Holland, T. P. 1973. 'Organizational structure and institutional care', *Journal of Health and Social Behavior*, 14, 3, 241–51.

Hood, C., O. James, C. D. Scott. 2000. 'Regulation of government: Has it increased, is it increasing, should it be diminished?', *Public Administration*, 78, 2, 283–304.

Hood, C. C., C. D. Scott, O. James, G. W. Jones and T. Travers. 1999. *Regulation inside government*. Oxford: Oxford University Press.

Hrebriniak, L. G. and W. F. Joyce. 1984. *Implementing strategy*. New York: Macmillan.

Hughes, G., R. Mears and C. Winch. 1997. 'An inspector calls? Regulation and accountability in three public services', *Policy & Politics*, 25, 3, 299–13.

Humphrey, J. 2002. 'A scientific approach to politics? On the trail of the Audit Commission', *Critical Perspectives on Accounting*, 13, 1, 39–62.

Hyndman, N. and R. Eden, 2001. 'Rational management, performance targets and executive agencies: Views from agency chief executives in Northern Ireland', *Public Administration*, 79, 4, 579–98.

Inkpen, A. and N. Choudhury. 1995. 'The seeking of strategy where it is not – Towards a theory of strategy absence', *Strategic Management Journal*, 16, 4, 313–23.

James, O. 2000. 'Regulation Inside Government: Public Interest Justifications and Regulatory Failures', *Public Administration*, 78, 2, 327–43.

James W. and K. Hatten. 1994. 'Evaluating the performance effects of Miles' and Snow's strategic archetypes in Banking', *Journal of Business Research*, 31, 2/3, 145–54.

Jarley, P., J. Fiorito and J. Thomas Delaney. 1997. 'A structural contingency approach to bureaucracy and democracy in U.S. unions', *Academy of Management Journal*, 40, 4, 831–61.

Jasinski, J. L. 2000. 'Beyond high school: An examination of Hispanic educational attainment', *Social Science Quarterly*, 81, 1, 276–90.

Johnson, G. and K. Scholes. 2002. *Exploring corporate strategy*, 6th ed. Harlow: Prentice-Hall.

Johanson, J-E. 2009. 'Strategic formation in public agencies', *Public Administration*, 87, 4, 872–91.

Johnson, G. 2000. 'Strategy through a cultural lens: Learning from managers' experiences', *Management Learning*, 31, 4, 403–26.

Joldersma, C. and V. Winter. 2002. 'Strategic management in hybrid organizations', *Public Management Review*, 4, 1, 83–99.

Joyce, P. 1999. *Strategic management for the public services*. Buckingham: Open University Press.

Kelley, E., A. Gamble-Kelley, C. H. T. Simpara, O. Sidibe and M. Makinen. 2003. 'The impact of self-assessment on provide performance in Mali', *International Journal of Health Planning and Management*, 18, 1, 41–8.

Ketchen, D. J. Jr., J. B. Thomas and R. R. Jr. McDaniel. 1996. 'Process, content and context: Synergistic effects on organizational performance', *Journal of Management*, 22, 2, 231–57.

Kim, S. 2002. 'Participative management and job satisfaction: Lessons for management leadership', *Public Administration Review*, 62, 2, 231–41.

Ladd, H. F. 1992. 'Population growth, density and the costs of providing public services', *Urban Studies*, 29, 2, 273–95.

Lane, J-E. and J. Wallis. 2009. 'Strategic management and public leadership', *Public Management Review*, 11, 1, 101–20.

Lindblom, C. 1959. 'The science of muddling through', *Public Administration Review*, 19, 2, 79–88.

Lindell, M. K. and D. J. Whitney. 2001. 'Accounting for common method variance in cross-sectional designs', *Journal of Applied Psychology*, 86, 1, 114–21.

Lipsky, M. 1980. *Street-level bureaucracy: Dilemmas of the individual in public services*. New York: Russell Sage Foundation.

Loewenthal, K. M. 1996. *An introduction to psychological tests and scales*. London: UCL Press.

Long, E. and A. L. Franklin. 2004. 'The paradox of implementing the Government Performance and Results Act: Top-down direction for bottom-up implementation'. *Public Administration Review*, 64, 3, 309–19.

Luginbuhl, R., D. Webbink and de I. Wolf. 2009. 'Do inspections improve primary school performance', *Educational Evaluation and Policy Analysis*, 31, 3, 221–37.

Lynch, M. 1995. 'Effect of practice and patient population characteristics on the uptake of childhood immunizations', *British Journal of General Practice*, 45, 393, 205–8.

Martin, P. Y. and B. Segal. 1977. 'Bureaucracy, size and staff expectations for client independence in halfway houses', *Journal of Health and Social Behavior*, 18, 4, 376–90.

Martin, S. J. 2010. 'Regulation'. In R. Ashworth, G. A. Boyne and T. Entwistle (eds), *Public service improvement: Theories and evidence*. pp. 36–59. Oxford: Oxford University Press.

Maynard-Moody, S. and M. Musheno. 2003. *Cops, teachers and counsellors: Stories from the front lines of public service*. Ann Arbor: University of Michigan Press.

Maynard-Moody, S., M. Musheno and D. Palumbo. 1990. 'Street-wise social policy: resolving the dilemma of street-level influence and successful implementation', *Western Political Quarterly*, 43, 4, 833–48.

McCrone, T., P. Rudd, S. Blenkinsop, P. Wade, S. Rutt and T. Yesahnew. 2007. *Evaluation of the impact of Section 5 inspections*. London: NFER.

McMahon, J. T. 1976. 'Participative and power-equalized organizational systems', *Human Relations*, 29, 3, 203–14.

Meier, K. J. and J. Bohte 2003. 'Not with a bang but a whimper: Explaining organizational failures', *Administration & Society*, 35, 1, 1–18.

Meier K. J., G. A. Boyne, L. J. O'Toole Jr., R. M. Walker and R. Andrews. 2010. 'Alignment for results: Testing the interaction effects of strategy, structure, and environment from Miles and Snow', *Administration & Society*, 42, 2, 160–92.

Meier, K. J. and J. L. Brudney. 2002. *Applied statistics for public administration*. Orlando: Harcourt College.

Meier, K. and L. J. O'Toole. 2001. 'Managerial strategies and behaviour in networks: A model with evidence from U.S. public education', *Journal of Public Administration Research and Theory* 11, 3, 271–93.

Meier, K. J. and L. J. Jr. O'Toole. 2002. 'Public management and organizational performance: The impact of managerial quality', *Journal of Policy Analysis and Management*, 21, 4, 629–43.

Meier, K. J. and L. J. Jr. O'Toole. 2004. 'Managerial strategies and behaviour in networks: A model with evidence from U.S. public education', *Journal of Public Administration Research and Theory*, 11, 3, 271–93.

Meier, K. J. and L. J. Jr. O'Toole. 2006. *Bureaucracy in a democratic state*. Baltimore: Johns Hopkins.

Meier, K. J. and O'Toole Jr., L. J. 2008. 'Management theory and Occam's Razor: How public organizations buffer the environment,' *Administration & Society*, 39, 8, 931–58.

Meier, K. J., L. J. O'Toole Jr., and Hicklin, A. 2008. 'I've seen fire and I've seen rain: Public management and performance after a natural disaster', *Administration & Society*, 41, 8, 979–1003.

Meier, K. J. and L. J. Jr. O'Toole, G. A. Boyne and R. M. Walker 2007. 'Strategic management and the performance of public organizations: Testing venerable ideas again recent theories', *Journal of Public Administration Research and Theory*, 17, 3, 357–77.

Meyer, J., R. Scott and D. Strang. 1987. 'Centralization, fragmentation and school district complexity', *Administrative Science Quarterly*, 32, 2, 186–201.

Miles, R. E. and C. C. Snow. 1978. *Organizational strategy, structure and process*. New York, McGraw-Hill.

Miller, D. 1986. 'Configurations of strategy and structure: Towards a synthesis',*Strategic Management Journal*, 7, 3, 233–49.

Miller, D. and P. H. Friesen. 1983. 'Strategy making and environment: The third link', *Strategic Management Journal*, 4, 3, 221–35.

Miller, S. 1997. 'Implementing strategic decisions: Four key success factors', *Organizational Studies*, 18, 4, 577–602.

Mintzberg, H. 1979. *The structuring of organizations*. Englewood Cliffs, NJ: Prentice-Hall.

Mintzberg, H. 1994. *The rise and fall of strategic planning*. New York: Prentice-Hall.

Mintzberg, H, 2000, *The rise and fall of strategic planning*. New York: Free Press.

Mintzberg, H., B. Ahlstrand and J. Lampel. 1998. *Strategy safari*. London, Prentice Hall.

Moore, M. H. 1995. *Creating public value: Strategic management in government*. Cambridge, MA: Harvard University Press.

Moore, M. 2005. 'Towards a confirmatory model of retail strategy types: An empirical test of Miles and Snow', *Journal of Business Research*, 58, 5, 696–704.

Montgomery, C. A. 2008. 'Putting leadership back into strategy', *Harvard Business Review*, 86, 1, 54–60.

Moynihan, D. 2006. 'Managing for results in state government: Evaluating a decade of reform', *Public Administration Review*, 66, 1, 77–89.

Moynihan, D. P. and S. K. Pandey. 2005. 'Testing how management matters in an era of government by performance management', *Journal of Public Administration Research and Theory*, 15, 3, 421–39.

National Assembly for Wales. 2003. *Circular 8/2001, Local Government Act: Guidance on Best Value performance indicators 2001–2002*. Cardiff: National Assembly.

National Assembly for Wales. 2003. *National Assembly for Wales performance indicators 2001–2002*. Cardiff: National Assembly.

National Assembly for Wales. 2004. *National Assembly for Wales performance indicators 2002–2003*. Cardiff: National Assembly.

Negandhi, A. R. and Reimann, B. C. 1973. 'Task environment, decentralization and organizational effectiveness', *Human Relations*, 26, 2, 203–14.

Niskanen, W. A. 1971. *Bureaucracy and representative government*. Chicago: Aldin.

Noble, C. H. 1999. 'The eclectic roots of strategy implementation research', *Journal of Business Research*, 45, 2, 119–34.

Nunnally, J. C. 1978. *Psychometric theory*, 2nd ed. New York: McGraw Hill.

Nutt, P. 1986. 'Tactics of implementation', *Academy of Management Journal*, 29, 2, 230–61.

Nutt, P. 1987. 'Identifying and Appraising How Managers Install Strategy', *Strategic management Journal*, 8, 1–14.

Nutt, P. and R. Backoff. 1993. 'Organizational publicness and its implications for strategic management', *Journal of Public Administration Research and Theory*, 3, 2, 209–31.

Nutt, P. 1989. 'Selecting tactics to implement strategic plans', *Strategic Management Journal,* 10, 2, 145–61.

Nutt, P. 1999. 'Surprising but true: Half the decisions in organizations fail', *Academy of Management Executive,* 13, 4, 75–90.

Odeck, J. and A. Akadi 2004. 'The performance of subsidized urban and rural public bus operators: Empirical evidence from Norway', *Annals of Regional Science,* 38, 3, 413–31.

Odom, R. and W. Boxx. 1988 'Environment, planning processes and organizational performance of churches', *Strategic Management Journal,* 9, 2, 197–205.

Organization for Economic Cooperation and Development (OCED) 2005. *Modernizing government. The way forward.* Paris: OCED.

Office for National Statistics. 2003. *Census 2001: Key statistics for local authorities.* London: The Stationery Office.

Office of Public Service Reform, 2003. *Leading from the front-line.* London: Office of Public Service Reform.

Office of Public Service Reform. 2002. *Reforming our public services. Principles into practice.* London: Office of Public Service Reform.

Office of the Deputy Prime Minister 2004. *Learning from the experience of recovery.* London: Office of the Deputy Prime Minister.

Okumus. F. 2003. 'A framework to implement strategies in organizations', *Management Decision,* 41, 9, 871–82.

Olson, E. M., S. F. Slater and G. T. M. Hult. 2005. 'The performance implications of fit among business strategy, marketing, organization structure, and strategic behaviour', *Journal of Marketing,* 69, 3, 49–65.

Osborne, S. P. and N. Flynn. 1997. Managing the innovative capacity of voluntary and non-profit organizations in the provision of public services. *Public Money and Management,* 17, 4, 31–39.

O'Toole L. J. Jr. 2000. 'Research on policy implementation: Assessment and prospects', *Journal of Public Administration Research and Theory,* 10, 2, 263–88.

O'Toole L. J. Jr. and K. J. Meier. 1999. 'Modelling the impact of public management: Implications of structural context', *Journal of Public Administration Research and Theory,* 9, 4, 505–26.

O'Toole L. J. Jr. and K. J. Meier. 2004. 'Public management in intergovernmental networks: Matching structural networks and managerial networking', *Journal of Public Administration Research and Theory* 14, 4, 469–94.

Ouchi, W. G. 1980. 'Markets, bureaucracies and clans', *Administrative Science Quarterly,* 25, 1, 129–41.

Pandey, S. K. and B. E. Wright. 2006. 'Connecting the dots in public management: Political environment, organizational goal ambiguity, and the public manager's role ambiguity', *Journal of Public Administration Research and Theory* 16, 4, 511–32.

Panzar, J. C. and R. D. Willig. 1977. 'Economies of scale in multi-output production', *Quarterly Journal of Economics,* 91, 3, 481–93.

Parsa, H. G. 1999. 'Interaction of Strategy implementation and power perceptions in franchise systems: An empirical investigation', *Journal of Business Research,* 45, 2, 173–85.

Payne, R. and R. Mansfield. 1973. 'Relationships of perception of organizational climate to organizational structure, context and hierarchical position', *Administrative Science Quarterly,* 18, 3, 515–26.

Perry, J. and H. G. Rainey. 1988. 'The public–private distinction in organization theory: A critique and research agenda', *Academy of Management Review,* 13, 2, 182–201.

Pettigrew, A. 1973. *The politics of organizational decision-making.* London: Tavistock.

Pettigrew, A., E. Ferlie and L McKee. 1988. *Shaping strategic change: Making change in large organizations. The case of the National Health Service.* London: Sage.

Pettigrew, A. M., R. W. Woodman and K. S. Cameron. 2001. 'Studying organizational change and development: Challenges for future research', *Academy of Management Journal,* 44, 4, 697–713.

Pfeffer, J. 1981. *Power in organizations.* London: Pitman.

Pfeffer, J. and G. Salancik. 1978. *The external control of organizations: A resource dependence perspective.* New York: Harper & Row.

Phillips, L. W. 1981. 'Assessing measurement error in key informant reports: A methodological note on organizational analysis in marketing', *Journal of Marketing Research,* 18, 4, 395–415.

Pinto, J. K. and J. E. Prescott. 1990. 'Planning and tactical factors in the project implementation process', *Journal of Management Studies* 27, 3, 305–27.

Podsakoff, P. M. and D. W. Organ. 1986. 'Self-reports in organizational research: Problems and prospects', *Journal of Management,* 12, 4, 531–44.

Poister, T. and G. Streib. 1999. 'Strategic management in the public sector', *Public Productivity and Management Review,* 22, 3, 308–25.

Poister. T. D. Pitts and L. Hamilton Edmunds. 2010. 'Strategic management research in the public sector: A review, synthesis and future directions', *American Review of Public Administration* 40, 5, 522–45.

Pollitt, C. and G. Bouckaert. 2000. *Public management reform: A comparative analysis.* Oxford: Oxford University Press.

Pollitt, C. and G. Bouckaert. 2004. *Public management reform: A comparative analysis,* 2nd ed. Oxford: Oxford University Press.

Porter, M. 1980. *Competitive strategy: Techniques for analyzing industries and competitors.* Free Press: New York.

Potoski, M. and Prakash, A. 2005. 'Covenants with weak swords: ISO 14001 and facilities' environmental performance', *Journal of Policy Analysis and Management,* 24, 4, 745–69.

Power, M. 1997. *The audit society.* Oxford: Oxford University Press.

Priem, R., A. Rasheed and A. Kotulic. 1995. 'Rationality in strategic decision processes, environmental dynamism and firm performance', *Journal of Management,* 21, 6, 913–29.

Pugh, D. S., D. J. Hickson, C. R. Hinings and C. Turner. 1968. 'Dimensions of organization structure', *Administrative Science Quarterly,* 13, 1, 65–105.

Purcell, J. 1999. 'Best practice and best fit: Chimera or cul-de-sac?', *Human Resource Management Journal,* 9, 1, 26–41.

Quinn, J. 1980. *Logical incrementalism.* Homewood, Illinois: Richard D Irwin.

Rajagopalan, N. and A. M. A. Rasheed. 1995. 'Incremental models of policy formulation and non-incremental changes: Critical review and synthesis', *British Journal of Management,* 6, 4, 289–302.

Rainey, Hal G. 1989. 'Public management – recent research on the political context and managerial roles, structures and behaviors', *Journal of Management,* 15, 2, 229–50.

Rainey, H. G. 2003. 'A theory of goal ambiguity in public organizations'. In J. L. Perry (ed), *Research in Public Administration,* 2, 121–66.

Rainey, H. G. 2010. *Understanding and managing public organizations.* San Francisco: Jossey-Bass.

Rainey, H. G. and P. Steinbauer. 1999. 'Galloping elephants: Developing elements of a theory of effective government organizations', *Journal of Public Administration Research and Theory,* 9, 1, 1–32.

Ramaswamy, K., A. Thomas, R. Litschert. 1994. 'Organizational performance in a regulated environment: The role of strategic orientation', *Strategic Management Journal,* 15, 1, 63–74.

Ramos-Rodrigiez, A. and J. Ruiz-Navarro. 2004. 'Changes in the intellectual structure of strategic management research. A bibliometric study of the Strategic Management Journal 1980–2000', *Strategic Management Journal,* 25, 10, 981–1004.

Rhodes, G. 1981. *Inspectorates in British government.* George Allen & Unwin, London.

Riccucci, N. M. 2005. *How management matters: Street-level bureaucrats and welfare reform.* Washington, D.C.: Georgetown University Press.

Richardson, H. A., R. J. Vanderberg, T. C. Blum and P. M. Roman. 2002. 'Does decentralization make a difference for the organization? An examination of the boundary conditions circumscribing decentralized decision-making and organizational financial performance', *Journal of Management,* 28, 2, 217–44.

Richter, F. D. and D. Tjosvold,. 1980. 'Effects of student participation in classroom decision-making on attitudes, peer interaction, motivation, and learning', *Journal of Applied Psychology,* 65, 1, 74–80.

Ring, P. S. and J. Perry. 1985. 'Strategic management in public and private organizations: Implications of distinctive contexts and constraints', *Academy of Management Review,* 10, 2, 276–86.

Rosenthal, L. 2004. 'Do school inspections improve school quality? Ofsted inspections and school examination results in the UK', *Economics of Education Review,* 23, 2, 143–51.

Rowan, B. 1982. 'Organizational structure and the institutional environment: The case of public schools', *Administrative Science Quarterly* 27, 3, 259–279.

Ruekert, R. W. and O. C. Jr. Walker. 1987. 'Marketing's interaction with other functional units: A conceptual framework and empirical evidence', *Journal of Marketing,* 51, 1, 1–19.

Salmon, P. 1987. 'Decentralisation as an incentive scheme'. *Oxford Review of Economic Policy,* 3, 2, 24–43.

Schmid, H. 2002. 'Relationships between organizational properties and organizational effectiveness in three types of nonprofit human service organizations', *Public Personnel Management,* 31, 3, 377–95.

Scholz, J. T. and W. B. Gray. 1997. 'Can government facilitate cooperation? An Informational model of OSHA enforcement', *American Journal of Political Science,* 41, 3, 693–717.

Scott, W. R. 2001. *Institutions and organizations,* 2nd ed. London: Sage.

Scott, W. R. 2003. 'Introduction to the transaction edition: Thompson's bridge over troubled waters'. In J. D. Thompson (ed.), 3rd ed. *Organizations in action.* New Brunswick, NJ: Transaction.

Segev, E. 1987. 'Strategy, strategy-making, and performance in a business game', *Strategic Management Journal*, 8, 6, 565–77.

Segev, E. 1989. 'A systematic comparative analysis and synthesis of two business-level strategic typologies', *Strategic Management Journal*, 10, 5, 487–505.

Shah, S. M. and Cook, D. G. 2008. 'Socio-economic determinants of casualty and NHS direct use', *Journal of Public Health*, 30, 75–81.

Sharpe, L. J. and K. Newton. 1984. *Does politics matter?* Oxford: Clarendon.

Shaw, I., D. P. Newton, M. Aitkin and R. Darnell. 2003. 'Do OFSTED inspections of secondary schools make a difference to GCSE results?', *British Educational Research Journal*, 29, 1, 63–75.

Shortell, S. M. and Zajac, E. J. 1990. 'Perceptual and archival measures of Miles and Snow's strategic types: A comprehensive assessment of reliability and validity', *Academy of Management Journal*, 33, 4, 817–32.

Siciliano, J. I. 1997. 'The relationship between formal planning and performance in nonprofit organizations', *Nonprofit Management and Leadership*, 7, 4, 387–403.

Simon, H. A. 1976. *Administrative behavior: A study of decision-making processes in administrative organization*, 3rd ed. London: Macmillan.

Slater, S. F. and E. M. Olson. 2001. 'Marketing's contribution to the implementation of business strategy: An empirical analysis', *Strategic Management Journal*, 22, 11, 1055–67.

Snow, C. C. and L. G. Hrebiniak. 1980. 'Strategy, distinctive competence, and organizational performance', *Administrative Science Quarterly*, 25, 2, 317–36.

Spanos, Y. E. and G. Zaralis and S. Lioukas. 2004. 'Strategy and industry effects on profitability: Evidence from Greece', *Strategic Management Journal*, 25, 2, 139–65.

Starbuck, W. H. 1976. 'Organizations and their Environments'. In M. D. Dunnette (ed.), *Handbook of industrial and organizational psychology*. pp. 1069–1123. Chicago: Rand McNally.

Starbuck, W. H. and P. C. Nystrom (eds). 1981. *Handbook of organizational design. Volume 1: Adapting organizations to their environments*. Oxford: Oxford University Press.

Staw, B. M. and L. D. Epstein. 2000. 'What bandwagons bring: Effects of popular management techniques on corporate performance, reputation and CEO pay', *Administrative Science Quarterly*, 45, 3, 523–56.

Stevens, J. M. and R. P. McGowan. 1983. 'Managerial strategies in municipal government organizations', *Academy of Management Journal*, 26, 3, 527–34.

Stewart, J. and P. Kringas. 2003. 'Change management: Strategy and values in six agencies from the Australian public service', *Public Administration Review*, 63, 6, 675–88.

Tam, M. Y. S. and G. W. Bassett. 2004. 'Does diversity matter? Measuring the impact of high school diversity on freshman GPA', *Policy Studies Journal*, 32, 1, 129–143.

Tannenbaum, A. S. 1962. 'Control in organizations: Individual adjustment and organizational performance', *Administrative Science Quarterly*, 7, 2, 236–57.

Taylor, Frederick W. 1911. *The principles of scientific management.* New York: Harper & Bros.

Thompson, J. D. 1967. *Organizations in action: Social science bases of administrative theory.* New York: McGraw Hill.

Thompson, J. R. 2000. 'The reinvention laboratories. Strategic change by indirection', *American Review of Public Administration,* 30, 1, 46–68.

Thorpe, E. and R. Morgan. 2007. 'In pursuit of the "ideal approach" to successful marketing strategy implementation', *European Journal of Marketing,* 41, 4/5, 659–77.

Tiebout, C. 1956. 'A pure theory of local expenditure', *Journal of Political Economy,* 64, 5, 416–24.

Tolbert, P. and L. Zucker. 1983. 'Institutional sources of change in organizational structure: The case of civil service reform, 1880–1930', *Administrative Science Quarterly,* 23, 1, 22–39.

Tourangeau, R., L. J. Rips and K. Rasinski. 2000. *The psychology of survey response.* Cambridge: Cambridge University Press.

Tullock, G. 1965. *The politics of bureaucracy.* Washington, D.C.: Public Affairs Press.

Veliyath, R. and S. M. Shortell. 1993. 'Strategic orientation, strategic planning system characteristics and performance', *Journal of Management Studies,* 30, 3, 359–81.

Wade, J. B., A. Swaminathan and M. S. Saxon. 1998. 'Normative and resource flow consequences of local regulations in the American brewing industry, 1845–1918', *Administrative Science Quarterly,* 43, 4, 905–35.

Walker, R. M. and G. A. Brewer. 2008. 'An organizational echelon analysis of the determinants of red tape in public organizations', *Public Administration Review,* 68, 6, 1112–27.

Walker, R. M. and G. A. Brewer. 2009. 'Can management strategy minimize the impact of red tape on organizational performance?', *Administration & Society* 41, 4, 423–48.

Walker, R. M. and G. Enticott. 2004. 'Using multiple informants in public administration: Revisiting the managerial values and actions debate', *Journal of Public Administration Research and Theory* 14, 3, 417–34.

Walker, R. M. and G. A. Boyne. 2006. 'Public management reform and organizational performance: An empirical assessment of the U.K. Labour government's service improvement strategy', *Journal of Policy Analysis and Management* 25, 2, 371–93.

Walker, R. M., G. A. Boyne and G. A. Brewer. 2010. *Public management and performance: Research directions.* Cambridge: Cambridge University Press.

Walker R. M., R. Andrews, G. A. Boyne, K. J. Meier and L. J. O'Toole Jr. 2010. 'Wake up call: Network alarms, strategy and performance', *Public Administration Review,* 70, 5, 731–741.

Wall, T. B., J. Michie, M. Patterson et al. 2004. 'On the validity of subjective measures of company performance', *Personnel Psychology,* 57, 1, 95–118.

Weber, M. 1947. *The theory of social and economic organizations.* Glencoe, Ill: The Free Press.

Wechsler, B. and R. Backoff. 1986. 'Policy making and administration in state agencies: Strategic management approaches', *Public Administration Review,* 46, 4, 321–27.

West, A., H. Pennell, T. Travers and R. West. 2001. 'Financing school-based education in England: Poverty, examination results, and expenditure', *Environment and Planning C: Government and Policy*, 19, 4, 461–471.

Western, B. 1995. 'Concepts and suggestions for robust regression analysis', *American Journal of Political Science*, 39, 3, 786–817.

Whetten, D. A. 1978. 'Coping with incompatible expectations: An integrated view of role conflict', *Administrative Science Quarterly*, 23, 2, 254–71.

Whittington, R. 2001. *What is Strategy – and does it matter?* Padstow, Cornwall: Thompson.

Wilkinson, R. G. 1997. 'Socioeconomic determinants of health: Health inequalities: Relative or absolute material standards?', *British Medical Journal*, 314, 591.

Williams, C. 2003. 'Harnessing social capital: Some lessons from rural England', *Local Government Studies*, 29, 1, 75–90.

Wilson, W. J. 1991. 'Studying inner-city social dislocations: The challenge of public agenda research', *American Sociological Review*, 56, 1, 1–14.

Withers, S. D. 1997, 'Demographic polarization of housing affordability *in situ* major United States metropolitan areas', *Urban Geography*, 18, 4, 296–323.

Wolf, P. J. 1993. 'A case survey of bureaucratic effectiveness in U.S. cabinet agencies: Preliminary results', *Journal of Public Administration Research and Theory*, 3, 2, 161–81.

Woodside, A. G., D. P. Sullivan and R. J. Trappey. 1999. 'Assessing relationships among strategic types, distinctive marketing competencies, and organizational performance', *Journal of Business Research*, 45, 2, 135–46.

Woolridge, B. and S. Floyd. 1990. 'The strategy process, middle management involvement and organizational performance', *Strategic Management Journal*, 11, 3, 231–41.

Xu, K. T. 2006, 'State-level variations in income-related inequality in health and health achievement in the US', *Social Science & Medicine*, 63, 2, 457–64.

Yang, K. and J. Hseih. 2007. 'Managerial effectiveness of government performance measurement', *Public Administration Review*, 67, 5, 861–879.

Zahra, S. A. and J. A. Pearce. 1990. 'Research evidence on the Miles–Snow typology', *Journal of Management*, 16, 4, 751–58.

Zajac, E. J. and S. M. Shortell. 1989. 'Changing generic strategies: Likelihood, direction and performance implications', *Strategic Management Journal*, 10, 5, 413–30.

Index